Theology Without Walls

Thinking about ultimate reality is becoming increasingly transreligious. This transreligious turn follows inevitably from the discovery of divine truths in multiple traditions. Global communications bring the full range of religious ideas and practices to anyone with access to the internet. Moreover, the growth of the "nones" and those who describe themselves as "spiritual but not religious" creates a pressing need for theological thinking not bound by prescribed doctrines and fixed rituals. This book responds to this vital need.

The chapters in this volume each examine the claim that if the aim of theology is to know and articulate all we can about the divine reality, and if revelations, enlightenments, and insights into that reality are not limited to a single tradition, then what is called for is a theology without confessional restrictions. In other words, a Theology Without Walls. To ground the project in examples, the volume provides emerging models of transreligious inquiry. It also includes sympathetic critics who raise valid concerns that such a theology must face.

This is a book that will be of urgent interest to theologians, religious studies scholars, and philosophers of religion. It will be especially suitable for those interested in comparative theology, interreligious and interfaith understanding, new trends in constructive theology, normative religious studies, and the global philosophy of religion.

Jerry L. Martin has served as Chair of the National Endowment for the Humanities and of the Philosophy Department at the University of Colorado at Boulder and has also taught at Georgetown University and the Catholic University of America. He has published on issues in epistemology, philosophy of mind, phenomenology, transreligious theology, and public policy. In 2014, he founded the Theology Without Walls project, which meets with the American Academy of Religion. He is the author of *God: An Autobiography, as Told to a Philosopher* (2016).

Routledge New Critical Thinking in Religion, Theology and Biblical Studies

The *Routledge New Critical Thinking in Religion, Theology and Biblical Studies* series brings high quality research monograph publishing back into focus for authors, international libraries, and student, academic and research readers. This open-ended monograph series presents cutting-edge research from both established and new authors in the field. With specialist focus yet clear contextual presentation of contemporary research, books in the series take research into important new directions and open the field to new critical debate within the discipline, in areas of related study, and in key areas for contemporary society.

Theologising Brexit
A Liberationist and Postcolonial Critique
Anthony G. Reddie

Vision, Mental Imagery and the Christian Life
Insights from Science and Scripture
Zoltán Dörnyei

Christianity and the Triumph of Humor
From Dante to David Javerbaum
Bernard Schweizer

Religious Truth and Identity in an Age of Plurality
Peter Jonkers and Oliver J. Wiertz

Envisioning the Cosmic Body of Christ
Embodiment, Plurality and Incarnation
Aurica Jax and Saskia Wendel

Theology Without Walls
The Transreligious Imperative
Jerry L. Martin

For more information about this series, please visit: www.routledge.com/religion/series/RCRITREL

Theology Without Walls
The Transreligious Imperative

Edited by
Jerry L. Martin

Routledge
Taylor & Francis Group

LONDON AND NEW YORK

First published 2020
by Routledge
2 Park Square, Milton Park, Abingdon, Oxon OX14 4RN

and by Routledge
52 Vanderbilt Avenue, New York, NY 10017

Routledge is an imprint of the Taylor & Francis Group, an informa business

First issued in paperback 2021

British Library Cataloguing-in-Publication Data
A catalogue record for this book is available from the British Library

Library of Congress Cataloging-in-Publication Data
A catalog record for this book has been requested

ISBN: 978-0-367-02871-8 (hbk)
ISBN: 978-1-03-208863-1 (pbk)
ISBN: 978-0-429-00097-3 (ebk)

DOI: 10.4324/9780429000973

With grateful thanks to my teachers
Richard McKeon
Henry Veatch
Philip Wheelwright

Contents

Figures

Tables

Acknowledgements

I would like to thank Christopher Denny, John Thatamanil, and Wesley Wildman for encouraging and helping to conceptualize this volume. Christopher Denny earned my double gratitude for generously and capably supervising the final stages of the editing process. I also owe a deep debt of gratitude to all my colleagues who have contributed to the vibrant dialectic of Theology Without Walls, including those not represented in this volume: John Becker, John Berthrong, Susan Power Bratton, Kenneth Cracknell, Hans Gustafson, Jan-Olav Henriksen, Joyce Ann Konigsburg, Michael McLaughlin, Anselm Min, Hugh Nicholson, Thomas Jay Oord, Michelle Voss Roberts, Wm. Andrew Schwartz, Rita Sherman, Bin Song, Leonard J. Swidler, Jon Paul Sydnor, Wilhemus (Pim) Valkenberg, and Anthony J. Watson.

Contributors

Francis X. Clooney, SJ is Parkman Professor of Divinity and Professor of Comparative Theology at Harvard Divinity School. His primary areas of scholarship are theological commentarial writings in the Sanskrit and Tamil traditions of Hindu India and the developing field of comparative theology, a discipline distinguished by attentiveness to the dynamics of theological learning deepened through the study of traditions other than one's own. He has also written on the Jesuit missionary tradition, particularly in India, and the dynamics of dialogue in the contemporary world. Professor Clooney is the author of numerous articles and books, most recently *The Future of Hindu-Christian Studies: A Theological Inquiry* (Routledge, 2017) and *Learning Interreligiously: In the Text, in the World* (2018) and *Reading the Hindu and Christian Classics: How and Why Deep Learning Still Matters* (University of Virginia, 2019). During 2010–2017 he was the Director of the Center for the Study of World Religions at Harvard Divinity School. He has received honorary doctorates from four institutions, and in 2010 he was elected a Fellow of the British Academy. He is currently Vice President of the Catholic Theological Society of America.

Johan De Smedt is a postdoctoral fellow at Saint Louis University, working in the philosophy of cognitive science, philosophy of religion, and philosophy of art/aesthetics. He has co-authored, with Helen De Cruz, *A Natural History of Natural Theology* (MIT Press, 2015) and is currently co-writing *The Challenge of Evolution to Religion* under contract with Cambridge University Press.

Helen De Cruz holds the Danforth Chair in Philosophy at Saint Louis University, working mainly in the philosophy of cognitive science, philosophy of religion, and experimental philosophy. She is the author of *Religious Disagreement* (Cambridge University Press, 2019) and has co-edited, with Ryan Nichols, *Advances in Religion, Cognitive Science, and Experimental Philosophy* (Bloomsbury, 2016).

Christopher Denny is an associate professor in the Department of Theology and Religious Studies at St. John's University in New York, where he teaches undergraduate and graduate courses in historical theology from the patristic to the modern era. Denny is the author of *A Generous Symphony: Hans Urs von Balthasar's Literary Revelations* (Fortress, 2016); the coeditor, with Patrick Hayes and Nicholas Rademacher, of *A Realist's Church: Essays in Honor of Joseph A. Komonchak* (Orbis, 2015); and the coeditor, with Jeremy Bonner and Mary Beth Fraser Connolly, of *Empowering the People of God: Catholic Action before and after Vatican II* (Fordham University Press, 2014). Other recent publications include articles in the journals *Horizons, Journal of Interreligious Studies, Journal of Hindu-Christian Studies*, and *Christianity and Literature*. Denny is the recipient of best-article awards from the Catholic Press Association, the College Theology Society, and the Conference on Christianity and Literature.

Jeanine Diller is an associate professor in the Department of Philosophy and Program on Religious Studies at the University of Toledo with a PhD in philosophy from the University of Michigan. She teaches and researches in philosophy of religion and religious studies, concentrating especially on the nature of ultimate reality, the diversity of traditional and secular views of religion, and the power of religion to change the world for ill and for good. She co-edited *Models of God and Other Alternative Ultimate Realities* (Springer, 2013); authored several articles; and worked in the federal legislative, state executive, and local nonprofit sectors. She lives in Ann Arbor with her husband and two sons.

Peter Feldmeier is Murray/Bacik Endowed Professor of Catholic Studies at the University of Toledo. He received his PhD in Christian spirituality at the Graduate Theological Union in Berkeley, California. Feldmeier's scholarship has focused on Christian spirituality, comparative theology, and Buddhist-Christian dialogue. He is the author of numerous articles and book chapters as well as nine books, the most recent being *Experiments in Buddhist-Christian Encounter: From Buddha-Nature to the Divine Nature* (Orbis, 2019).

Paul Hedges is Associate Professor in Interreligious Studies at the Studies in Interreligious Relations in Plural Societies Programme at the S. Rajaratnam School of International Studies (RSIS), Nanyang Technological University, Singapore. He has previously worked for other universities in Asia, Europe, and North America, and been a consultant or trainer for the media, faith groups, nongovernmental organizations, and governments. He has published a dozen books and over 60 papers. Recent books include *Comparative Theology: Critical and Methodological Perspectives* (Brill, 2017), *Towards Better Disagreement: Religion and Atheism in Dialogue* (Jessica Kingsley, 2017), and *Contemporary Muslim-Christian*

Encounters (Bloomsbury, 2015), and his next book, provisionally entitled *Understanding Religion: Method and Theory for Exploring Religiously Diverse Societies* (California University Press, due 2020), should be out soon. He is co-editor of *Interreligious Studies and Intercultural Theology* and *Interreligious Relations* (occasional paper series) and sits on the editorial board of a number of other international journals and book series.

S. Mark Heim is Samuel Abbot Professor of Christian Theology at Andover Newton Seminary at Yale Divinity School. His books include *Salvations: Truth and Difference in Religion* (Maryknoll, NY: Orbis Books, 1995), *The Depth of the Riches: A Trinitarian Theology of Religious Ends* (Grand Rapids: Eerdmans, 2001), *Saved From Sacrifice: A Theology of the Cross* (Grand Rapids: Eerdmans, 2006) and *Crucified Wisdom: Christ and the Bodhisattva in Theological Reflection* (New York: Fordham University Press, 2018). He is a member of the American Theological Society and has co-chaired the comparative theology group in the American Academy of Religion. An ordained American Baptist minister, he has represented his denomination on the Faith and Order Commissions of the National Council of Churches and the World Council of Churches, and served on various ecumenical bodies, including the Christian–Muslim relations committee of the National Council of Churches.

J. R. Hustwit is Professor of Philosophy and Religion at Methodist University in Fayetteville, North Carolina. His research specialties are philosophical hermeneutics, interreligious dialogue, and comparative theology. He is the author of *Interreligious Hermeneutics and the Pursuit of Truth* (Lexington Books, 2014).

Paul Knitter is the Emeritus Paul Tillich Professor of Theology, World Religions, and Culture at Union Theological Seminary, New York, as well as Emeritus Professor of Theology at Xavier University in Cincinnati, Ohio. He received a Licentiate in theology from the Pontifical Gregorian University in Rome (1966) and a doctorate from the University of Marburg, Germany (1972). Most of his research and publications have dealt with religious pluralism and interreligious dialogue. More recently, his writing and speaking engagements have focused on what Christians can learn in their dialogue with Buddhists, which is the topic of his 2009 book, *Without Buddha I Could Not Be a Christian* (Oneworld), and of his 2015 co-authored book with Roger Haight, SJ, *Jesus and Buddha: Friends in Conversation* (Orbis).

Hyo-Dong Lee is Associate Professor of Comparative Theology at Drew University Theological School and its Graduate Department of Religion. A native of South Korea, he holds a PhD from Vanderbilt University and is the author of *Spirit, Qi, and the Multitude: A Comparative Theology for the Democracy of Creation* (Fordham University Press, 2014) and numerous articles, including "Ren and Causal Efficacy: Confucians and Whitehead on the Social Role of Symbolism" (in *Rethinking Whitehead's Symbolism*, Edinburgh University Press, 2017) and "Confucian Democracy and a Pluralistic Li-Ki Metaphysics" (*Religions* 9, no. 11 [2018]).

Jeffery D. Long is Professor of Religion and Asian Studies at Elizabethtown College, where he has taught since receiving his doctoral degree from the University of Chicago Divinity School in 2000. He is the author of *A Vision for Hinduism* (IB Tauris, 2007), *Jainism: An Introduction* (IB Tauris, 2009), and the *Historical Dictionary of Hinduism* (Rowman & Littlefield, 2011) and is editor of *Perspectives on Reincarnation: Hindu, Christian, and Scientific* (MDIP, 2019) and co-editor of the *Buddhism and Jainism* volumes of the *Springer Encyclopedia of Indian Religions* (Springer, 2017). He also edits the Lexington Books series, *Explorations in Indic Traditions: Ethical, Philosophical, and Theological*. In 2018 he was given the Hindu American Foundation's Dharma Seva Award in acknowledgment of his work to promote accurate and sensitive portrayals of Hindu traditions in the American education system and popular media. His forthcoming book projects include *Indian Philosophy: An Introduction* and *Hinduism in America: A Convergence of Worlds*, both from Bloomsbury.

Jerry L. Martin has served as chair of the National Endowment for the Humanities and of the Philosophy Department at the University of Colorado at Boulder, and has also taught at Georgetown University and the Catholic University of America. He has published on issues in epistemology, philosophy of mind, phenomenology, transreligious theology, and public policy. In 2014, he founded the Theology Without Walls project, which meets with the American Academy of Religion. He is the author of *God: An Autobiography, as Told to a Philosopher* (Caladium Publishing Company, 2016).

Rory McEntee is a philosopher and interspiritual theologian working at an intersection of spirituality, education, social justice, and culture. Through his work with influential teachers and his own writings, Rory is considered one of the architects of the New Monastic and Interspiritual movements. Rory is co-author, with Adam Bucko, of *The New Monasticism: An Interspiritual Manifesto for Contemplative Living* (Orbis Books, 2015) and Executive Director of *The Foundation for New Monasticism and InterSpirituality*. Rory has done doctoral work in Mathematics and Theological and Philosophical Studies. Among other endeavors, Rory can be found writing in his hermitage, snowboarding, playing with his niece and nephew, and trekking in the Himalayas.

Linda Mercadante, PhD, is *Distinguished Research Professor* and former Straker Professor of Historical Theology at Methodist Theological School in Ohio. Specializing in theology and culture, Mercadante's most recent book is *Belief without Borders: Inside the Minds of the Spiritual but not Religious* (Oxford University Press, 2014). The author of five books and hundreds of articles dealing with a theological analysis of culture, her topics include spirituality, addiction recovery, Shaker gender imagery, faith and film, moral injury, trauma, reproductive loss, and spiritual geography. She is ordained in the Presbyterian Church in the United States.

Robert Cummings Neville is quite old, having begun giving out grades in 1961. In the course of that time he has taught at Yale, Fordham, SUNY Purchase, SUNY Stony Brook, and Boston University. He is the author of the *Philosophical Theology* trilogy (*Ultimates*, 2013; *Existence*, 2014; *Religion*, 2015) published by SUNY Press. He is a member of the American Philosophical Association, the New Haven Theological Discussion Group, the American Academy of Religion, the Metaphysical Society, the International Society for Chinese Philosophy, the Boston Theological Society, the Institute for American Religious and Philosophical Thought, the American Theological Society, and the Charles S. Peirce Society; in all but the first two he has been the chief officer.

Richard Oxenberg received his PhD in Philosophy from Emory University in 2002, with a concentration in Ethics and Philosophy of Religion. He is the author of numerous articles on interreligious theology and the philosophy of spirituality. His book, *On the Meaning of Human Being: Heidegger and the Bible in Dialogue,* has been recently published by Political Animal Press. Richard currently teaches at Endicott College in Beverly, Massachusetts.

Kurt Anders Richardson, DTh (Basel), is a comparative theologian at Dallas International University and at Toronto/McMaster universities. He specializes in Abrahamic Studies: the historic and contemporary intersection of Jewish, Christian, and Muslim exegetical and theological practices. He is the co-founder of the Society of Scriptural Reasoning, comparative theology groups, and steering committee member of the Theology Without Walls group in the American Academy of Religion. His recent collaborative projects include studies in comparative messianism, concepts of divine being, and open-field theology. Richardson's ongoing fieldwork in the Middle East and Asia explore fruitful venues for theological reasoning and encounter through emerging interdisciplinary approaches of anthropology.

Peter Savastano is Associate Professor of Anthropology and Religious Studies at Seton Hall University in South Orange, New Jersey. An anthropologist of religion, consciousness, sexuality, and gender, Peter Savastano is also a theologian and a scholar of mysticism, most especially in the Abrahamic traditions. He teaches courses on Religions of the World, Thomas Merton, Catholic Mystics and Mysticism, Folklore and Mythology, and

Consciousness. He is also an ordained Episcopal Clergyperson with a deep attraction to Judaism and Islam, most especially Kabbalah and Sufism, the mystical traditions of these two Abrahamic religions. Peter Savastano is the editor of the forthcoming volume in the Thomas Merton Series published by FonsVitae Press, entitled *Merton and Indigenous World Wisdom* (anticipated fall 2019).

John J. Thatamanil is Associate Professor of Theology and World Religions at Union Theological Seminary in the City of New York. He is the author of *The Immanent Divine: God, Creation, and the Human Predicament* (Fortress Press, 2006) and the forthcoming *Circling the Elephant: A Comparative Theology of Religious Diversity* (Fordham University Press). Thatamanil works at the intersection of theologies of religious diversity and comparative theology with special interest in Christian, Hindu, and Buddhist traditions.

Jonathan Weidenbaum teaches courses in philosophy, ethics, and world religions at Berkeley College, New York City. With a PhD in Philosophy (University at Buffalo), Jon concentrates on topics in the philosophy of religion. He draws upon figures and themes from the Continental, Eastern, and classical American philosophical traditions. The cultural diversity of Jon's students, along with his regular travels through Asia, nurtures both his thinking and writing. His essays may be found in *The Journal of Liberal Religion, Transcendent Philosophy, The Journal of Speculative Philosophy, Open Theology*, and in a number of other journals and several books.

Wesley J. Wildman is Professor of Philosophy, Theology, and Ethics at Boston University. He is a philosopher of religion specializing in the scientific study of complex human phenomena. His research and publications pursue a multidisciplinary, comparative, trans-religious approach to topics within religious and theological studies, a venture whose underlying theory of rationality is systematically presented in *Religious Philosophy as Multidisciplinary Comparative Inquiry: Envisioning a Future for the Philosophy of Religion* (State University of New York Press, 2010). For further information, see www.WesleyWildman.com.

Introduction

Jerry L. Martin

The coming wave of thinking about ultimate reality is transreligious. The transreligious turn follows ineluctably from the discovery, profound in its depth and implications, of divine or ultimate truth in multiple traditions. At the forefront of this turn are scholars associated with Theology Without Walls. This approach is based on the following syllogism: If the aim of theology is to know and articulate all we can about the divine or ultimate reality, and if revelations, enlightenments, and insights into that reality are not limited to a single tradition, then what is called for is a theology without confessional restrictions, a Theology Without Walls (TWW). Any approach that omits the insights of traditions other than one's own falls short of being adequate to the ultimate reality. Any approach that insists on translating those insights into the terms of one's own tradition risks narrowness, distortion, and misappropriation.

It is a question of subject matter. The subject matter of theology is ultimate reality, not one's own tradition. One way to put it is that, in addition to Christian theology, Hindu theology, Islamic theology, etc., there is just Theology, the *logos* of *theos*, of ultimacy. It is not that we do not stand somewhere, but our sense of our goal is not limited to where we stand at the outset. All available terms, including "divine or ultimate reality" and "theology" itself, must be provisional, giving a sense of direction to thought without precluding surprising advances and revisions. In TWW, works of literature, philosophy, psychology, anthropology, and the natural and social sciences, as well as personal experience, may become important sources of theological insight. A major achievement of the past half-century has been the development of increasingly adequate concepts and methods for comparison and dialogue conducive to theologizing across traditions.

Is TWW a form of religious pluralism? No, pluralism is a concept within confessional theology of religions. It is a thesis about the religions, not about ultimate reality. It is an answer to the question that arises within a tradition about the status – particularly the soteriological effectiveness – of other traditions, about whether they can deliver what "our" religion does. TWW poses questions more radically: What should our soteriological aim

DOI: 10.4324/9780429000973-1

be? What is the fundamental human predicament that soteriology should address? Indeed, is soteriology even the central concept in our relationship with ultimacy?

Is TWW a form of comparative theology? Yes, if it is understood as a Comparative Theology Without Walls. But it is an alternative to those forms of comparative theology that are essentially confessional, seeking to enhance one's own theology by studying another tradition. The most natural mode of TWW may not involve comparison or side-by-side reading. Whereas comparative theology tends to anchor studies in the religions, TWW is open to taking evidences wherever they are found, including sources quite outside religion as historically defined. Its theologians can look to literature or to psychology or to evolutionary biology for insight into the human condition and, from there, into the soteriological solution to that condition. The familiar metaphor for comparative theology in a confessional mode is "passing over" and "returning home." For TWW, "returning home" is a possibility, not a necessity. Any place truth can be found is home.

Is the aim to find what is common among all the major religions? No, noting commonalities may make a useful contribution, but the aim is to understand what is truly ultimate and, hence, in the end, to be selective. There is no guarantee that every religion dubbed as "major" is, even in essential aspects, right on target with regard to ultimate reality. Or that those religions not identified as major lack evidential value. We have to use spiritual discernment, philosophical reflection, personal experience, and transreligious insight to sort that out.

Is it possible to sort out or evaluate insights from traditions not our own? In fact, we do this already. When we seriously study other traditions, we frequently find deep insights there. We do not find them in every aspect of every tradition, but in certain texts, practices, spiritual disciplines, and iconic figures that strike us as revelatory or evidential. However accounted for, this is a human spiritual capability, without which religion itself would hardly be possible.

Is the aim of TWW to arrive at a single, encompassing theological worldview? No more than any other field of inquiry. Disagreement is fruitful.

Is engaging in TWW compatible with a commitment to one's own confession? Yes, just as a Jungian psychotherapist can take in insight from other thinkers and acknowledge that psychology itself is a wider field of inquiry, one can, like Huston Smith, be a participating Presbyterian while holding a much wider religious worldview. Some essays in this volume discuss how the spiritual life might be lived in a transreligious context.

TWW might, however, have an impact on religious traditions. They might come to regard themselves as offering truth, but not the only truth. Participants may become willing and interested to learn from other traditions. The religions themselves could evolve toward greater spiritual openness.

That Theology Without Walls is necessary – if theology is to live up to its goal of explicating ultimate reality as fully as possible – does not ensure that it is achievable. Theology as we know it has been, almost by definition, the articulation of religious truths as held by a particular tradition. It is that tradition that provides the canonical texts, hermeneutical strategies, theological questions, proffered answers, methods for assessing and modifying them, and even institutional authorities for ruling certain answers in or out. In addition, such traditions provide the full-bodied religious life that their theologies serve.

What are, for TWW, the theological issues, debates, and methods of interpretation and of resolution? These issues are already being sorted out in interreligious scholarship and discussion of such matters as the role of mystical and other religious experience, the role of religious authorities, which spiritual practices are effective and what they achieve, alternative ontologies, and rival hermeneutical strategies. More fundamentally, theologies must address the enduring questions of human life and death, felicity and suffering, love and compassion, justice and mercy, and so on.

This volume explains and argues for this new approach to theology. It includes scholars from a range of religions and spiritual orientations and of disciplines whose research clarifies the scope and conditions of valid religious theorizing. Some contributors make the case for transreligious theologizing or for their own approaches to it. Some discuss particular issues, such as dual religious belonging or the relation of TWW to confessional commitment. The volume includes sympathetic critics whose serious concerns indicate challenges TWW must face. Finally, to ground the project in examples, the volume includes emerging models of transreligious inquiry.

TWW presents an obvious challenge to traditional theology, but its importance is not limited to scholars, or even to religious professionals. The wider public is involved. We no longer live in villages or neighborhoods where everybody has the same religion. There are ashrams and mosques in the same towns as churches and synagogues. Global communications bring the full range of religious ideas and practices into our homes and offices. Moreover, the growth of the "nones" and those who describe themselves as "spiritual but not religious" creates a pressing need for theological thinking not bounded by prescribed doctrines and fixed rituals, yet subject to the rigor of a search for truth. TWW responds to this vital need.

At the outset, transreligious theology should be considered an exploratory program, at best a "research programme" in Imre Lakatos's sense. "One must treat budding programmes leniently," he writes, since, early on, the obstacles will be more obvious than their fruitfulness. Meanwhile, we must exercise "methodological tolerance." We cannot allow procedural worries to block the path of inquiry. Models are beginning to emerge. Concepts for transreligious discourse are increasingly well-developed. We will learn the best methods by engaging in the process.

TWW calls upon each theologian to seek truth, wherever it can be found, and to articulate it even when methods and concepts are still in the process of being developed and are not, or not yet, ready at hand. Consider these essays forays into ultimacy. Gandhi named his autobiography, *The Story of My Experiments with Truth*. That is what all our lives are, including our theological lives. They are experiments with truth.

Part I

Why Theology Without Walls?

Introduction

Jerry L. Martin

The most comprehensive systematic transreligious theology is presented in Robert Cummings Neville's three-volume *Philosophical Theology*. The first volume is called *Ultimates* and contains a précis of the whole. Neville establishes a metaphysical structure within which the various "ultimates" represented by or symbolized through various traditions find their place. His accomplishment, requiring a philosophical sophistication and cross-cultural erudition few possess, can be daunting, rather than empowering, for emerging theologians. For that reason, he was asked to reflect on "how to become the next Robert Neville." He does that by telling his own story, which goes back to the age of four and is still ongoing.

Why Theology Without Walls (TWW)? Because, says Neville, there are inescapable questions about "what is ultimate and how it is ultimate" with respect to the "problematic" aspects of life and the universe. "No one really trusts walled-in answers to them." In fact, "theologies *with walls* reduce to sociological claims" – this is what my tradition "believes." In spite of his own metaphysical grounding and comprehensive interreligious scope, Neville reminds us that "theologians need to make their own decisions." He recognizes that, in spite of powerful arguments on its behalf, his way is not the only way to engage in Theology Without Walls. Other ways, some quite different, are also represented in this volume.

For theologians to make thoughtful choices based on years of study is one thing; for everyone to shop casually among religious and nonreligious offerings is quite another. Scholars from Robert Bellah to Christopher Smith have lamented the rise of the loosely affiliated "Sheila" as a cultural type. For Christopher Denny, teaching Catholic theology in a Catholic university, it came as a shock to realize to what extent we live in an age of casual shoppers in the spiritual supermarket. But the shock prompted an insight that, contrary to the concerns of Bellah and Smith, in religious as well as secular life, "there is a human agent making the choice." The great religions themselves resulted from human choices and, in our more democratic and egalitarian times, these choices are open to a larger population. He concludes that "the recognition of preferences provides theology with a new starting point from which to engage the bewildering array of religious options." The

DOI: 10.4324/9780429000973-2

phenomenon of choice does not imply relativism. He quotes Kurt Richardson: "The self as the locus of truth does not mean the self as the source of truth." Not every choice, Denny says, will be "intellectually coherent, morally defensible, or spiritually attractive to others." This is true whether we choose a traditional path or a personal one. "Whatever mistakes we make, they will be our own," he concludes. "In that sense, we are all Sheilas."

As radical as Denny's argument may seem, Richard Oxenberg argues that a transreligious thrust is implied by the theological project itself and, surprisingly, "forecast by Jesus himself." He begins by exploring the reasons for theology *within* walls. He answers that "faith requires understanding in order simply to fulfill itself as faith." He quotes Jesus's warning about hearing the message but failing to understand it. Oxenberg argues that TWW "*also* has its basis in revelatory experience; a revelatory experience more and more of us are having in the context of the global encounter of the world religions with one another." We are seeing "divine truth" outside our home traditions. Dogmatic faith gives way to "Socratic faith," which requires humility rather than claims of infallibility. It involves the dialectical examination of the revelations themselves. He goes further: TWW "*itself* betokens a new revelation of the divine," one that has its own soteriological power, namely, to overcome tribalistic rivalries and "thereby bring us closer to a recognition of the divine as *One*."

In place of a world of fixed religions, maintaining their own stable doctrines and devotions, we face a world of contending, unpredictable individual choices. In such a world, Kurt Anders Richardson argues, TWW creates a hermeneutical space for "open-field" theology, a meta-discourse about theological practices and their contexts in relation. It seeks to "coordinate discursive spaces with no theological limitations" while respecting "the inviolate mind, conscience and body of every human being." Thus "any discursive handling of divine or ultimate topics . . . qualify as kinds of theology." TWW as a hermeneutic open-field theology creates a "community field of discourse where multiple rationalities and theological priorities can find concourse" without having to agree to "common ground" or "common problems." Put simply, it provides the "working space" for theology suitable to our times.

1 Paideias and programs for Theology Without Walls

Robert Cummings Neville

Editor Jerry L. Martin asked me to explain how I became the kind of theologian without walls that I am. The first thing to say about that is that there are many kinds of theologians without walls, not just mine. Many different starting points exist, and there are many different kinds of theological problems in which to be interested. I myself am a systematic philosophical theologian, and I take myself to be accountable to any thinker in any tradition, religious or secular, who has an interest in the outcome of my inquiry. My inquiry has a number of parts, and at the beginning of my career I could not develop any of them very well. But I kept working on them all together and gradually became more sophisticated. It would be great to be deeply and evenly sophisticated, although I do not expect that! Here are some of the parts of my systematic philosophical inquiry. Note that this is the first time I have been asked to write in an avuncular voice: if I wobble between braggadocio and patronizing, remember it is a first attempt.

Knowledge of religion

I was born in 1939 in St. Louis, Missouri, and raised there through public schools until I left for college in 1956.[1] My family was active in a rather liberal Methodist church. Most of our neighbors and my classmates were Roman Catholic; the more established German and Irish Catholics were resentful of the newly arrived Italians. When I was about 14, I edited our congregation's weekly newsletter and decided to write a series of 500-word columns about world religions. Based on encyclopedia articles, my columns dealt sequentially with Buddhism, Confucianism, Christianity, Daoism, Judaism, Hinduism, and Islam (in alphabetical order). This was not high scholarship and certainly had no peer review. Notice that Christianity was presented as one religion among many. No one gave me any grief for that. I'm proud that my first "publications" were about world religions.

In college I roomed with a Greek Orthodox and a Jew, never having met representatives of those religions before (my St. Louis neighborhood was rather homogeneous). I majored in philosophy, but we studied only Western philosophy, no Indian, Chinese, or Islamic. Not until I was teaching

DOI: 10.4324/9780429000973-3

at Fordham University did I begin to study non-Western philosophies and religions, under the prodding of Thomas Berry. He taught me Sanskrit and arranged for me to learn a little Chinese; moreover he arranged for me to teach both Indian and Chinese philosophy, which I have done ever since until I retired in the spring of 2018. Although I cannot keep up with a well-trained historian of any religion, I am literate in frontline research in those fields and can talk with scholars from most religious traditions. I'm recognized as a contemporary progressive Confucian philosopher (Neville 2000). I think it is possible for a theologian without walls to grow slowly from a position of naiveté and bias about religions to enough erudition to be conversant with thinkers from most traditions and to be relatively expert in those of personal interest.

Systematic thinking

In college I was taught that system in philosophy means the development of a group of connected categories in terms of which everything can be represented as a specification. Hegel, Peirce, and Whitehead were the model systematic thinkers, and I thought a lot about Whitehead's criteria for a philosophical system: consistency, coherence, adequacy, and applicability (Whitehead 1978). At my college, Yale, systematic thinking was encouraged, not discouraged, as would have happened at nearly any other college in those days. My senior thesis on interpretation and nature was my first attempt at a system.

Nevertheless, systems are based on core ideas, and my first core philosophical-theological idea came when I was in kindergarten. One of my classmates told me that God is a person. I checked with my father who said that, although Jesus was a person, God is more like light or electricity. I understood that idea at a five-year-old level and began working on it. My current theological naturalism is a more sophisticated version of my father's hypothesis. I never had a serious commitment to a personal God that I would have to get over in order to deal with Brahman or the Dao. About the time I was editing the church newsletter, one of my high school teachers said to me, "You know, Bob, that God is not in space or time." I understood immediately what he meant and agreed with it. I also immediately knew that understanding that idea was an unusual kind of thinking, to which I decided to dedicate my life. So my systematic theology of creation *ex nihilo* began in high school and became the topic of my PhD dissertation (1963), which was revised and published in 1968 as *God the Creator* (Neville 1968, 1992). That is a real systematic book, although not half as sophisticated as my recent systematic statement, *Ultimates: Philosophical Theology Volume One* (Neville 2013).[2]

The moral I draw about this part of my inquiry is that it is important to begin as soon as possible with systematic thinking and grow from naïve and brash to more sophisticated and intelligent. Do not wait until you have mastered everything that systems need and then try to put them together. People I've known who waited until old age to put things together in a systematic way simply did not develop the tastes and skill of system making. Good systems have multiple layers, and really good ones allow you to see through many layers and interconnections at once. So I think you have to start young, duck your head when critics cry "juvenile," and just make your system more complex and transparently simple.

Comparative theology

It is one thing to learn a lot about many religions and another to be able to compare them. Comparison usually begins by noting some at least surface similarities between the religious positions and then inquiring into just how similar and different they are. Progress in comparison, however, requires hard work identifying exactly the respects in which the comparison is being made. Comparison is always "with respect to something." The respects in which things can be compared are comparative categories, and they are astonishingly hard to develop. Often what looks like a similarity between two positions turns out to be thinking at cross purposes. Some years ago, for instance, some comparativists got excited about the similarities between sunyata in Buddhism and kenosis in Christianity. But upon examination, the similarities boiled down to the fact that both translate as "emptiness" in English: Buddhist sunyata is a metaphysical characteristic of things as experienced by enlightened people, and Christian kenosis is Christ's or a person's taking on a humble station. There was no respect in which they can be compared except the accident of translation into English. The question of gods is an interesting comparative one. But in what respects is it important to compare them? Whether religions believe in one, several, or thousands? How many are male, female, both, ungendered? Do the gods squabble in ways that affect humans? Are there divine hierarchies? What is at stake in these comparisons, all of which can be made? I suspect that continued reflection on gods gives rise to the comparative category of what is ultimate and how is it ultimate. Monotheisms identify the ultimate with one God, however differently that God might be understood among and within monotheisms. Polytheisms, even those with a top God in a hierarchy, do not consider the ultimate to be a god with intentional agency, but some deeper principle. Some religions like Buddhism, many forms of Hinduism, Confucianism, and Daoism in their early forms believed that the world is populated with many kinds of supernatural beings but that they were not ultimate at all. Confucianism and Daoism do not use many personalistic metaphors for ultimacy, but rather look to metaphors of spontaneous emergence. The important categories for comparing theological positions emerge only slowly with the process of learning and systematizing.

In my own experience, the categories that emerge as important for theological comparison, the respects in which it is important to compare religious positions, turn out to be the categories that are important for the system in philosophical theology. I think that there are five problematics that any seriously developed theological tradition must address: why there is something rather than nothing; how human choice determines not only what happens sometimes but also the character of the chooser; how to have a good self; how to relate to other people, institutions, and nature on their own terms; and what the meaning of life and existence is. These are extremely complicated problematics, and religions say many different things about them. But the problematics can be sorted through to develop important categories for comparative theology. Of course, the religious positions are often in wild disagreement.[3] Theologians without walls need to make their own decisions about how to evaluate the positions compared.

The moral here is that the development of important comparative categories for theology is a long, evolving, and critical process. It is not that the theologian can first get categories for comparison and then work for years filling in how the theological positions compare. Rather, every comparative category is itself an hypothesis about the important respects in which to compare theological positions and should be kept vulnerable to correction throughout a comparative theologian's continuing inquiry. Start young and correct yourself.

Programs of teaching

I assume that most theologians without walls are teachers at the high school, undergraduate, or perhaps graduate levels. Some of us are retired from all that, and it is possible to be a serious theologian without walls without an academic career at all. Nevertheless, teaching helps one become a better theologian without walls. We all know that trying to explain something to students who do not know it makes you figure out just what you understand and what you do not.

I recommend that, to as great an extent as circumstances allow, we should teach courses about the three topics I have already mentioned, namely courses on different religions, courses on systematic theology aiming to say what you think is true, and courses in comparison where you lead students to understand both the nature of religion and what should be said about the most important theological topics. I have been fortunate that in my 57 years of teaching I have taught all three kinds of courses. Some people, of course, teach in religious schools where discussion of other religions is discouraged or forbidden. Some teach in schools where it is forbidden to say what you think is true on theological topics or admit to having a theological system. Some teach in places where there is no leisure for complicated discussions about the nature of comparison. But we should hope to teach the elements of theology without walls to as great an extent as possible.

Furthermore, we should teach these courses again and again, revising and improving them. Some changes in evolving curricula come from the changing nature of the students. Here I am advocating repetitive improvements based on what can be learned from teaching. In my 31 years at Boston University, I have been fortunate to teach a sequence of three advanced systematic courses nine times. Each sequence is a little different from the one before, and sometimes there are radical changes in the readings. Teaching this sequence again and again has led me to the publication of my three-volume philosophical theology based on some comparative erudition and aimed at an audience of anyone interested in the outcome of the inquiry. Teaching for many years is a great good fortune. I personally could have stopped grading papers 15 or 20 years ago, but the classroom is always fresh.

Professional colleagues

Another crucial part of the ongoing paideia for a theologian without walls is the cultivation of professional contacts. This is not likely to be done by having a whole department of theologians without walls, although Wesley Wildman advocates "academic theology" in colleges and universities as theology without walls (Wildman 2010). More likely is the possibility of developing collaborative friendships and close involvements with professional societies that are relevant to the many parts of theology without walls.

The professional societies can be of many sorts. For the sake of developing a philosophical system, I have been fortunate to be part of the Metaphysical Society of America from my graduate school days. It was founded by Paul Weiss, who was on my dissertation committee and who published my first professional philosophy paper in *The Review of Metaphysics*, which he founded and edited for many years. My own kind of philosophical heritage owes very much to American pragmatism, and I have long belonged to the Institute for American Religious and Philosophical Thought. More recently I have been involved with the Charles S. Peirce Society. For comparative work, my main interest has been in Confucianism, and I have been a multidecade member of the International Society for Chinese Philosophy. Theology without walls has flourished mainly in the American Academy of Religion to which I have belonged for most of my career. I have frequently given papers at these groups and have commented on others. They provide long-term communities of critics and encouragers. I have been involved with their administrations and have served as the president of each of them, engaging as a Confucian scholar-official.

Friends are perhaps the most important collaborators in developing a rich theology without walls over the long haul. Some friends come from special projects with which we can become involved. Others become the special friends that grow with you over the years. I myself have been greatly fortunate in friendships and am convinced that philosophical friendships, rather than the philosophical rush to refutation in which I was raised by analytic philosophers, are the proper venues for cultivating the openings into the depths of the soul.

Publication

As Boston's Mayor Curley said about voting, publish early and often. Do not wait until you have a perfectly polished piece of theology before you submit it for publication. Do not be afraid to grow in the press, publishing improved renditions of your ideas as they come to you. Find the publishing venues amenable to your work and pursue them. If the peer-review process elicits good criticisms, figure out where they are coming from and accept them selectively.

The more original your work, the less likely it is to be understood by reviewers and editors. When I first started out, my first book was rejected by a number of publishers before it was finally accepted after three years by the University of Chicago Press. During that dry period all of my articles were rejected as well. In frustration, I sent the rejected articles to Wilfrid Sellars, one of my graduate professors, and asked what to do. He wrote back that the philosophy I was doing was different from what was recognized in the assorted philosophical Balkans and that when my book was finally published, it would establish an audience for my work. That is pretty much what happened.

Theology without walls will not be recognized as legitimate theology by people who think theology is always based within some faith community. It will also not be recognized by most philosophers who do not like theology because they think it is always apologetic for some faith community. So we need to be patient in developing venues for the publication of theology without walls. Keep up the courage to sustain many rejections.

Two principal reasons exist for hope for the paideia and programs of theology without walls. First, theologies *with* walls reduce to sociological claims: this is what Thomists, Advaita Vedantins, and Confucians "believe" in their theologies. Most theologians cannot be satisfied with that and want their claims to be true, not just part of the grammar of a select group. Second, the world, especially colleges and universities, needs disciplined people to address the big theological questions: Why is there something rather than nothing? Why are human beings obligated and how? What is the nature of an ideal self, and how can that be achieved? How can we relate to others while respecting their perspectives? What is the meaning of life and existence? Many other first-order questions have rung the bells for centuries. Those questions cut across all religions and the assorted secularities. No one really trusts theologically walled-in answers to them. Colleges and universities need to make places for theology without walls, because those are the most basic and important questions.

I am a philosophical realist and believer that we get feedback from reality on ultimate theological questions, particularly, the feedback that says, "Why aren't you answering these questions?" Let's get to it.

Notes

1 You will find an account of my childhood at www.robertcummingsneville.com, including embellishments of some of the stories I tell here.
2 That is part of the now larger system that includes Neville (2014) and Neville (2015).
3 See Neville (2014, 2015) to track some of these wild differences.

References

Neville, Robert C. 1968. *God the Creator: On the Transcendence and Presence of God.* 1st ed. Chicago: University of Chicago Press.

Neville, Robert C. 1992. *God the Creator: On the Transcendence and Presence of God.* rev. ed. Albany, NY: State University of New York Press.

Neville, Robert C. 2000. *Boston Confucianism: Portable Tradition in the Late Modern World.* Albany, NY: State University of New York Press. doi:10.1525/nr.2004.7.3.105

Neville, Robert C. 2013. *Ultimates: Philosophical Theology Volume One.* Albany, NY: State University of New York Press.

Neville, Robert C. 2014. *Existence: Philosophical Theology Volume Two.* Albany, NY: State University of New York Press.

Neville, Robert C. 2015. *Religion: Philosophical Theology Volume Three.* Albany, NY: State University of New York Press.

Whitehead, Alfred N. 1978. *Process and Reality: An Essay in Cosmology, Corrected Edition*, edited by Donald W. Sherburne and David Ray Griffin. New York, NY: Macmillan/Free Press.

Wildman, Wesley J. 2010. "Afterword: Religious Philosophy in the Modern University." In *Religious Philosophy as Multidisciplinary Comparative Inquiry: Envisioning a Future for the Philosophy of Religion*, edited by Wesley J. Wildman, 307–318. Albany, NY: State University of New York Press.

2 In spirit and truth

Toward a Theology Without Walls

Richard Oxenberg

Introduction: spirit and truth

In the Gospel of John, we are told the story of a Samaritan woman who asks Jesus whether the proper place of worship is on the holy mountain of Samaria or in the Temple of Jerusalem. These were the centers of two rival, antagonistic religious institutions. Jesus responds:

> Woman, believe Me, an hour is coming when neither in this mountain nor in Jerusalem will you worship the Father . . . an hour is coming, and now is, when the true worshippers will worship in spirit and truth; for such people the Father seeks to be His worshippers. God is spirit, and those who worship Him must worship in spirit and truth.
>
> (Jn 4:21–24)

"Spirit and truth," of course, are neither places nor institutions. "Spirit" – *pneuma* in New Testament Greek – refers to that which animates life and gives it meaning. "Truth" – *aletheia* in Greek – might better be rendered as "truthfulness." It refers here not to the correctness of abstract propositions, but to the earnestness that is the mark of the true spiritual aspirant. Jesus is saying that the true worshiper of God is not one whose primary allegiance is to one or another religious institution, but one who genuinely seeks the divine in heart and mind. Whether on the Samaritan mountain or in the Jerusalem Temple, the one who worships in "spirit and truth" worships rightly.

Those of us pursuing a "theology without walls" aspire to do theology in "spirit and truth"; that is, in a manner not confined to any particular religious institution or tradition, but grounded simply in an earnest search for the divine. This aspiration constitutes a new and distinctive way of approaching theological pursuits; one forecast by Jesus in the earlier passage but fully realizable only in our time.

To make this clear, it will be helpful, first of all, to consider why theology has traditionally been done *within* walls and then to consider why and how some of us now feel called upon to pass beyond such walls in pursuit of a fuller approach to the divine.

DOI: 10.4324/9780429000973-4

Theology within walls

We might begin by considering the peculiar relationship of theology to religion. Religions do not arise in response to theological reflection; rather, theology arises as an attempt to understand and apply religious experience. Religion as a communal and spiritual practice is prior to theology as an intellectual discipline. This priority of religion to theology is reflected in the classical designation of theology as "faith seeking understanding." If we say that faith *seeks* understanding, we imply that faith exists prior to understanding. Theology is not the basis of faith; rather, faith is the basis of theology.

What, then, is the basis of faith? The religions of the world have emerged not from theological reflection, but from an encounter or, anyway, a perceived encounter, with the divine. I use the word "divine" here to refer to that which is ultimate in meaning and value – what Paul Tillich calls our "ultimate concern." This might be a personal God, as in the Abrahamic religions, or it might be an exalted or awakened state of being, as in Buddhism. Nevertheless, whether we think of divine reality as a highest person or as a supernal state of awareness, religions have their origin in some direct encounter, or purported encounter, with this divine reality. Theology, then, emerges as the endeavor to reflect upon this encounter, to appropriate it cognitively and work out its implications for ordinary life. This, indeed, is what distinguishes theology from philosophy. Philosophy begins with mundane experience and seeks to arrive at universal truths through rational reflection, extrapolation, and generalization. Theology begins with an experience of the divine, or reports of such experience, and seeks to make sense of that experience at the cognitive level.

In this regard, theology is rooted in what John Thatamanil has called "first-order knowledge" of the divine. First-order knowledge is direct knowledge, experiential knowledge; it is "knowledge of" rather than "knowledge about." As Thatamanil puts it, a person who never swims can nevertheless acquire a great deal of information (i.e., "*second*-order knowledge") *about* swimming, but only the swimmer can have first-order knowledge of what it *is* to swim (Thatamanil 2016).

It is such first-order knowledge, reflected in a particular body of revelation – as recorded in scripture and/or passed down by tradition – that constitutes the primary source material for theology. The theologian who takes up the task of interpreting a given body of revelation does so, presumably, because he or she has had a taste of such first-order knowledge with respect to it. In Tillich's language, the theologian is "grasped" by an ultimate concern and feels called to the task of making cognitive sense of that by which he or she is grasped. In this respect, theology is "hermeneutical" in the most basic, etymological sense of the word: Just as the messenger-god Hermes was charged with the task of communicating divine messages to human beings, so the theologian seeks to "hear" the divine message and translate it into conceptual terms for reception by our cognitive faculties.

This makes it clear why theology has traditionally been done "within walls." It emerges in response to a particular body of revelation and thus, quite naturally, confines itself to that body. Theology is done within the walls of a given revelatory tradition because it is born within those walls and within those walls has its meaning and function.

But one thing more needs to be added. We might ask *why* faith seeks understanding. Why isn't faith content with itself, *sans* understanding? There is, of course, an important practical reason for this. Encounter with the divine seems never, or rarely, to be an experience whose purpose is fully consummated in itself. The divine makes demands concerning how we are to live, what we are to value, and how we are to relate to one another. Theology is needed to understand the tenor of these demands and to apply them to the concrete circumstances of life.

But beyond this, faith requires understanding in order simply to fulfill itself as faith. In the Gospel of John, Jesus says to his disciples, "I no longer call you servants because a servant does not *know* his master's business. Instead, I have called you friends, for everything I have learned from my Father I have made *known* to you" (Jn 15:14–15, my emphasis). Consummated relation with the divine – "friendship" with the divine – requires some understanding of the divine purpose, or *telos*. Indeed, flawed understanding can imperil faith itself. Again, in the words of Jesus: "Whenever someone hears the message about the kingdom and fails to understand it, the evil one comes and snatches away the word that was sewn in his heart" (Mt. 13:19).

Faith seeks understanding, then, in order to secure itself and fulfill itself as faith. Faith *sans* understanding is half-formed, inchoate, immature, and subject to distortion and error.

Theology without walls

If this is an accurate account of the roots and purposes of traditional theology – theology *within* walls – we might next ask: What are the roots and purposes of a theology *without* walls? Does theology without walls also have its roots in an encounter with the divine, a revelatory experience, or is it more like philosophy, examining the particular religions as they appear to mundane experience and, through comparative analysis, extrapolation, and generalization, seeking to extract from them something of universal import?

I suggest that theology without walls *also* has its basis in revelatory experience; a revelatory experience more and more of us are having in the context of the global encounter of the world religions with one another. What many of us are seeing – and I do believe "seeing" is the right word here – is that divine truth is to be found outside the bounds of our home tradition. In some cases, we see that the revelations of another tradition shed a light on our own that allows us to understand our own more fully. In other cases, we see that the teachings or practices of another tradition speak to, or awaken, a dimension of ourselves – of our "ultimate concern" – that our home tradition does not touch upon or speak to as profoundly. In still other cases, we see corrections for the distortions and limitations of our home tradition in the traditions of others. In all these cases, we see that our encounter with other traditions helps us to broaden, deepen, and solidify our experience and understanding of the divine.

I use the word "see" here because I do not believe these recognitions are the result of a purely intellectual calculus. They do not arise from a simple, conceptual, contrast and compare. On the contrary, at the strictly conceptual level many of the world religions seem to have very little in common. Steven Prothero makes this point in his book *God Is Not One*. There is nothing, or very little, that would allow us to conceptually identify the attributes of the God of Abraham as presented in the Bible, for instance, with the attributes of the state of Nirvana as presented in Buddhist tradition. When we confine our thought to this level, we find more differences than commonalities, even apparently irreconcilable differences.

But many of us – more and more of us – have sensed, or intuited, or directly experienced that at the level of encounter, at the level of *first-order knowledge*, there are similarities, complementarities, and correspondences between the spiritual state one enters when one feels oneself in touch with the God of Abraham and the spiritual state of the Hindu bhaktic or the Buddhist arhat. This is not to say that such states are identical, but rather that they bear a meaningful correspondence to one another, such that we are led to believe, or perhaps, stated more cautiously, to suspect, that all these experiences of the divine have their roots in a common ontological ground.

This is an exciting thought. The religious pluralist John Hick analogizes it to the excitement Newton must have felt when he suddenly recognized that the same force that makes an apple fall to the ground also makes the planets revolve around the sun. The excitement itself, I would say, has a certain revelatory import and power. It calls us forth, it bids us on, it impels us to seek to make sense of these correspondences and commonalities, not merely for the sake of promoting religious tolerance, but much more fundamentally, as a way of more fully apprehending the divine ground from which the diverse religions spring. In this respect, it is the spiritual drive itself that calls us to do theology without walls.

Of course, a planet revolving around the sun and an apple falling to the ground are not the same thing. That they are both manifestations of the same force, or of the same natural law, does not make them identical, nor does it imply that apples should "convert" to planets or planets to apples, nor that both apples and planets should somehow, impossibly, become gravity. These correspondences, in other words, do not imply that religions should shed their distinctions and merge into one. But they do give us a new understanding of the relationship of the religions to one another and to the divine ground that is their source. We come to see the different religions as brethren rather than rivals and are able to recognize the commonality of purpose – of "spirit and truth" – underlying all genuine religious pursuits.

Thus, theology without walls entails a new understanding of the relationship of the religions to one another and to the divine ground from which they spring. We can further explore the nature of this new understanding by examining what I will call "the three suspicions" of theology without walls.

Three suspicions

Theology Without Walls (or what has also been called "transreligious theology") is, as I see it, predicated upon three assumptions, or what we might better call three "suspicions," about the nature of the religions to one another and to the divine.

The first suspicion is that there is indeed a singular divine reality to which human beings respond and have responded variously throughout their history. As noted earlier, we mean by "divine reality" that which is ultimate in meaning and value – in Paul Tillich's terminology, that which presents itself to us as the object of our "ultimate concern." This divine reality is conceived, and indeed experienced, differently in different cultures, different religions, and different historical epochs. Indeed, as even a superficial review of the world's religions makes clear, profound differences are to be found even within the *same* religious tradition: Protestant and Catholic Christians, Mahayanist and Theravadin Buddhists, Sunni and Shia Muslims, each have distinctive, and often conflicting, views of the meaning and import of their common religious heritage. It seems to be the very nature of the divine to become *refracted* upon entering human experience, somewhat as white light is refracted when passing through a prism. Some will see the light as blue, some as red, some as yellow – but all are experiencing aspects of the same white light.

This observation leads us to our second suspicion: that the divine reality expresses itself, for the most part, *through* human beings, rather than directly *to* human beings. Thus, what we see when we look at the scripture, creeds, and practices of any given religious tradition are *products* of the divine–human encounter, not the divine as it is in and of itself. If you pour the ocean into a vial, the ocean will, of necessity, take upon itself the shape of the vial. Similarly, the religions of the world are manifestations of the divine as "poured into" a particular people at a particular historical moment, shaped by the specific concerns and conditions that characterize that people at that moment. This is what accounts for the great diversity we see across religious traditions, and, indeed, within them.

The third suspicion, a correlate of the second, is that the various religions of the world are *imperfect* products of this divine–human encounter – "imperfect" in the sense that they do not afford us an unmediated and unmitigated view of the divine *as such*, but rather contain, in their diverse and limited ways, what we might call "evidences" of the divine, evidences that we must tease out, sort through, and make sense of in order to achieve a fuller understanding.

This way of thinking about religion stands in decided contrast to the view that some one religion has been directly, and uniquely, revealed by God and that, therefore, all other religions are, at best, pale reflections, or, at worst, demonic imposters, of the one and only true religion.[1] Our suspicion is that this exclusivist view is itself but one way of experiencing the divine – a way shaped by the particular interests and concerns of the people who have adopted it.

I believe that strong arguments can be made for these three suspicions, arguments that appeal not only to religious phenomena as they have appeared throughout the centuries but also to the authoritative writings of many of the traditional religions themselves when we read them with discernment. Wilfred Cantwell Smith, John Hick, and other religious pluralists have cogently presented such arguments, and so I won't rehearse them here. What we might next consider, however, are the implications that acceptance of these suspicions has for the practice of theology. How do we engage in a "theology without walls?"

The practice of theology without walls

The purpose of theology in general is to provide the cognitive framework for our spiritual pursuits. If, again, we understand spiritual life as the endeavor to put us in touch with the object of our "ultimate concern," then we turn to theology in order to answer three basic questions regarding this endeavor. *First*: What is the true character of our "ultimate concern," that is, what is it we seek when we seek "the divine?" *Second*: What is the true nature of the *object* of our ultimate concern? What *is* "the divine?" *Third*: In what way (or ways) can genuine communion with the divine be achieved? How can our ultimate concern be satisfied? Clearly, the purpose of answering the first two questions is for the sake of answering the third.

As we have discussed, the way these questions have been traditionally approached is through appeal to the authoritative teachings of whatever religious tradition one happens to subscribe to. Thus, Theravadin Buddhists, appealing to the Four Noble Truths, will identify our ultimate concern with the need to overcome the suffering (*dukkha*) that arises from clinging to the ephemeral; they will identify the object of ultimate concern with the nirvanic state in which such clinging is eradicated; and they will identify the way to communion with the object of ultimate concern (in this case, the way to nirvana) as the Eightfold Path.

Likewise, Christians, appealing to Scripture, will identify our ultimate concern with the desire for eternal life; they will identify the object of ultimate concern as the triune God, revealed through Christ; and they will identify the way to communion with that object as faith in Christ, however this may be envisioned.

The underlying assumption of these theological approaches is that the authoritative teachings and writings of one's particular tradition are, indeed, *legitimately* authoritative. This is an assumption that is, for the most part, accepted on the basis of faith. The theologian's aim is not so much to question, or even evaluate, the legitimacy of these authoritative teachings and writings, but to interpret them cogently and apply them effectively. Of course, one may also question their legitimacy, but to do so is generally to step outside the theological circle of one's own tradition and risk being labeled a heretic or apostate.

But if the suspicions of theology without walls are correct, this approach, though appropriate within its limits, will tend to obscure the greater picture of the divine–human encounter. What is needed, then, is a sea change – or what John Hick has called a "Copernican revolution" – in the way we think about religion and approach theology. As Hick expresses it, traditionally each religion has tended to see itself at the center of the religious universe. The Copernican revolution he calls for involves recognizing that the divine itself is at the center and that each religion revolves around this center, receiving what light it does in a manner accordant with its distinctive orientation to it.

When we take the assumptions, or suspicions, of theology without walls seriously, we realize that we must change our understanding of both the *locus* and the *weight* of religious authority. These changes entail a shift from what might be called "dogmatic faith" to what I have come to think of as "Socratic faith." Let's take a closer look at the nature of this shift.

The locus and weight of religious authority: toward a "Socratic faith"

Let's first consider the *weight* of religious authority. If religious scripture is now understood as the imperfect product of the divine–human encounter, we must abandon doctrines that claim the inerrancy or infallibility of scripture. A theology without walls must advance a doctrine of scriptural and doctrinal *fallibility*. This does not mean that we must cease to regard scripture as inspired in some sense. But we must recognize that inspired scripture will partake of the flaws and limitations of the inspired human beings who produce it. Such a doctrine would lead to what might be called a *dialectical*, as opposed to a dogmatic, engagement with scripture.

In a dialectical approach we wrestle with scripture, question scripture, challenge scripture, and allow what we find in scripture to challenge and question us. The aim of the dialectic is not to finally reconcile ourselves to whatever we find in scripture, but to allow the dialectical process itself to conduct us into a fuller communion with the divine. Perhaps, in the course of this, we will find passages that we must reject as inadequate, or even perverse. We may reject such passages after due consideration, understanding that our final allegiance is to the divine and not to this or that imperfect reflection of the divine.

Such an approach naturally opens one to engagement with religious traditions beyond one's own, through which one can expand and enrich one's dialectical practice. Thus, one might consider the relationship between the Buddhist idea of *tanha* (craving, clinging) and the Christian idea of *concupiscence*, or the relationship between *nirvana* and *eternal life* as spiritual aspirations.

The purpose of such comparisons is not merely to promote understanding between religions, but, more fundamentally, to seek the nugget of divine truth that may be contained in these different traditions and thereby achieve a more complete apprehension of that truth.

But it may be asked: Where are we to find the *locus* of authority in such an approach? How are we to know, what criteria are we to bring to bear in deciding, whether or not we are moving closer to truth or further away?

This question, it might be noted, is as salient for traditional theology as for theology without walls. How does the traditional theologian know that his or her theological interpretations are apt? Even the dedicated dogmatist will have to give an account, if she is at all reflective, of the grounds upon which she accepts what dogma she does. Such an account, if it is to avoid tautology, cannot simply appeal to dogma for its justification. Ultimately, then, it is *we* who must function as the locus of authority for the truth claims we accept; that is, our intuitions, our discernment, our analyses, our honest assessments of what is true and good – which, ideally, we do not adhere to uncritically, but submit to the dialectical process through which we hope to make them progressively better.

But it may be asked: How can we trust to our fallible selves what is of *utmost* importance, of *ultimate* concern?

It is here, I would say, that something like faith comes in. Just as theology without walls entails a particular understanding of the locus and weight of religious authority, so it entails a particular kind of faith. The faith demanded by a theology without walls is what I have come to think of as *Socratic faith*. At his trial, Socrates was accused of denying the gods of Athens, a charge leveled against him in response to his skeptical questioning of traditional Athenian beliefs. But he disputes this charge. He responds, "I do believe that there are gods, and in a far higher sense than that in which any of my accusers believe in them" (Plato 1973, 464–465). But what can this mean? Are there higher and lower ways to believe in the gods?

I suggest that the "higher sense of belief" to which Socrates here refers is not belief as *affirmation* of this or that propositional claim, but belief as *dedication* to what is ultimately true and good; a dedication that entails, at the same time, the humble admission that one's apprehension of the true and the good, at any given moment, is incomplete and fallible and therefore in constant need of critical evaluation and correction.

At his trial, Socrates tells the famous story of being designated the wisest man in Athens by the Oracle at Delphi, but only because he is the only one who "knows that he doesn't know." Socrates says, "The truth is, O men of Athens, that God only is wise; and in this oracle he means to say that the wisdom of men is little or nothing" (Plato 1973, 452).

But it must be immediately pointed out that this conclusion does not lead Socrates to a resigned skepticism or nihilism. On the contrary, for Socrates, the continual pursuit of a wisdom that can never be perfectly seized is itself a form of worship, a sublime mode of engagement with the divine. And indeed, he does admit to having what he calls "a certain sort of wisdom . . . If you ask me what kind of wisdom, I reply, such wisdom as is attainable by man, for to that extent I am inclined to believe that I am wise" (Plato 1973, 450).

The sort of wisdom attainable by human beings is approximate wisdom, tentative wisdom, wisdom that must be ever open to review, reevaluation, supplementation, and correction. For Socrates, this confession of uncertainty does not make one less but more open to the divine, for it frees us from the idolatry of taking our own limited representations of the divine as sacrosanct.

Socrates thus takes it to be his divinely ordained mission to probe and question, critique and scrutinize: "For this is the command of God, as I would have you know, and I believe that to this day no greater good has happened to the state than my service to the God" (Plato 1973, 459). His faith is that the divine endorses this (necessarily) error-prone approach and accepts us in our limitations and fallibilities. Its demand of us is not that we cling to this or that dogmatic formula in denial of our limitations, but that we humbly pursue the true and the good in an honest and genuine way.

Finally, it might be noted that this mode of faith does not at all exclude full-fledged involvement and investment in one particular religious path. To recognize that there are many paths is not at all to imply that one should abandon the path one is on. But it does entail a new understanding of the status of one's path, especially in its relation to others. Should this new understanding gain acceptance, should the religions of the world come to see themselves as different movements in response to the same divine reality, this itself would have a transformative effect upon religion in general. It would bring us that much closer to an appreciation of the universality of truth proclaimed by all the major religious traditions.

Conclusion: in spirit and truth

Let us conclude then by recalling the story of the Samaritan woman who asks Jesus whether the proper place of worship is in Samaria or Jerusalem. The Samaritans and the Jews were hostile religious antagonists, each group claiming exclusive possession of the divine truth bequeathed to the ancient Israelites at Sinai, each accusing the other of distortion, corruption, error, and bad faith. Of course, the rivalry between the Samaritans and the Jews is but one instance of a great legion of such religious rivalries – rivalries that have plagued humanity over the long course of its religious history.

But if we posit that divine truth is *One*, at least in in its ultimate nature, then these antagonistic schisms between (and within) the different religions – violent antagonisms that have led such critics as Christopher Hitchens to deem religion itself "poisonous" – must be seen as some indication of revelatory failure, that is, the failure of revelation to communicate itself effectively to human beings. Such religious rivalries and antagonisms appear symptomatic of our failure to orient ourselves rightly to the divine.

From this perspective, theology without walls may be seen as inspired by a new revelatory moment, a moment that calls us to abandon our narrow parochialism and open ourselves to the wide expanse of the divine–human encounter. My suggestion, in other words, is that theology without walls as a practice and, indeed, as a commitment *itself* betokens a new revelation of the divine, one that, like all such revelations when they are authentic, has its own soteriological power: in this case, the power to resolve the tribalistic rivalries and chauvinistic hostilities that have plagued religious humanity for so long and thereby bring us closer to a recognition of the divine as *One*.

And, as we have seen, we can find the seeds of this new moment already embedded within the traditional religions themselves: "An hour is coming when neither in this mountain nor in Jerusalem will you worship the Father," says Jesus, "An hour is coming, and now is, when the true worshippers will worship in spirit and truth; for such people the Father seeks to be His worshippers. God is spirit, and those who worship Him must worship in spirit and truth."

To worship in spirit and truth is to transcend the boundaries that condition religious hostility. Those who do so, Jesus suggests, will come to see the contingent nature of such boundaries and will rise above them to a fuller and more genuine encounter with the God who would be "All in All."

Note

1 Karl Barth writes, for instance, that only Christianity has the authority "to confront the world of religions as the one true religion, with absolute self-confidence to invite and challenge it to abandon its ways and to start on the Christian ways" from *Church Dogmatics*, as quoted in Hick (1982, 8).

References

Hick, John. 1982. *God Has Many Names*. Philadelphia: The Westminster Press.

Plato. 1973. "Apology." In *The Republic and Other Works*, trans. Benjamin Jowett, 450, 452, 459, 464–465. Garden City: Anchor Press/Doubleday.

Thatamanil, John. 2016. "'True To and True For': The Problem and Promise of Religious Truth for a Theology Without Walls." *Journal of Ecumenical Studies* 51 (4): 456. doi:10.1353/ecu.2016.0041

3 Revisiting Bellah's Sheila in a religiously pluralist century

Christopher Denny

Scholars of religion only know her by her first name, Sheila, which is just as well because Sheila is a pseudonym, a cipher, a symbol for a phenomenon that has been described in different terms since Sheila came to the attention of readers over 30 years ago. For scholars influenced by the work of Philip Rieff (1987), Sheila's worldview may be judged to encapsulate "the triumph of the therapeutic" in which psychology subverts the older strictures of religiosity. Sheila probably qualifies as one of the baby-boomer seekers profiled in the writings of Wade Clark Roof (1993, 1999). Then again, with her fusion of spirituality and individualism Sheila would be amenable to being typecast as one of those who are "spiritual but not religious" analyzed in the work of sociologist Robert Fuller (2001). Finally, even though she predates the advent of the millennial generation, Sheila certainty seems like one of the "nones," that growing cohort of young adults who in the early twenty-first century self-consciously decline to affiliate themselves with organized religion (Drescher 2016).

To know Sheila Larson is to judge her, because that is how Robert Bellah and his co-authors presented her to readers in their influential 1985 book *Habits of the Heart* – as a person to be judged and found wanting. Recounting the presentation in Chapter 9 of the book, readers are given the following information. Sheila states that she believes in God but cannot remember when she last went to church. She has faith in her own little voice, an internal guide that tells her to love herself and to be gentle with herself. Sheila's little voice urges her to remember that we are supposed to "take care of each other." Sheila describes her faith in the most individualized and self-centered term possible – Sheilaism. In Bellah's telling, Sheila is "sufficiently paradigmatic" to be employed as a composite sketch for the privatization of religion in the United States in the latter half of the twentieth century. Moreover, Bellah asserted that many churchgoing Protestants and Catholics are "Sheilaists" who do not see either the Christian Bible or church traditions as normative and authoritative in the way in which they live their religious lives.

DOI: 10.4324/9780429000973-5

"How do we, in a pluralist society," Bellah asked an audience in 1986, "avoid the radical individualism expressed by Sheila?" For Bellah, individualism is a problem, especially for religion:

> Just the notion that religious belief ought to be a purely internal thing, and then you go to the church or synagogue of your choice, shows how deeply ingrained a kind of religious privatism is, which turns the church into something like the Kiwanis Club or some other kind of voluntary association that you go to or not if you feel comfortable with it – but which has no organic claim upon you.
>
> (Bellah 1986)

What is interesting is that in *Habits of the Heart* Bellah and his co-authors came to a mixed appraisal of individualism in American life, recognizing it as a social force that had shaped American religion since its founding. For the authors, individualism, with its exaltation of self-reliance and hard work, had a place in our country so long as it is checked by offsetting social trajectories that nurture the afflicted while providing civic unity. In this line of thought, the "biblical tradition" and the religious communities that have fostered it are tasked with orienting their members towards a transcendent reality that gives a moral justification for our national experiment in ordered liberty. The authors of *Habits of the Heart*, then, prescribed a specific cultural role for religion in late twentieth-century American life, and Sheila did not help religion perform that necessary pedagogical role of counterbalancing the rough-and-tumble world of individualistic capitalist acquisition. Given these expectations for religion, Bellah was correct in sensing a threat to the biblical tradition's place in our national social fabric.

Every crisis presents itself simultaneously as a problem and as an opportunity. Rather than joining in the chorus of those who see religious individualism and the decline of churches' social influence primarily as a problem, I choose to see the Sheilas of the world as providing contemporary societies with opportunities as well, and the Theology Without Walls (TWW) initiative outlined in this present book's contributions seconds that hope. It does adherents of traditional religion little good to complain about the rise of individualism if they hope to change this state of affairs in the future. In what follows I offer two personal anecdotes and accompanying theological reflection that illustrate how religious individualism can manifest itself in ways that point groups to a different type of unity than the "civil religion" outlined in Bellah's (1967) work. In each case my encounter with a student upset cherished scholarly approaches to categorizing religious differences and enabled me to see pluralism in new ways for which I was unprepared.

First encounter: moving beyond positions to people

Years ago during my first year in graduate studies I worked as a research assistant and was asked to proofread and review a very long dissertation on the recent history of ecumenical dialogue in the United States between representatives of the Roman Catholic Church and a mainline Protestant denomination that I will not name now in order to keep the dissertation's author anonymous. Over the course of hundreds of pages, the author detailed the times, places, delegation members, and program titles of successive meetings between the theologians designated to carry out a particular rapprochement in the years immediately succeeding the Second Vatican Council's close in 1965. In workmanlike prose, the dissertation included details about hotel venues, meeting schedules, and alternating responses to conference prompts. After reading halfway through the dissertation, I noticed that many of the Catholic participants in these meetings either left the priesthood or the Catholic Church over the years during which the dialogue proceeded in the 1960s and 1970s, to be replaced by other representatives. I began to ask myself why in this dissertation there was no direct reference to this trend and no examination of the reasons for the systemic departure of many of the Catholic participants in this series of ecumenical dialogues.

To fault the student for this omission would be short sighted, for both the genre of the dissertation itself and the assumptions undergirding most interreligious dialogues justified this caesura. The dominant framework of most formal ecumenical and interreligious dialogues conducted since the start of the ecumenical era in the early twentieth century posits the stable existence of two or more reified religious communities whose goal is to achieve at least tolerance, hopefully respect, and maybe – if the dialogue is really ambitious – intercommunion or an institutional merger. Each side in these dialogues comes to the table in order to reconcile past traditions and normative doctrines, assumed as a given, with openness to new developments and the experiences of others outside the home church. The participation of dialogue partners is sanctioned by authorities within their respective communities. When seen in this manner, interreligious dialogue is basically analogous to a summit meeting between leaders and ambassadors of two sovereign nations, with a heavy dollop of public relations and face-saving techniques required. When one or more of the dialogue groups in such activity is Christian, ecclesiocentric interpretations of religious and theological traditions are privileged as a matter of course. As an example of this "summit" understanding of interreligious dialogue, consider Roman Catholic magisterial documents such as *Dialogue and Mission* and *Dialogue and Promulgation*, published in 1984 and 1991 by the Secretariat for Non-Christians, which promote interreligious dialogue. These texts, however, are mostly focused upon developing the Catholic Church's own self-understanding. When the Congregation for the Doctrine of the Faith published *Dominus Jesus: On the Unicity and Salvific Universality of Jesus Christ and the Church* in 2000, this inward-looking ecclesial trend became even more apparent (Pontifical Council for Interreligious Dialogue 1984, 1991; Congregation for the Doctrine of the Faith 2000; Denny 2017).

An examination of dialogue from the standpoints of the existential experiences of the partners, maybe even a partner like Sheila, however, would yield a very different account of such dialogues. Granted, such dialogues would no longer qualify as official ecumenical conversations, given that the Sheilas of the world generally abjure representing any spiritual view other than their own. Structuring dialogues instead around the axes of individual persons' search for truth and ultimacy, deliberately subordinating concerns about institutional boundaries and doctrinal consistency with the past, removes the need to save face. Or to put the matter in a different frame of reference, dialogue in a TWW does not begin by presuming the theological stability of competing doctrinal boundary markers as *a priori* obstacles that need to be reconciled through logical consistency. This is not because the TWW initiative shuns logic or the need for clear thought. Rather, the issue that TWW chooses to begin with is relevance, not consistency. In a world marked by religious individualism, ensuring that ecumenical and interreligious dialogue is relevant to the lives of people today must be the initial issue in learning to converse across religious boundaries. Not to begin with the concrete existential situations of contemporary people risks creating more dialogues like the one I encountered in the dissertation draft decades ago: officially structured formal conversations whose value becomes less compelling, even to those taking part in the dialogue.

Kurt Richardson has identified the necessity within our current interreligious situation very well. He writes:

> Heightened by our current deinstitutionalized situation, a central place is taken by religious experience – the experience of faith disengaging more than ever from institutional forms and ritual structures in favor of authenticity – something approaching "first-order" experience of God . . . This situation of disaffiliation is a hermeneutical condition for "theology without walls" or "trans-religious" theology.
>
> (Richardson 2016, 508)

Much of the impulse for beginning interreligious dialogue with doctrines and institutional prerogatives stems from the Enlightenment-era development, termed confessionalization by historians, by which different Christian churches distinguished themselves from one another by developing creedal formulations and competing structures of ecclesial authority. Within the milieu of early modern Europe, uniform definitions of belief were the intellectual currency of the age, and personal religious experience was denigrated as idiosyncratic, superstitious, and backward. When Gotthold Lessing (1956, 53; emphasis in original) could levy his famous charge, *"accidental truths of history can never become the proof of necessary truths of reason,"* the unrepeatable singularity of personal experience was discredited as well, as post-Cartesian Western religion sought to pattern itself after the recurring standardized proofs of mathematics and the measurable laws of natural science.[1] Bellah's Sheila does not expect anyone else to replicate her own spiritual worldview, but there are others who haven't given up hope that religious experience may be something more than a noncognitive realm. Richardson asserts, "The self as locus of truth is not of necessity relativistic at all," and he makes this claim in light of his additional position: "The self as locus of truth does not mean the self as the source of truth" (Richardson 2016, 511, 512). Perhaps Sheila's personal credo emanates from a source outside her? Adjudicating this issue leads me to the next turning point in my religious conversion.

Second encounter: embracing one's inner religious consumer

The second major turning point in my spiritual journey involving an encounter outside my home tradition was at first glance a very prosaic one and didn't involve any famous thinkers or profound world-historical transformation. In fact, it did not entail an encounter with another religious tradition in the familiar sense, but rather an experience that I think marks a challenge to all religious traditions as we have known them. The year was 2004, and I was in my first semester teaching at St. John's University in New York City. I had been assigned to teach Theology 2210: Perspectives on the Church before my arrival, and as a freshly minted PhD I came armed with a detailed lesson plan for the course. Much of our time was devoted to examining the role of the Church in salvation and ecumenism. Towards the semester's end we studied different soteriological typologies along the lines of the now well-known schema set forth by Alan Race and followed by many others in the theology of religions – exclusivism, inclusivism, and pluralism (Race 1983). Those familiar with the Roman Catholic magisterial approach to these paths since Vatican II know that its overall judgment on these positions is exclusivism, bad though dominant through most of the Church's history; inclusivism, good; pluralism, very, very bad, especially if you are a Catholic theologian teaching at a Catholic university. Eager to have students weigh in on this debate in the latter half of the course, I gave them the following assignment:

> Vatican II's Decree on Ecumenism states that division among Christians should be a cause for scandal, as it is a contradiction of God's plan of salvation. For your **final paper** I would like you to enunciate what you yourself identify as the principal causes of religious division, not merely among Christians, but among all peoples. Do you think that the multiplicity of churches and religions is a good thing? Or do you perceive it to be a stumbling block that we must overcome? Do you have any concrete ideas as to how religious divisions can be healed? As a student in New York City three years after September 11, in what ways do you think greater cooperation and harmony between peoples of different religions can be achieved?

There was a student in this course whom I will call Derek (not his real name). Derek was, by conventional standards, anything but a model student – his attendance was sporadic, he failed exams, and his essays were poor. During most classes he sat by himself near a window with his feet propped up on an adjacent chair. He ended up failing the course. Yet Derek transformed the trajectory of the class through his participation in our discussions on this assigned topic. Not having applied the insights I gleaned from my reflections on the very long dissertation on ecumenical dialogue I've already mentioned, I burst onto the teaching scene in my new academic home expecting students to have a personal stake in arguments pitting inclusivism against pluralism. I expected the students to assess the ecumenical landscape from the well-worn perspective of institutional unity vs. diversity. Rahner vs. Hick. Robert Bellarmine vs. Paul Knitter (Bellarmine 2016; Rahner 1966, 1976, 1979; Hick 1982; Knitter 1985). Derek, and the students whom he managed to persuade in the course of the semester, torpedoed my assumptions about ecumenical and interreligious relations and convinced me that much of the scholarship on the theology of religions from the 1970s and 1980s was not only dated but also obsolete.

So, what was Derek's trailblazing contribution to Theology 2210? Derek didn't see the unity or diversity of religions or their soteriological efficacy as an issue. That is not simply to say that he didn't understand religious unity or religious pluralism as the *primary* issue in interreligious dialogue. Rather, Derek judged that this issue was downright irrelevant; what mattered instead according to Derek was each individual's preferences in religious belief and practice, nothing more. Ecumenical efforts to achieve religious unity were a waste of time for him and those peers adopting his articulated stance. If everyone wanted the same religion, so be it. If no one preferred a religious path, hey, who was to judge anyone else? Prodding the class in our final few weeks of the semester, I asked them if such a stance reduced religion to the level of a commodity or a consumer good, and I hoped that by phrasing the issue in this way they might reconsider. But, lo and behold, they seized upon this analogy, which I had intended to be derogatory, and agreed enthusiastically with this comparison: yes, professor, that's it, religion is a lifestyle choice just like that.

Now for those familiar with the sociological work of Christian Smith, whose recent work has traced the path by which Protestant Christianity in the United States has moved from post-Reformation denunciations of works-righteousness to what Smith calls "moralistic therapeutic deism," Derek's assertion will be familiar. Smith, along with William Cavanaugh and others, have derided this development over the past two decades (Miller 2003; Smith and Denton 2005; Cavanaugh 2008). There are many Dereks now, and the consumerist approach to religion calls into question basic assumptions about religious unity and diversity that governed academic research in these fields right up until the end of the last century.

It may be offensive to religious studies scholars and practitioners of religion to suggest that there is a positive side to the marriage between consumerist ideology and interreligious dialogue. I understand that, and I emphatically reject any necessary connections between this recognition – and the near-inevitable trajectory of this development in secular capitalist postmodern societies – and prescriptive consequences for political and economic practice. But I ask you, doesn't Derek have a point? If we are to appreciate the value of individual autonomy in religious inquiry, shouldn't we recognize that there is a common denominator between choosing a religion and choosing a brand of cereal – namely, that in both cases there is a human agent making the choice? This is the point at the heart of the rational-choice theory of religion offered by scholars such as Rodney Stark, Roger Finke, and Laurence Iannaccone (Stark and Bainbridge 1985, 1996; Iannaccone 1998; Finke and Stark 2005). And if we acknowledge the inescapable reality of agency and transformative constructions of religious worldviews in light of human choice, might the turn to the consumer in late modernity prompt us to invert the *ordo* of much comparative theology? Why do people who are able to do so choose one spiritual path over another? Why do they choose to follow one route on their spiritual map and not others that might lead to the same destination? Sincere guardians of tradition like Smith and Cavanaugh bemoan this consumerist development, but we must recognize that all the so-called great religious traditions are in large part the result of choices made by influential leaders and their followers. Now more democratic forms of politics and more egalitarian social structures make these choices less constricted for a wider segment of the human population, including people like Robert Bellah's eponymous Sheila.

Unlike relativism, TWW need not concede that all religious preferences are equal in existential value or, if we choose to introduce this framework, soteriological efficacy. Participants in a theology without walls can come to think that certain theological options are dead-ends or meandering one-lane roads that are unhelpful or inefficient in spiritual journeys. By not precluding the possibility that a participant in religious dialogue can come to the table without representing any group or institution beyond himself or herself, however, TWW need not be threatened by the metaphor of the spiritual marketplace. We can see the marketplace as a place of possibility, not as a prison governed by ironclad rules of determinism or economic efficacy. In a 1974 address, "Map Is Not Territory," the late Jonathan Z. Smith called for a critical reassessment of reified notions of sacred space, claiming that an earlier generation of scholars in the history of religion had often uncritically conflated experience and interpretation (Smith 1978). A map may be all we have to find our way, Smith said, but all maps are necessarily interpretive documents.

If this is so in the realm of geography, it is all the truer in matters of religious agency. No religion has ever existed upon earth without religious adherents constructing its traditions, rituals, and doctrines; appealing to divine or superhuman origins for such facets of religion does not obviate this assertion, as whatever origin to which religious practitioners appeal is inevitably mediated through human interpretation. Adapting Richardson's formulation noted earlier, the self is a locus of truth even when the source of truth may lie elsewhere. To formulate a theology of religions without fore-grounding human choice is to regress to a naïve religious era in which the role of human subjectivity was often passed over in silence and in which religious traditions were reified without an appreciation of historical conscious-ness and the processes of sociological change. Because one's "spiritual map" is not composed from a God's-eye perspective surveying the whole of reality, the recognition of preferences provides theology with a new starting place from which to engage the bewildering array of religious options available to us as we push our existential shopping carts through the aisles of reality. We can even, to extend the metaphor, push our carts through the walls of exist-ing traditions. In doing so, there is no guarantee our spiritual choices will be intellectually coherent, morally defensible, or spiritually attractive to others. My metaphor of the shopping cart is not designed to defend the content of our spiritual choices, but rather to acknowledge that the spiritualities we carry forth in our lives are there because we placed them in our carts. This is true whether we choose to adopt a classic religious tradition or forge a new idiosyncratic path. Whatever mistakes we make, they will be our own. In that sense, we are all Sheilas.

Note

1 For an argument that identifies diminishing theological returns on the strategy of confessionalization, see Buckley (2004).

References

Bellah, Robert N. 1967. "Civil Religion in America." *Daedalus, Journal of the American Academy of Arts and Sciences* 96 (1): 1–21.

Bellah, Robert N. 1986. "Habits of the Heart: Implications for Religion," lecture at St. Mark's Catholic Church, Isla Vista, California, February 21. www.robertbel lah.com/lectures_5.htm (accessed September 4, 2019).

Bellarmine, Robert. 2016. *On the Church Militant.* Trans. Ryan Grant. Post Falls, ID: Mediatrix Press.

Buckley, Michael J. 2004. *Denying and Disclosing God: The Ambiguous Progress of Modern Atheism.* New Haven: Yale University Press.

Cavanaugh, William T. 2008. *Being Consumed: Economics and Christian Desire.* Grand Rapids, MI: Eerdmans University press.

Congregation for the Doctrine of the Faith. 2000. "Declaration 'Dominus Iesus': On the Unicity and Salvific Universality of Jesus Christ and the Church." www.vatican. va/roman_curia/congregations/cfaith/documents/rc_con_cfaith_doc_20000806_ dominus-iesus_en.html.

Denny, Christopher. 2017. "Religiones Antiquae: Reviving Nostra Aetate to Expand the Scope of Salvation 'History'." *The Journal of Interreligious Studies* 20: 29–37.

Drescher, Elizabeth. 2016. *Choosing Our Religion: The Spiritual Lives of America's Nones*. New York: Oxford University Press. doi:10.1093/acprof:oso/97801 99341221.003.0001

Finke, Roger, and Rodney Stark. 2005. *The Churching of America, 1776–2005: Winners and Losers in Our Religious Economy*. rev. ed. New Brunswick, NJ: Rutgers University Press. doi:10.1086/ahr/99.1.288

Fuller, Robert C. 2001. *Spiritual, but Not Religious: Understanding Unchurched America*. New York: Oxford University Press. doi:10.1086/427015

Hick, John. 1982. *God Has Many Names*. Philadelphia: Westminster.

Iannaccone, Laurence. 1998. "Introduction to the Economics of Religion." *Journal of Economic Literature* 36 (3): 1465–1495.

Knitter, Paul. 1985. *No Other Name? A Critical Survey of Christian Attitudes toward the World Religions*. Maryknoll, NY: Orbis.

Lessing, Gotthold. 1956. "On the Proof of the Spirit and Power." In *Lessing's Theological Writings*, edited by Henry Chadwick, 53. Stanford: Stanford University Press.

Miller, Vincent J. 2003. *Consuming Religion: Christian Faith and Practice in a Consumer Culture*. New York: Continuum.

Pontifical Council for Interreligious Dialogue. 1984. "Dialogue and Mission." www.pcinterreligious.org/search?str=dialogue+and+mission.

Pontifical Council for Interreligious Dialogue. 1991. "Dialogue and Proclamation." www.vatican.va/roman_curia/pontifical_councils/interelg/documents/rc_pc_inte relg_doc_19051991_dialogue-and-proclamatio_en.html.

Race, Alan. 1983. *Christians and Religious Pluralism: Patterns in the Christian Theology of Religions*. London: SCM Press. doi:10.1017/s0034412500016474

Rahner, Karl. 1966. "Christianity and the Non-Christian Religions." In *Theological Investigations*, vol. 6, *Later Writings*, trans. Karl H. Kruger, 115–134. Baltimore: Helicon.

Rahner, Karl. 1976. "Observations on the Problem of the 'Anonymous Christian'." In *Theological Investigations*, vol. 14, *Theology, Anthropology, Christology*, trans. David Bourke, 280–294. New York: Seabury.

Rahner, Karl. 1979. "The One Christ and the Universality of Salvation." In *Theological Investigations*, vol. 16, *Experience of the Spirit: Source of Theology*, trans. David Morland, 199–224. New York: Seabury.

Richardson, Kurt. 2016. "Theology Without Walls: Toward a Hermeneutics Without Boundaries?" *Journal of Ecumenical Studies* 51 (4): 506–516. doi:10.1353/ecu.2016.0046

Rieff, Philip. 1987. *The Triumph of the Therapeutic: Uses of Faith After Freud*. 2nd ed. Chicago: University of Chicago Press.

Roof, Wade Clark. 1993. *A Generation of Seekers: Spiritual Journeys of the Baby Boom Generation*. San Francisco: Harper San Francisco.

Roof, Wade Clark. 1999. *Spiritual Marketplace: Baby Boomers and the Remaking of American Religion*. Princeton: Princeton University Press. doi:10.11 77/004057360205900131

Smith, Christian, and Melinda Lundquist Denton. 2005. *Soul Searching: The Religious and Spiritual Lives of American Teenagers*. New York: Oxford University Press. doi:10.1080/00344080701657931

Smith, Jonathan Z. 1978. "Map Is Not Territory." In *Map Is Not Territory: Studies in the History of Religions*, edited by Jonathan Z. Smith, 289–310. Chicago: University of Chicago Press.

34   *Christopher Denny*

Stark, Rodney, and William Sims Bainbridge. 1985. *The Future of Religion: Secularization, Revival, and Cult Formation.* Berkeley, CA: University of California Press. doi:10.2307/3165483

Stark, Rodney, and William Sims Bainbridge. 1996. *A Theory of Religion.* New Brunswick, NJ: Rutgers University Press.

4 Theology Without Walls as open-field theology[1]

Kurt Anders Richardson

Although all theologies are perspectival, "hermeneutical theology" intends a meta-discourse about theological practices and their contexts in relation. Theology Without Walls (TWW) seeks simultaneously to coordinate discursive spaces with no theological limitations while at the same time tolerating no intrusions upon the natural "walls" of the inviolate mind, conscience, and body of every human being, of every theologian. I regard TWW as a hermeneutical space or field of discourse that explores twenty-first-century conditions of doing theology where Christian "religion" and particularly "denomination" (of institutions, creeds, and canons) was historically enlisted to define and to implement theological sovereignty over other connected institutions as government, particularly over the fields of law and science. This hermeneutical space "without walls" makes possible something like open-field theology (OFT) to indicate the constructive hermeneutical project of "theology" as a comprehensive, nonprescriptive association of theologians. TWW/OFT, in contrast to theological programs of "openness," "process," "naturalistic" or "traditional," etc., presupposes only that theologians might find "theology as an open field" a helpful and ultimately fruitful way to do any kind of theology: apophatic or cataphatic, theist or atheist, exclusivist or pluralist. By contrast, historic theologies imagine, through cultural memory, nostalgia, and various "traditionalisms" and "fundamentalisms" a recovery of such sovereignty as best for faith and religious life. TWW would come to the aid of many theologians from such backgrounds (there are many parallels of sovereign theology throughout the "world religions") who wish either to be free of such ambitions or at least wish to develop strategies of constructive theological engagement with contemporary theological conditions and trajectories. For some time TWW/OFT has been explored as a descriptive title, along with others such as "transreligious theology." Here, OFT is offered as a way that respects the very problem of "religion" as an increasingly inadequate term for all the ways that humans devote themselves to the divine or to the ultimate and to one another, often expressed through rational and systematic constructions as "theology" in the broadest possible terms. In this context, any discursive handling of divine or ultimate topics – across spectra of affirmations

DOI: 10.4324/9780429000973-6

and denials – qualify as kinds of theology. The theological commitments of the present author include TWW/OFT as an advantageous way of pursuing those commitments, confessional and otherwise.

One impetus to TWW/OFT is that many theological traditionalists argue for some fundamental reestablishment of these historic sovereignties and theologically reimagined "historic norms." This sovereign role of theology was, and for some still is, the canonically controlled mediation of divine revelation in the world. But such perspectives discount the long development of the principle of reform for theological flourishing that respects the irreducible diversity communities (denominations) of each of the religions. The reasons for hankering for sovereignty seem to be obvious, because government, law, and science are such powerful regulatory institutions that once included concepts of authority that included infallibility and absolute certitude of religious knowledge. But what happens when meta-discourses of science and law are forced to incorporate fallibility as essential to cognitive development and applied success? How are all theological practices to incorporate fallibility in their hermeneutical and conceptual models? TWW/OFT would propose theologies find their best environment in something like an open field of reflective anthropology where human perceptions and traditions of divinity and ultimacy can advance the work of those within traditions, as well as those who claim no religion.

The present author approaches its subject from the standpoint of a "lived theology" that is "ecumenically evangelical," "comparative," "Abrahamic," "postcolonial," and global in the pluralistic sense. TWW/OFT is open-ended and amenable to the challenge of rival interests and contrary opinions on the way to realizing benefits to any individual or collective theological endeavor. The very eclectic theological practices indicated in TWW/OFT are areas of serious exploration and learning for me. Each point of engagement in some way enriches the other and the "theological-self-in-community": interactive exposure, rational interchange, and imaginative engagement can take place with one's own tradition and in conversation with theologians of other or no traditions. I would add that the historical-theological frame of reference in this chapter is one aspect that TWW/OFT practitioners need to heed. Realizations as to the creative and influential futures of theology come by means of noticing how ancient TWW/OFT is. Trajectories in earlier theological movements provide us with plotlines that continue to contemporary construction.[2] Lived theology is more and more a matter of incorporating a spectrum of theological sources and goals. Hence, the hermeneutical desirability for a community field of discourse where multiple rationalities and theological priorities can find concourse, with no prescription for identifying "common ground," let alone solving "common problems." Within the religious liberty environments of the world, theology no longer provides a sovereign or regulative function for sociopolitical majorities through state-sponsored, privileged religions. Instead, the plural reality that began with the irreducible internal diversity of Christian theologies in the sixteenth century is now giving way to the irreducible external diversity of religions, each with its own internal theological diversity. TWW/OFT proposes that "external" theological learning is incumbent upon all theologians who would speak intelligibly about their own theological practices but also those of proximate others. TWW/OFT provides the working space for that proximity.

One helpful starting point for TWW/OFT is the nearly undefinable word "religion," from its Latin root "*religio*" ("to bind together") and the consequent boundaries constructed by religious belief, practice, identity, and state sponsorship. Theology is a form of discourse that specializes in discerning complex conceptualities that would "bind together" the divine and the human, the human and the human, the human and the nonhuman. Whereas theologies' deities are the transcendent, infinite being or real [p]³resence, all theology is human, from first to last a human enterprise. The very humanness of religions and their theologies subjects the history of human discourse on the divine with the problematic charge of anthropomorphizing and hypostatizing the infinite [m]ystery or being or existence.

Most of the participants currently in TWW/OFT are Western, mostly "Christian" in terms of theological traditions and their institutions of learning, quite "Western" in terms of sociopolitical models of human and communal ethics – insofar as the latter reflect theological reasoning. One of the most interesting and earliest of the boundary crossings of ancient Christian and Jewish theologies consisted of assertions against classical theologies of being and "supreme Being" and raises the issue of the divine as capable of novelty, rejecting the rejection of novelty according to its absolutely immutable "perfections."[4] Another boundary to be deconstructed in late antiquity (ca. fifth century BCE to the eighth century CE) was the Aristotelian categorization of the human female as ontologically inferior to the human male. Yet another dimension, still contested,[5] is the reality of divine and human volition – human decision making and the reality of choice as over and against any model of determinism. Finally, the eschatological assertion that the cosmos is on a pathway of amelioration rather than sheer annihilation is afforded helpful space by TWW/OFT.

The history of sovereign theologies for the regulation of legal and scientific reasoning is a massive legacy of the Christianized Roman Empire that exercises continuous, if much diminished, influence in theology. This was the original context for "political theology" – a theology for the polity and often mirroring the polity of religious majorities. Similar trends are visible in many different religious contexts. Certainly, one of the most seriously limiting walls in the history of Christian theology was its polemical theologies aimed at bringing the highly diversified Christian, Jewish, and other religious theological movements of late antiquity into "catholic order" of "orthodox" insiders and heterodox outsiders. By the sixth century, very intentional boundaries barred "interrituality" in order to separate Christians from all Jewish ritual observances as asserted on pain of excommunication. Creating and attaching to every Jewish person and community the theologically defined charge of "deicide" was certainly the nadir of the entire theological heritage of so-called "religious crimes" defined by Roman law on behalf of its *religio licita* ("legal religion"). What began with antiheretical (*contra haereticos*) literature for the early construction of anti-Jewish theology (tractates known as "*Contra Iudaios*") was part of and yet distinct from the larger branch of polemical theology known as "*Contra Gentes* (/*Gentiles*)" – which included multiple tractates opposed to and condemning the religion of Islam. The religious monotheism adopted by Rome, as well as other polities, that constitutionally established Christianity endures into the twenty-first century.[6] This heritage of sovereign theology (Yelle 2018), along with many other dimensions of the "world's largest religion," presents multiple ongoing barriers to critical and constructive theological practices.

Political, legal, and scientific boundaries not only define but also plague most theologies, internally and externally. Although the deities, anthropologies, and cosmologies of the religions betray striking differences, many of their hermeneutical moves, especially as each interacts with other religions and theologies, are quite similar, as comparative theology has shown. As a Hindu or Jewish scripture scholar works with a constellation of beliefs about the divine origin of a sacred text, the humanity of the reader/listener, and the relation between human cognition and its "divine" or "ultimate" referent, one must ask about the critical and constructive purpose of theology. Crucial to this assessment is the recognition of the radical resources that the history of theology can hint at. But these efforts are moot if the expansive and varied potentialities of theology are curtailed through the imposition of constrictive, even destructive, boundaries preventing genuinely liberative and life-enhancing theological construction.

"Revelation," legal and scientific walls, and OFT

The history of every theology begins with a revelation claim of some sort – the deity has conveyed its presence through some natural mediation, usually oracular or prophetic, the presence of the divine, and the divine word and image. Conveying "divine revelation" and epistemologies that included "revelation claims" correlates very closely with transcendent philosophical claims of illumination and higher-order perceptions and knowledges. Plato's "Allegory of the Cave"[7] is a kind of narrative theology of revelation and revelatory experience. In Scripture, "prophets" narratives, via multiple genres but all metaphorically and stylistically rich, have become "inscripturated" forms of the immediately revealed word and image. Revealed word and image, regarded as captured in sacred scriptures and ritual objects, required constant interpretation in reinterpretation in successive generations of believing communities. The history of "modern theology" of the last five centuries globally displays hermeneutical and even substantive learning and borrowing across religious and cultural boundaries. One of the attractions of comparative theology is to trace whatever can be detected of these commonalities, however they have made themselves apparent – in my case, particularly in monotheisms and messianisms in the Abrahamic and non-Abrahamic religions and their theologies. Time and again, however, the larger and more complex theological systems are found to have reified claims of a complete and perfect revelation, a revelatory "deposit" in sacred histories inseparable from the sacred texts and objects themselves, preserved by a perfect community. In Western Christian traditions, these sacred histories come most often by means of an "originalist" hermeneutic: reconstructions of the original revelatory events and first-generation community, or "medievalist" or other authoritative "scholastic" hermeneutic – reconstructions of a golden age of religious achievement in every aspect of communal life. Each of these traditions is distinguished by strategies of "repristination": theology as an exercise in recovery of a "pristine" religious condition of communication and practice. Theology becomes an exercise as much in historical imagination as one of engaging theologically one's own audience in real time.

In many ways, theology as a "science" (*scientia* as in "way of knowledge") reflects an ancient oracular or mystical dimension as well as the knowledge of law. Whether theorizing based upon experimental insight regarding "natural law" or "human law" on the way toward the "rule of law," the penchant for believing in the authoritative perception of an idea or argument for some exclusive claim stems from the ancient monotheism that refuses to relativize truth claims that regulate nature or human beings. With scriptures, especially in view of earlier predictions and later "fulfillments" often relayed through obscure texts, every word of the text could potentially contain truths to be distilled into authoritative propositions, whether legal or scientific. The stakes became exceedingly high early on. Internally, the texts and their adherents established bodies of knowledge and tests for "good law" and "good science." As early as Origen in the third and Augustine in the fourth to fifth centuries, appeal against naïve interpretations of, say, the creation narratives of Genesis were already rather well argued.

Ancient scriptures are *sui generis* – they are neither law nor science nor a broad range of literary conventions. Although their genres were very familiar to their original audiences, their purposive and traditional receptions were always distinct. Often, the scriptures are *sui generis* in relation to one another. The conception of Christianity as a sect of Judaism and Islam as inseparable from both unites their scriptures in a unique fashion and gives much credence to the Abrahamic studies projects that have emerged in recent years, tapping into centuries of "Abrahamic" reasoning among the three. When we consider non-Abrahamic scriptures and their traditions, particularly in ethics, there is much commonality and probably cross-fertilization. There is much overlap in the way in which they reason theologically, liturgically, ethically, scientifically, and juridically – particularly through the massive migration of scriptures and methods of interpretation since the eighteenth century. But their status as revelation, and therefore sacred, bridges the immanent and transcendent worlds and brings their audiences into binding relationships that they would not otherwise express. Their texts and their genius are such that they produce an unabated history of interpretation and application. Theological literature in the last 50 years has burgeoned in forms and complexity. This is reason enough to suggest that theology might best be done according to an "open field" principle. Their potential has proven to be almost unlimited, and although they provide no more detail than fundamental distinctions for law (protecting persons but not defining virtue) and science (the intelligibility of the cosmos), their greater aid is narrating the mixed bag that is human life and behavior.

Externally, however, once an ecclesial ruling in law or science had become "incorrigible" according to institutional claims of historical authority and unreformability, rejecting extra-theological criteria resulted in retrograde "science" or no science at all. In this and other ways, the problem of an account of revelation as supplying the purest distillation of truth about God and the world, and the resulting history of interpretation and its errors, sometimes of the worst sort, plague the history of theology. Even worse is the conceit of correcting, if not eliminating, other revelation claims and theologies. In virtually all the major Christian traditions, the commitments to compatibility between the Graeco-Roman and biblical cosmologies always leaves the neutral reader with a sense that the exercise is more one of apologetics than a theological reasoning that follows an unbiased path.

One of the greatest points of reference for Christian theologians in general is undoubtedly the theology of Vatican II and constructive engagement with it. The council adopted of the doctrine of religious liberty[8] – that without freedom from all religious sovereignties, the necessary exercise of the liberty of conscience and deep persuasion in faith is undermined and the necessary condition of religious decision making by each human being is blocked. These ideas were rooted in the ideas of the early American theologian, Roger Williams, and updated by the Jesuit theologian, John Courtney Murray. The historic shock over precisely this canon from Vatican II, qualifying definitively as "development of doctrine" (Newman 1845), becomes a fascinating movement of theological aggiornamento – a theological "opening," a key trajectory toward TWW/OFT. Parallel to this opening were a series of papal addresses to the United Nations at least once during the papacy of each pope since 1948. The speeches have reflected a theology opening a field of learning beyond the confines of tradition and institution, seeking to embrace new insights without contradicting tradition and institution. John Paul II, Benedict XVI, and Francis I have each in their own way kept Vatican II as their frame of reference (United Nations Headquarters 2015). Most importantly, all the Christian denominations were regarded as "instruments of salvation," despite the claim to being "the one true church," an inclusive statement long in coming but definitive (Congregation for the Doctrine of the Faith, 2007).[9] The multiple religious "ends" of the theologies among the many human communities make impossible any conflating or reducing of the diversity of necessary or ultimate doctrines among the religions. What we see from the Roman Catholic example of theological development is its own gradual moving to a place where boundaries and open spaces are quite compatible, even "normative."

The earliest expressions of theological openness within communal boundaries is quite ancient. The fascinating history of the Hellenization of Judaism through the first translation of any scripture signaled an intentional engagement with Greek culture and cosmology after the sixth century BCE – something which had already happened in Babylon and the Jewish Persian academies that would develop there. Due largely to Christian persecution, Medieval (Masoretic) Judaism attempted to consign Hellenistic Judaism and its traditions to heresy, apostasy, and oblivion. Indeed, it will require the first critical edition of the Tanakh (Hebrew Bible), which is currently in production, to reveal crucial knowledge about its textual traditions in times where, even among the strictest Jewish communities such as Qumran, Tanakh and Septuagint were read side by side. Although the Athenian Academy had long abandoned the theologies of Plato and Aristotle, their arguments are revived by Hellenistic Judaism and Christianity in marshalling precedents for their perceived monotheisms considered entirely compatible with the biblical accounts of the divine being – especially the *locus classicus* of the Bible, Exodus 3:14, the self-determining, noncontingent deity, the "I am that I am." The great advancement and problem is that the meanings captured in the Greek translation are highly constructive extrapolations of the Hebrew/Aramaic texts. Scripture translation is a constructive and comparative theological process in itself. One telling example is the radical extraction of Christological "facts" from highly metaphorical gospel narratives. By the end of the seventh century, virtually nothing from the "life of Jesus" remained in the ontological paradigm of "divine and human" in the two-natures doctrine. Doctrinal theology is utterly rooted in this tradition and is difficult to reconcile with narrative gospel interpretation. TWW/OFT provides an open field that yields new possibilities for reconciling doctrine with neglected narratives.

TWW/OFT in some ways has been a descriptive rather than a constructive hermeneutical exercise. As an American project TWW/OFT begins with Protestant and Catholic theologians as constructive educators and takes stock of the ever-expanding diversity of theological schools and approaches. It then encompasses theological interactions with the historical churches: Catholic, Orthodox, Oriental, African, and contacts with the quarter billion Christians of new churches and movements with no denominational connections at all. In all, the salvation history narratives of scripture and the normative creeds arising from particular theologies of modernity up to our moment follow traditional patterns but also construct new pathways. Theology is primarily expositional, responding to "revelation" or "knowledge of the ultimate," correcting or rendering more persuasive inherited theological statements or pioneering new ones and, finally, channeling these insights in multiple contexts of learning and faith practices. Theology grounds the constant pursuit of human and planetary flourishing but ultimately articulates human hopes and visions of redemption, even when cosmology is understood from a religious naturalism perspective, agnostically or even atheistically. TWW can encompass even a theology of religious atheism. "There is no God" or "The God of religion is nonexistent" can be heard theologically according to the personal confession of God as unknown, unknowable, or unexperienced, or critically as inescapably tied to violence – although one wonders if "religious entanglements" were somehow genetically removed, any appreciable decrease in human violence would result.

Theology when it fully flowers is a divine or ultimate cosmological narrative or model: Creator–creation; God–world—humanity; continuum (with or without a beginning). Communication in such forms, even the naturalistic with no deity, is theological and speculative, following, for example, apophatic or cataphatic hermeneutical trajectories: one is characteristic of the unknowability of God and the other of the divinity of all things. What is important is the comprehensibility of all theological discourses (even atheistic theologies) in OFT. In the apophatic direction, by the end of the first millennium of Christian theology, the best theologians had concluded that the being of God and its infinite attributes, "God of God," were unknowable, because what can be known is entirely determined by the characteristics of human cognition. From the apophatic angle, the unknowability of God could cover the widest possible range of agnostic or atheistic modeling. Indeed, there is little difference between the speculative knowledge claim of God's nonexistence and the apophatic cognitive impossibility of knowing the being of the God that is known by revelation. From the cataphatic angle, however, theology follows the affirmations of its diverse traditions and trajectories, but in common context where the diversity that was once, at most, intrareligious is now interreligious, due to the global nearness of every theologian to every other.

We can now see "perfect being theology" from a new hermeneutical perspective. Based in part upon mathematical ideals, the perfect being was subjected to "infinity modelling" with regard to divine (fore)knowledge (as "exhaustive"), eternal existence, ultimacy as "source" of all things, "perfection" as a moral quality, and desperate strategies for grounding ethics and law, as well as the coherence and intelligibility of the universe – explanatory of the derivation of all things. These ideals are also reflected in naturalistic models as "grand unified theory" agendas – some kind of "system" that gives integration or unity to everything. Perfect Being Theology in any system begins with a certain perfection of either the law of noncontradiction or even tautology (the most "perfect" formulation) and extrapolates from there. Historically, various "perfect" forms, numbers, or proportionalities become nodes of reasoning about the [p]erfect "exhaustively," as in divine foreknowledge. The implied qualifier "at least" is constantly begging the question of the models of divinity – even the Platonic or Hindu originals.

Either the systems of perfection beg questions as to the narratives of revelation where such models are not offered or the patent inappropriateness of the models to begin with, trying to generate a model that is implied by near-infinite multiplications of physical conditions in some cosmologies founded upon replicating behaviors in the quantum world. Given the complexity of the quantum world, even the catchphrase, "infinite in all directions" doesn't catch, doesn't capture a set of coordinates by which a satisfactory model of the infinite perfections of divinity can be represented. Atheism protests the models of the divine being – none even approach being satisfactory from their starting points, let alone their *teloi*, or "ends." Perfect being as infinite being becomes "optative" – an "if–only" plea for the knowledge of infinite being identical to the models of revelation. Acknowledging the inadequacy of models of the divine being does not remove the warrant for affirming the infinite reality of Anselm's "that than which nothing greater can be thought," but it reminds us this concept is a contentless placeholder for the infinite existent and real ultimacy, yet unknowable as such by finite knowers, however reflective of the divine being of revelation they may be, yet always not reflective of [the] being that is nothing other than infinite.

"Open-field" and theological trajectories

Hermeneutical theology that would foster the open field of theological practice asks no questions of pluralism, inclusivism, or exclusivism, because technically, it would only provide warrant for their coexistence within the same field. TWW/OFT places theological communities in some kind of coexistence in theological space. Theological commitments other than hermeneutical privilege some particular religious aspect, even purported general or pluralistic ones: traditional, confessional, ecumenical, mystical, "religious belonging," naturalist, "the Real," etc. Each is better pursued in something of a "democratic," "universal," "level playing field"–based hermeneutical theological community than being performed on separated ("separatist") bases. Even exclusivist theologies are better formulated under the conditions of TWW/OFT.

What is the range or register of "open field" in terms of theology? There are perspectives that offer something that are similar: "open and relational theology" or "open theology"; "process" and "naturalistic" models of [g]od or the [r]eal or naturalist/materialist models. The point about "field" is that it pursues a kind of "level playing field" approach to what are historically rival exclusivisms in religious doctrine and practice. But such a "field" approach, while not only removing the possibility of privilege and ranking among the theologies and a-theologies, is much more about discursive and hermeneutical conditions of the freedom of inquiry, reconstructing and reframing theologies through encounter, inclusive of the "postconfessional," "postreligious," "postsecular" world. By orienting theology according to field of inquiry rather than a particular tradition that has opened its boundaries or a model of God in relation, TWW can do its work theologically as an anthropological exercise of many related disciplines and perspectives.

Post-Constantinian, postdenominational and postconfessional trends in theology already present in the nineteenth century were represented by some of the greatest modern theological minds: Soren Kierkegaard and Franz Overbeck can be seen as on the way to Bonhoeffer's "religion-less Christianity." The institutional dominance of theology, let alone institutions of government, law, or science, are replaced by theological engagement and dimensionality for a "lived theology" in the context of multiple voices and irreducible diversity. Most moderate to liberal academic thinking has been gesturing toward TWW for some time. The student is free to pursue relatively unbounded inquiry apart from those courses of study leading to ordination. Theologies in the developing world are especially needful of TWW/OFT because so many new movements do not have any connections to creedal denominations. Missional theology must respond more and more to "insider movements" which syncretically absorb Christian orientations within non-Christian communities, often with highly expressive forms of spirituality. Indeed, "spirituality" has become part of the taxonomy of human wellness and flourishing, no matter how secular or postreligious the context.

At the same time, hyper-politicization can be detected in branches of Jewish, Christian, Muslim, Hindu, and Buddhist communities. The already massively stressed "ultra-orthodox" subgroups vie in their claims for infallibility in knowledge and perfection in practice. It is sometimes difficult to locate the boundary between a zealotry that begets religious violence and a zealotry that foreswears it. Examples include American evangelical theologians with no theological critique of the new nationalism and racism in its midst, Al Azhar University of Cairo refusing to condemn the teaching of ISIS, Modi of India refusing to condemn Hindutva ideology, Aung San Suu Kyi refusing to condemn her government's genocide of the Muslim Rohingya in Rakhine, and even China's absolutist president Xi refusing to acknowledge the massive internment camps for Muslims. These and many similar examples reflect the aggressive and often violent instrumentalization of religion.

Through the previous century, theological schools moved toward shedding strict denominational boundaries (although in Germany, Catholic and Protestant PhD students are not allowed cross-denominational supervisors). These predominantly Christian institutions have accommodated different kinds of Christian identity and constructed new forms centered on ethics and critical biblical studies decoupled from creedal controls in the interest of contextual understanding and innovative applications.

One of the highest levels of literacy is religious, for example, being able to perceive theological meanings across the range of literatures and the arts – scripture or commentary, classic or contemporary theology; ethics;

liturgy; music, visual and other performative arts. Theologizing is a capacity among readers and writers to communicate about the divine/human referents in religious discourse and to discern assertions and arguments with focused religious intention and advocacy. Indeed, to be a theologian without walls implies a capacity to make informed theological judgements outside, although not necessarily antithetical to, any particular religion or denomination. TWW grapples with the best of the heritage through comparative practice and multiple religious interactions, involving dialogue, composition, and literacy. Student and faculty expectations and formulations are already reflecting this postconfessional reality.

If we look closely at the twenty-first-century developments and those just prior, we see the final retreat of a dogmatic world where the common property of the Abrahamic tradition's best legacies can be accessed, weighed, and applied in new forms and venues, such as comparative scripture/theological study across the interreligious frontiers. A crucial development is the "postmetaphysical" trend in modern theology – but this must be understood in a precise way. Theological texts are also texts of metaphysics. But the characteristic of "objective science" going back to the axial age (fifth century BCE) of prophets, scriptures, and sages are the constructions of cosmology based political systems. The origins of the meta-narrative are both humanistic and scientific. Indeed, the best way to read natural theology and speculations of "natural religion" (from Spinoza to Hick) is as some primal religion – an ancient idea.

We need to take seriously postdenominational yet postsecular trends to recognize how new expressions of theology are arising through nontraditional avenues of scripture study and spirituality. Why this deference to scriptures? They represent the inspired sources of sources. Theologically, there are many "sources," and one can certainly begin from the history of a tradition or a critical or reductionistic, even atheistic response, because a-theology is still dealing with the transcendent/ultimate category of reflection. What is characteristic across the board is the distancing from "religious authority" as institutionalized through fellow human mediation. The "without walls" of this theology is the resistance to any connection between spiritual truths and any appropriation by political, historical, and cultural authorities to justify privilege or exclusion. In their place, an unbounded/un-walled theological conversation has broken upon us and our world of many human and nonhuman lives.

Although early twenty-first-century developments in Western religiousness are marked by a "postsecular" trend, this is matched by a "postreligious" trend as well. Both terms require vagueness and wide applicability to be serviceable as well as linked together. Indeed, in a postdogmatic age – dogma meaning the religious bases in legal reasoning that once sustained the protection of religious institutions through the legislation and execution of religious laws and the punishment of religious crimes – this world of religious law no longer exists among Christians and Jews and many Muslims; persons of many other large religions are moving in this direction.

The import of "confession-less" Christian theology as a key trajectory behind TWW/OFT correlates with the "subjective turn" in the history of theology. Earlier models of God in many, if not all, of these traditions had to be replaced, for example, divine presence with divine "design," divine subjectivity and activity in some form of "relational" model of [g]od. The by-product has been personal individuation and identity formation.

TWW/OFT responds to the gradual abandonment of sovereign religion and the recognition of irreducible multiplicity. Boundaries there always will be, but these are, more than ever, the boundaries of voluntary association (e.g., denominations of religions, local communities, often connected but not wholly defining any "religion") and ultimately the inviolability of the individual person, religious or not. Indeed, in the radical period of the Reformation and ever after, a particular gospel verse and its interpretation as "church" was programmatically condemned by the traditionalists: "wherever two or more are gathered in my name" (Mt 18:20). Today, two or more in community is a "church" or spiritual community of any religion and yet not at all. Such community is not discounted by a wide variety of theological reasoners. There is a sense in which the multiplication of communities is finally a diversification down to the individual theologian, hopefully in conversation and constructive productivity, if nowhere else than in a TWW/OFT hermeneutical space.

Notes

1 TWW/OFT.
2 One immensely helpful comparative historical treatment: Stroumsa (2016).
3 The use of [] (e.g., [B]eing) in this chapter is meant to convey the alternating capital/lowercase letter depending upon use: the varying registers in theological discourse for such terms.
4 Otherwise known as "eternity of the world" cosmology and its consistent rejection by the vast majority of Abrahamic theologians; e.g., Philoponus, Maimonides, Avicenna, Bonaventure, and Aquinas.
5 Brilliantly debated by Hannah Arendt in her posthumously published *Willing* (1978).
6 Some 16 countries have constitutionally established national Christian churches, or "Christianity": Argentina, Armenia, Tuvalu, Tonga, Costa Rica, Kingdom of Denmark, England, Greece, Georgia, Iceland, Liechtenstein, Malta, Monaco, Vatican City, Papua New Guinea, and Zambia.
7 *Republic*, 514a – 520a.
8 Not to mention its theology of religions.
9 It includes a very clear affirmation of Vatican II as normative.

References

Arendt, Hannah. *Willing. The Life of the Mind*. New York: Harcourt, 1978.
Congregation for the Doctrine of the Faith. 2007. "Responses to Some Questions Regarding Certain Aspects of the Doctrine on the Church." www.vatican.va/roman_curia/congregations/cfaith/documents/rc_con_cfaith_doc_20070629_responsa-quaestiones_en.html (accessed February 23, 2019).

Newman, John Henry. *An Essay on the Development of Christian Doctrine.* Notre Dame, IN: University of Notre Dame Press, 1989.

Stroumsa, Guy. 2016. *The Scriptural Universe of Ancient Christianity.* Cambridge: Harvard University Press. doi:10.1017/s000964071800015x

United Nations Headquarters. 2015. "Address of the Holy Father." http://w2.vatican.va/content/francesco/en/speeches/2015/september/documents/papa-francesco_20150925_onu-visita.html (accessed January 6, 2019).

Yelle, Robert A. 2018. *Sovereignty and the Sacred: Secularism and the Political Economy of Religion.* Chicago: University of Chicago Press.

Part II

Experience and transformation

Introduction

Jerry L. Martin

Theology Without Walls encourages a greater emphasis on religious experiences and the transformations they engender. "Ultimate reality," John Thatamanil argues, "cannot be corralled or confined within the boundaries of . . . 'the religions.'" In Christian terms, "if God is the God of the whole world, traces of divinity will surely be found anywhere one thinks to look." The goal is interreligious wisdom, engaging not only the claims of other traditions but their ends and their means as well. This engagement requires "the pursuit of truth gained through the theologian's own transformation." The goal is to know God, not merely about God. "This *knowledge of* rather than *knowledge about* is driven by soteriological desire." "To be religious . . . is to search for comprehensive qualitative orientation." It seeks to order *human desiring* in ways true to the nature of reality. Interreligous wisdom requires "embodied knowing of reality as understood by means of the therapeutic regimes of more than one tradition." If the ultimate reality is "a multiplicity not an undifferentiated simplicity," then interreligious wisdom reveals "more than one dimension of ultimate reality."

Paul Knitter's book, *Without Buddha I Couldn't Be a Christian*, created something of a sensation. Here was a learned Catholic theologian immersing himself in Buddhism so much that he became rather equally committed to both traditions. If theology is, as he says, "spiritual experience trying to make sense of itself," how was he to make sense of his dual belonging? He starts with the difficult question, "Just how does Jesus save me?" Finding atonement theory unsatisfactory, he looked to a "functional analogy" in the Buddhist tradition: the saving role of Jesus is that of Guru Yoga, or "spiritual benefactor." The participant must "visualize and truly *feel* the presence of the Benefactor. The final phase is to let the images dissolve and merge non-conceptually into, in Buddhist language, the Essence Love. Or, as St. Paul puts it, 'It is now no longer I who lives; it is Christ living in/as me.'" This, Knitter says, is salvation – "not as an atoning process that takes place outside of oneself but as a transformative unitive experience." In another functional analogy, "both Buddha and Jesus can be considered 'liberators.'" Knitter explores what Buddhists can teach Christians and what Christians

DOI: 10.4324/9780429000973-7

can teach Buddhists about efforts at liberation and social justice. He concludes, "by realizing my Buddha-nature, I have been able to understand and to live my Christ-nature."

Questioning a "smorgasbord" approach to religion, Huston Smith once quoted a teacher in India, "If you are drilling for water, it's better to drill one 60-foot well than ten 6-foot wells." Peter Savastano reports from his own life a deep involvement with multiple traditions, reaching the level of a spiritual master in several. He has studied theology but, he says, "theory eventually hits the wall of personal experience." Seeking "knowledge of and through the heart," he engaged in a wide range of spiritual practices from multiple traditions. "By engaging these non-Christian practices," he says, "I have expanded my understanding and experience of the Abrahamic God." Is ultimate reality personal or impersonal? Sometimes one, sometimes the other, sometimes both at the same time, in his experience. "I continue to immerse myself more deeply in Christ-oriented experience although I do so 'interspiritually.'" There is a further movement "when my experience of the Divine surpasses all concepts and metaphors . . . an experience of the apophatic nature of The Great Mystery which I describe as 'the scaffolding falling away.'" The experience is "both elating and troubling." It is perhaps, he concludes, the prelude to what a Sufi psychologist calls the "final integration."

Rory McEntee begins with his experiences with Fr. Thomas Keating and the Snowmass Dialogues, which provided remarkably rich opportunities to study interspirituality. McEntee was influenced by Wayne Teasdale's belief that interspirituality could create "a continuing community among the religions that is substantial, vital, and creative." It would "make available to everyone all the forms the spiritual journey assumes." In the Snowmass discussions, theological disagreements would arise. "At the level of doctrine we find (perhaps) incommensurable 'accounts of reality.' However, in 'the religious quest as transformative journey,' we have found what Raimon Panikkar called 'homeomorphic equivalence.'" The interspiritual approach might be particularly valuable for the spiritual but not religious. Though coming from a particular tradition, he now finds that the interspiritual community is his home.

No philosopher has paid more nuanced attention to religious experience than William James. Jonathan Weidenbaum explores doing theology, to use James's phrase, "with open doors and windows," open to the full range of human experience. "Intuitions that are pathological, paranormal, and even drug-induced join religious experiences in possessing revelatory value for James." The encounter with another person that shatters our "prejudices and assumptions," can, James said, cause a "complete re-ordering of our inner lives." Reflection is important but should not erase "the freshness and immediacy of concrete experience." He finds mystical experiences to have a seemingly noetic quality as "states of insight into the depths of truth unplumbed by the discursive intellect." Indeed, the "overcoming of all the usual barriers between the individual and the Absolute is the great mystic achievement." At the same time, James celebrates diversity. If all religions were seen as, at some level, saying the same thing, "the total human consciousness of the divine would suffer."

5 Theology Without Walls as the quest for interreligious wisdom

John J. Thatamanil

Theology Without Walls (TWW) is not a single, highly integrated, and uniform research program but rather a family of kindred research projects. As TWW gains greater traction and more voices join in, the methodological diversity within TWW will only continue to expand. What binds these diverse projects together is the core conviction that theological truth is available, and therefore must be pursued, beyond the walls of any single religion. If there is (at least one) ultimate reality, there is no reason to suspect – confessional claims notwithstanding – that ultimate reality is accessible through a single tradition alone. Indeed, even exclusivist confessional thinkers typically insist that knowledge of God, even if to an inferior degree, is available to those outside the tradition, for example, in the book of nature and not just in the book of scripture. If such truth is, indeed, available, and if what is so available does not replicate what is already known within a single tradition, then theologians must commend investment in transreligious learning.

TWW investigators may seek knowledge of ultimate reality in literature, in the work of scientific cosmologists and evolutionary biologists, in comparative theology, or by way of experimentation with mind-altering psilocybin. Ultimate reality cannot be corralled within the boundaries of those domains of cultural life that some modern communities have taken to calling "the religions." What sort of self-respecting ultimate reality would that be? Speaking in traditional Christian theological terms, as God is the God of the whole world, traces of divinity will be found anywhere one thinks to look. Hence, a diversity of approaches and methods is inevitable for TWW.

In this chapter, I propose one particular conception of TWW that has for its goal interreligious wisdom gained by means of engagement with not just the *claims* of other traditions but also their *ends* and the *means* to those ends. I hold that at least some who engage in TWW will do so by way of multiple religious participation, that is by taking up practices drawn from the repertoire of more than one religious tradition, practices that provide access to the spiritual ends prized by the traditions in question. In what follows, I offer a rudimentary sketch of this version of TWW, commend its desirability and importance, and describe some of the unique conceptual and practical challenges that come with it. I have no intention of commending

DOI: 10.4324/9780429000973-8

its superiority to other modes of TWW. Not all will be drawn to the appeals and demands of this style of theological engagement. Nonetheless, I commend this account of TWW because it affords access to what I call interreligious wisdom, first-order knowledge of ultimate reality gained by drawing from the resources of more than one religious tradition.

Theology is more than making claims: on theological ends and means

Theological reflection within many contemporary forms of Christianity remains a resolutely cognitivist enterprise wedded to the labor of making and assessing claims about God and God's relation to the world and human beings.[1] There is nothing misguided about such a project. Theological work quite naturally seeks to think about how best to construe ultimacy. Is God a being among beings or rather the ground of being? Is ultimate reality personal, transpersonal, or perhaps even both in different respects? Is the relation between ultimacy and the world best understood within a pantheist, panentheistic, nondualist, or dualist metaphysics? Of course, these questions might also be taken up within the framework of philosophy of religion. What customarily renders these questions distinctively theological is the constraint that they are taken up with reference to the sources and norms of a particular tradition, a constraint that TWW rejects.

Might we entertain another conception of what makes thinking theological, a conception that hinges not on exclusivity – "Work within the parameters of this tradition alone!" – but instead understands theology as marked by existential commitment to the pursuit of religious truth gained through the theologian's own transformation, a transformation brought about by taking up the spiritual disciplines that serve as the *means* for reaching the distinctive spiritual *ends* of the tradition in question? True, Pierre Hadot has shown that within the history of the West, philosophy, too, was once understood to require spiritual discipline, but this particular conception of philosophy has largely fallen by the wayside (Hadot 1995). In this historical moment, theology seems better suited as the rubric for committed truth seeking gained through spiritual transformation.

Such theology would be attentive to far more than theological claim assessment but would instead seek to understand claims within the broader spiritual matrix from which they are often isolated for the sake of deliberation. Even within Christian circles, theology has not always been focused on claims to the exclusion of religious ends and the means by which those ends were reached. Recall one of the tradition's earliest definitions of the theologian by the fourth-century desert father, Evagrius: "The one who prays truly is the theologian; the theologian is one who prays truly" (Ponticus 1972, 65). For Evagrius, prayer makes the theologian, not the proposal and defense of this or that set of theological claims. The theologian is one who comes to intimate knowledge of the divine by means of the spiritual discipline of prayer, which is itself a gift of God. The theologian is the one who *knows God*, not merely knows *about* God. This *knowledge of* rather than *knowledge about* is driven by soteriological desire. The *end* of Christian life is knowledge, and love of God that sets human beings free from sin, death, and the devil, and that knowledge is to be gained by *means* of the spiritual discipline of prayer.

In the kind of TWW I am proposing herein, the theologian rejects denominational or traditional exclusivity but embraces Evagrius's insistence on the centrality of the religious means that aim at transformative truth. Evagrius's maxim reminds us that ancient Christian traditions affirmed an intimate and inseparable bond between religious ends and the means by which those ends are attained. The theologian's vocation and identity are secured, within such a framework, by commitment to spiritual disciplines and not by way of conceptual assessment alone.

What if, borrowing from and riffing on Evagrius, we proposed the following contemporary maxim: the interreligious theologian is one who prays *and* meditates truly; the one who prays and meditates truly is the interreligious theologian. Here, of course, "meditation" is a placeholder, a token for some specific set of disciplines for religious knowing commended by a non-Christian tradition. Theologians without walls, in my account, are those who seek to know ultimate reality not by rejecting the spiritual disciplines of their home tradition but by supplementing those disciplines with others responsibly borrowed from another tradition. Actually, this provisional definition needs further nuance because there is no reason to assume, from the first, that the theologian without walls has a single home tradition, let alone the Christian one. Religious affiliations, in our time, defy any predictable pattern. A theologian without walls or the transrreligious theologian is one who seeks to know the truth of ultimate reality by faithfully engaging in the spiritual disciplines of more than one religious tradition.

Some key terms, definitions, and operative assumptions

What are the fundamental assumptions that render such a definition of transreligious theology meaningful and desirable? I would like to lay out here a number of central terms, definitions, and operative assumptions that I bring to the work of transreligious theology. To begin with the basics, just what do we mean by the terms "religious" and "religions?" How can care with definitions correct for the doctrinal preoccupations of much contemporary theology? How can we strive to ensure that our definitions of religion do not build into themselves expectations that render singular religious belonging normative and multiple religious participation aberrant?

To be religious, in my account, is to search for comprehensive qualitative orientation. Religious persons and communities seek to take their place with respect to the whole of things, the nature of reality as such, in an affective key. Religious orientation, as opposed to, say, scientific orientation, seeks to order *human desiring* such that human desires are rendered true to the nature of reality. How should human desiring be ordered if reality is marked by impermanence and insubstantiality? What if, beyond all the finite goods given in experience, there is an infinite good upon whom all finite things depend? What would that entail for how desire is ordered? If reality is marked by radical interdependence, such that my well-being is inseparable from yours, then what should I do about deeply entrenched habits of self-seeking that presently mar my life with others? What are we to do about market-based regimes of shaping desire that teach that the collective good spontaneously emerges by maximizing individualistic acquisitive impulses? All of these questions about what to do with our desiring, when desires are situated within some account of the way things are, count as religious.

Nothing about this project to render human desiring true to the real implies an understanding of the religious as passive rather than activist in character. In order to render human desiring true to the nature of the real as such, one might well have to undo social orders that are marked by falsity, triviality, and destructivity. Religious comportment can and routinely does take on the work of world transformation.

The religious work of orienting desire within a cosmic frame has historically taken place within local and translocal communities whose lives have been shaped by a variety of traditions that we have taken recently to calling "religions" or "world religions." In much of the globe for much of human history, any given local community was informed by a variety of religious traditions. That such religious diversity marked East Asian and South Asian life is well known. Less well known is the presence of enduring multiplicity in "Christian lands." The presence of various indigenous and pagan customs and practices has diversely colored the Christianities of Ireland, Brazil, and even Italy. That is why even European Christianities have distinctive local flavors, flavors as distinctive as their respective cuisines. The work of comprehensive qualitative orientation thus routinely draws upon the repertoires of more than one religious tradition.

Religious traditions are historically deep repertoires of myths, rituals, practices, symbols, sacred objects, sacred sites, scriptures, institutions, norms, experiences, and intuitions. More precisely, traditions are arguments about what ought to be in a given tradition's repertoire and how that repertoire ought to be employed in the work of generating interpretive schemes and therapeutic regimes. Interpretive schemes are the means by which religious thinkers and their communities give an account of the nature of reality. Therapeutic regimes are the means by which personal and communal desiring is attuned to the nature of the real as depicted by an interpretive scheme. Therapeutic regimes include rituals, practices of worship, spiritual exercises, pilgrimages, and the like by which personal and communal lives are tutored and shaped so as to be rendered true to and true for the real.

Religious traditions *are not* interpretive schemes; they contain a plethora of interpretive schemes, and theologians, both elite and lay, continue to generate and debate a host of interpretive schemes. There is neither a single Christian nor Buddhist take on reality. There are historically fluid and geographically diverse Christian and Buddhist repertoires, which are then deployed in contested fashion by religious intellectuals and their communities.

The ingredients contained within a given religious repertoire are malleable and constantly subject to growth and subtraction, but not infinitely so. Certain items have historic staying power and come to be seen as essential to that repertoire because of symbolic power, entrenched habit, the backing of institutional elites, sheer antiquity, and a host of other reasons. It is just as difficult to imagine a Christian interpretive scheme that does not make use of the cross, baptism, or some account of the resurrection as it would be to imagine South Indian cuisine without cumin, coriander, turmeric, mustard seeds, or coconut milk. Not every ingredient is found in all curries, but there are recognizable continuities. Likewise, not every ingredient from the Christian repertoire is found in any particular Christian theological vision, but there are recognizable continuities that mark a Christian dish as Christian or a Buddhist dish as Buddhist. It is difficult to imagine a Christian therapeutic regime that takes leave altogether of prayer of some kind (intercessory, contemplative, etc.), although even so "central" an ingredient as the Eucharist is relatively marginal in some ecclesial families.

Not every Buddhist meditates or chants mantras – there is a vast difference between monastic and lay practice, for example – but, again, one recognizes important material historical continuities. A theory of the religious traditions must strike the right balance between continuity and creativity, a task well beyond the scope of this chapter. Emphasize continuity alone, and agency is stripped from religious actors; emphasize creativity alone, and the historical depth, heft, and binding power of traditions might be forgotten.

The appeal to the example of cooking in this context is not random. No two Kerala fish curries are identical, even when prepared by members of a single family. But you do generally know when you are having a Kerala fish curry. If the dish doesn't have some combination of tamarind, coconut milk, mustard seeds, curry leaves, turmeric, garlic, and a good many chilies, what you've concocted may taste good, but it is unlikely to be a Kerala fish curry. Tradition imposes constraints, but those constraints can themselves serve as the material basis for improvisational creativity.

For the purposes of this chapter, what must be reemphasized is that the work of comprehensive qualitative orientation cannot be accomplished by appeal to an interpretive scheme alone, no more than reading the ingredients from a recipe will satisfy hunger. Desires are configured in healing and life-giving fashion when they are shaped by means of the specific spiritual disciplines that enable human beings to accomplish the religious ends celebrated by the tradition in question. Human flourishing requires truing oneself to the nature of the real; religious orientation is, hence, a matter of comportment, when desires are in right accord with the reality rightly interpreted.

For most religious traditions, right comportment requires that human beings are rightly attuned to certain feature or features of reality that are taken to be ultimate. I speak of "features" in this context rather than a singular ultimate reality because it is not clear that all religious traditions maintain that a single ultimate reality exists. A given tradition might celebrate a plurality of Orishas or instead point to the fact that everything in reality whatsoever is empty (*sunya*) of self-existence (*svabhava*). The former is not a singular ultimate, and the latter is not easily characterized as an ultimate reality in the way that either God or Brahman might be.

Comportment requires that human beings are in right accord with ultimacy rather than merely know about ultimacy. Here, one might speak about first-order knowledge, *knowledge of*, rather than second-order knowledge, *knowledge about*. Consider, for example, the knowledge that Michael Phelps has of water as opposed to the nonswimmer who happens to be expert in fluid mechanics. The latter knows a very great deal *about* water, far more than Phelps, in fact, but as a nonswimmer, she would not be long for the world if she should happen to fall into the deep end of a pool.

First-order religious knowing, the kind that Evagrius commends, is acquired only by means of spiritual disciplines such as prayer and meditation. Without proper comportment, there is no true *knowledge of the* real. This is why generations of students in the nation's "Introduction to Buddhism" classes have not spontaneously awakened to wisdom upon a first hearing or reading of the Four Noble Truths. Enlightenment experiences are not recurring features of collegiate lecture halls even when staffed by brilliant lecturers. Reading the recipe is not cooking, let alone eating the dish.

Buddhist traditions customarily insist on the priority of spiritual disciplines. Zen students do not receive lectures on Dogen but are instead compelled to sit in Zazen. What there is to know about Zen is learned, first and foremost, by taking on a particular therapeutic regime that tutors the body to see as Zen what teachers want the student to see. Even dharma talks are not so much about the transmission of doctrinal or propositional information but are instead meant to elicit and evoke transformation. The upshot: if you want to know as Buddhists know, you must do as Buddhists do. There are no shortcuts.

Multiple religious participation as the precondition for interreligious wisdom

With these preliminary terms and definitions in place, we are now able to say just why multiple religious participation is necessary for one modality of TWW, namely that which strives at interreligious wisdom. But first, one additional definition is necessary, that of interreligious wisdom. Religious traditions account persons to be wise when they have, by means of right comportment, arrived at embodied knowing of ultimate reality as understood by the tradition in question. Persons are recognized to be wise when they have arrived at intimate first-order knowledge of ultimate reality by means of spiritual disciplines that have rightly attuned human desiring. It would follow that *interreligious wisdom* arises when human beings come into an embodied knowing of reality as understood by means of the therapeutic regimes of more than one tradition. In so doing, these persons will have inscribed into their bodies first-order knowledge of ultimate reality or ultimate features of reality as articulated by the interpretative schemes of traditions whose therapeutic regimes they have taken up. I have elsewhere spoken of such wisdom as a kind of binocular vision – the capacity to see the world through more than one set of religious lenses and to integrate what is seen thereby. I wish to argue that at least some theologians without walls must set themselves to the pursuit of such binocular vision by way of multiple religious participation.

But is such interreligious wisdom possible? What are the conditions for the possibility of such wisdom? And, if possible, is it desirable? What obstacles, if any, stand in the way of such wisdom? Who might interreligious wisdom be for? What communities might it serve? These are the questions that I take up in the remainder of this chapter. Let's address these questions in turn.

Proof of actuality is, of course, proof of possibility. We know that interreligious wisdom is possible precisely because we know of a host of religious luminaries who have successfully committed themselves to the cultivation of such wisdom. Consider, for example, Buddhist-Christian figures such as Ruben Habito, Maria Reis Habito, Sallie King, and Paul Knitter.[2] These thinkers are, in each case, not merely speculative students of Buddhist and Christian interpretive schemes considered in isolation from Buddhist therapeutic regimes. Each is grounded in years, even decades, of multiple religious participation, with recognized teachers in Buddhist traditions. In the case of Ruben Habito, his immersion in Buddhist practice is so thoroughgoing that he has received dharma transmission and is now a Buddhist teacher within a Zen lineage while remaining a Christian. These figures are Christians who have remained Christian even as they came to be deeply steeped in Buddhist traditions.

On the Hindu-Christian front, one can readily think of figures such as Raimon Panikkar, Swami Abhishiktananda, and Bede Griffiths, among others.[3] Particularly in the case of Abhishiktananada and Bede Griffiths, we have figures who immersed themselves in contemplative practice in the Advaitic strand of Hindu traditions. Their theological writings followed only after taking up the contemplative therapeutic regimen of Advaita Vedanta. The goal of such writing is to integrate, so far as possible, nondual wisdom with Christian devotional practice and wisdom, a meeting between wisdoms that takes place in "the cave of the heart." Questions about the Christian trinity and nonduality are taken up as they are illumined by the interspiritual experiences generated by practice and are not driven solely by a penchant for speculative theological ontology. The quest for such integration has to it an experiential intensity and rigor that, at least in the case of Abhishiktananda, proved to be soul-wrenching. It is no simple matter to integrate into one's life experience the competing appeals of nondualism and devotionalism when both have had an integral place within one's own spiritual life and orientation.[4]

No treatment of what these figures have come to know about ultimacy is possible herein, but a careful study of them would be an integral component in a research program that sought to think through the nature and possibilities for interreligious wisdom. What have such figures learned? What challenges have they faced? What is the relationship between their interreligious wisdom and wisdom as conventionally understood by each of the single traditions to which these figures made appeal? Such research would, I suspect, not just show that interreligious wisdom is a meaningful notion but also go a considerable way toward elucidating what interreligious wisdom is.

Let us turn now to the question, "What are the conditions for the possibility of interreligious wisdom, and why might such wisdom be desirable?" To answer that question, I posit the following propositions:

1   What we know of ultimate reality is intimately tied to how we come to know ultimate reality. The knower must become transformed so as to come into a knowing of ultimate reality in the respect that the seeker seeks to know it.
2   Ultimate reality is a multiplicity, not an undifferentiated simplicity.
3   Therefore, it follows that if different dimensions of the ultimate reality are to be known, they must be accessed by means of the specific spiritual disciplines that afford such access.
4   The bearer of interreligious wisdom, therefore, is one who has come to know more than one dimension of ultimate reality and has begun to integrate what has been so learned.

Interreligious wisdom is possible if these propositions hold.

First, we have already argued that first-order knowing of ultimate reality can be gained by means of the specific disciplines, the therapeutic regimes that make just such knowledge possible. Just as Michael Phelps undertakes the specific training regimens that create in his body the complex habitus that makes possible excellence in swimming, so, too, those who seek to know ultimate reality – not merely know about ultimate reality – must undertake specific disciplines. If no such disciplines exist, then there is no comportment to ultimate reality.

With that basic first presupposition in place, the possibility of interreligious wisdom requires the second supposition: that ultimate reality is a multiplicity and not just an undifferentiated simplicity.[5] Without that hypothesis, there is no reason to suppose that the various distinct disciplines of our religious traditions can augment and enrich knowledge gained by some primary practice. There must be more dimensions to the divine life that can be diversely accessed through diverse disciplines.

One other logical counterpossibility must be broached, namely that our various spiritual disciplines may be reduplicative. Remaining with the analogy of the swimmer, one might argue that nothing new is learned about water when a swimmer masters, in turn, the backstroke, the butterfly, and the breaststroke. What gain there is rests in the swimmer's fitness as different muscle groups are mobilized by way of these different strokes, but no new knowledge of water is gained. Water just is water. By extension, one might suggest that Zen practice grants no new knowledge of ultimacy that the Eucharist does not. The practitioner is spiritually fitter but has learned nothing more by spiritual cross-training.

This possibility must be entertained as a hypothesis, but if it holds without exception for all spiritual disciplines, then I do not see how a robust conception of interreligious wisdom can be defended. The different therapeutic regimes of our traditions would open no new vistas of vision, and the connection between religious means and the noetic ends that those means strive to access would be severed. In this account, the various spiritual disciplines would all be reduplicative, all paths up the same mountain but affording no new knowledge of it. The variety of disciplines may just be attributed to the contingent cultural-linguistic matrices from which the disciplines arise and yield no distinctive truth-bearing power.

Now, although it is certainly true that spiritual cross-training may well generate in practitioners a variety of spiritual excellences that are not directly tied to distinct dimensions of the divine life, there is every reason to believe that *at least some* disciplines are so connected. Some so shape persons and communities that distinctive insights are gained by means of diverse practices. We have reason to believe this because the traditions themselves tell us so. Christian life requires becoming the Kingdom-bringing egalitarian social body of the Christ. If you seek to become that body, you must eat that body's food; you must participate in the egalitarian sharing of the one bread and one cup, where Christians, in all their differences, come together and become one community of reconciled love-in-difference. In so doing, Christians become the Love that they are called to be. The discipline of Dzogchen, by contrast, is meant and employed for other purposes. The practice calls practitioners into recognition of the nature of mind itself as nondual, marked by spacelike clarity, unbounded, and intrinsically compassionate. Practice stabilizes in the practitioner this truth about their own nature; moreover, there is an inseparable connection between path and goal. What one practices is what one comes to know.

Those who seek interreligious wisdom need not posit that the practice of Eucharist and its goal are identical with the practice and goal of Dzogchen. Such assertions seem both implausible and unnecessary. Dzogchen practice operates within another ontological imaginary, one grounded in affirmation of the Buddha-nature of all beings and so operates within a different horizon of intelligibility. And it is precisely that difference which lends it desirability for some Christian practitioners. Indeed, one can only affirm the possibility of complementarity if one refuses to posit sameness – one must if interreligious wisdom is to be a cherished goal.

Christian Eucharistic practice, by contrast, is not rooted in nondual met-aphysical commitments. Difference matters. The uniqueness of the many gathered is affirmed in the singularity of each one, a singularity that is drawn without reduction or elimination into relation and community. And, of course and most obviously, the Eucharist is an act of worship of One who is not in every sense identical to those who worship. Here, of course, it is all too easy to become ontologically reductive. Christian theologies of God are all, without exception, aware that God is not a finite and countable object. To affirm that God is infinite is immediately to complicate every con-ventional depiction of the God–world relation as flatly akin to the relation between finite objects.

One need only remember, for example, Nicholas of Cusa's insistence that God is best understood as *non-aliud*, Not-Other, to realize that Christian the-ological imagination cannot be narrowly confined to a dialogical frame that is taken precisely to mirror dialogue as it takes place between two human interlocutors. Beginning with St. Paul, Christians have affirmed that the "dia-logical structure" of prayer is most peculiar. "Likewise the Spirit helps us in our weakness; for we do not know how to pray as we ought, but that very Spirit intercedes with sighs too deep for words" (Rom 8:26: NRSV). God prays to God in and through us; this is surely not dialogue as usual. Still, devotional life is marked by a longing for One who is not just or simply me, even if my longing for God is always already God's longing in me.

With these differences between Eucharist and Dzogchen sketched, albeit hastily, we are able to posit that the transreligious theologian might take up both practices with faithfulness, integrity, and some enduring continuity so as to be formed in depth by both practices and the matrices within which those practices are embedded. The wager is that differences matter, that there is an intimate noetic relation between the practices and what they seek to illuminate, and that each grants access to dimensions of ultimate reality that the other does not. The questions guiding the transreligious theolo-gian might include these: 1) Might there be dimensions of ultimate reality that correlate to the nondualism of Dzogchen and the complicated logic of singularity and relation present in Eucharist? 2) Might ultimate reality contain dimensions that are, on the one hand, nondually related to world and self *and* also dimensions that cannot be characterized as nondual and might even be meaningfully encountered as personal? 3) If so, how might one become maximally attuned, insofar as possible, to both dimensions and features of ultimate reality? 4) What kind of theological living and writing might follow from such transreligious living?

These questions, when taken together, point to the novelty and promise of transreligious theology as a quest for interreligious wisdom. What is sought is a practical braiding of spiritual disciplines, first, in the life of the practi-tioner and only then in the writing and teaching that might flow from such a life. Textual writing follows only after a writing into a flesh of the therapeutic regimes of specific traditions, which creates in the practitioner the long training that opens angles of vision that cannot be opened otherwise. The practitioner's primary goal is to arrive at a "sense and taste" for dimensions of ultimate reality by means of just these practices and then just this second set of practices. First-order intimacy is the cherished goal. The transformed theologian is the first product of transreligious theology imagined in this practical key; textual production follows next as an expression of what has been so learned.

Notes

1 The charge against a narrowly cognitivist-propositional account of theology was perhaps most famously made in contemporary theology by George Lindbeck in his brilliantly argued, *The Nature of Doctrine: Religion and Theology in a Post-liberal Age* (1984). My project is unlikely to be mistaken for his, but we do share a conviction that theological life is embedded within larger cultural-linguistic milieus. But there agreement ends. With other thinkers, most especially Kathryn Tanner in *Theories of Culture*, I reject the notion that religious traditions are unitary, tightly integrated, cultural-linguistic schemes with transhistorically enduring deep grammars. There are no nonporous boundaries between Christian metanarratives and non-Christian language games anywhere to be found because they do not exist. Human beings, Christians being no exception, live at the intersection of and navigate between multiple porous traditions, sacred and secular. We are, all of us, always already multiple; the question is only whether we are intentionally or accidentally so. On all these matters, it is impossible to exceed Tanner's work. See Tanner (1997).
2 For a discussion of these exemplary dual belongers, see Drew (2011).
3 For more about these figures, see Ulrich (2011) and (2004)
4 For a brief but illuminating account of the intensity of Swamiji's struggle, see Amaladoss (2016).
5 There is, of course, also the possibility that there may be more than one ultimate reality. This option has been proposed by a variety of thinkers, including, most prominently, David Ray Griffin and John Cobb. Griffin also points to Mark Heim as a kindred spirit and ally. For Griffin and Cobb, there are at least three: God, a personal ultimate; creativity, a transpersonal ultimate; and the world itself. Together, these three can account for personal religious experience, the transpersonal experiences of Hindu and Buddhist traditions, and the cosmic/naturalistic religiosities. See Griffin (2005).

References

Amaladoss, Michael. 2016. "Being Hindu-Christian: A Play of Interpretations – The Experience of Swami Abhishiktananda," pp. 89–98, in *Many Yet One? Multiple Religious Belonging*, edited by Peniel Jesudason, Rufus Rajkumar, and Joseph Prabhakar Dayam. Geneva: World Council of Churches.

Drew, Rose. 2011. *Buddhist and Christian? An Exploration of Dual Belonging.* New York: Routledge.

Griffin, David R., ed. 2005. *Deep Religious Pluralism.* Louisville: Westminster John Knox.

Hadot, Pierre. 1995. *Philosophy as a Way of Life: Philosophical Exercises from Socrates to Foucault*. Malden, MA: Blackwell.

Lindbeck, George. 1984. *The Nature of Doctrine: Religion and Theology in a Post-liberal Age*. Louisville: Westminster John Knox.

Ponticus, Evagrius. 1972. *Evagrius Ponticus: The Praktikos. Chapters on Prayer*. Kalamazoo, MI: Cistercian Publications.

Tanner, Kathryn. 1997. *Theories of Culture: A New Agenda for Theology*. Minneapolis: Fortress Press.

Ulrich, Edward T. 2004. "Swami Abhishiktananda and Comparative Theology." *Horizons* 31 (1): 40–63. doi:10.1017/s0360966900001067

Ulrich, Edward T. 2011. "Convergences and Divergences: The Lives of Swami Abhishiktananda and Raimundo Panikkar." *Journal of Hindu-Christian Studies* 24: 36–45. doi:10.7825/2164–6279.1486

6   My Buddha-nature and my Christ-nature

Paul Knitter

Although any statement that is supposed to apply to all religions is risky, I do believe that a case can be made that all wisdom traditions recognize, in one form or another, that *religions really don't know what they are talking about!* All of them insist that what they are seeking or what they believe they have come to experience, what many of them call ultimate reality, is *beyond all human comprehension.* No human being, and no human community of spiritual seekers, can grasp the fullness of God, or Tao, or Brahman, or Wakan Tanka. As a tee-shirt that someone gave me – and which would make an ideal gift for all theologians – puts it: "God is too big to fit into any one religion."

In my theology classes, I have used the image of ultimate reality or Truth as a universe surrounding us that, in its vastness and richness, is beyond all human sight. To see it, we need telescopes. But all such telescopes – in their varying power and specializations – do two things: they enable us to see more of the Truth that otherwise would be beyond our visual capacity; but they also limit what we can see, for focusing on one part of the universe of truth leaves out others. So in order to see more of the universe than what my telescope allows me to see, I need to look through other telescopes that are different in their abilities and specificities than mine.

The analogy is clear. If followers of the different wisdom traditions are convinced that they have encountered and come to know a Truth that has given meaning to their lives, they also know that there is more to the Truth than what they know. They know, but they also know that they don't know. What more and more followers of the religions are coming to realize in our interconnected, intercommunicating contemporary world is that they can discover and come to know more of the Sacred by using, as it were, the telescopes of other religions. In order to learn more of the Sacred, in order to overcome the limitations of one's own religion, one must engage the teachings and practices of other religious paths. As Raimon Panikkar put it with his typical edgy insightfulness: "To answer the question 'Who/what is my God,' I have to ask the question 'Who/what is your God'" (Panikkar 1979, 203).

DOI: 10.4324/9780429000973-9

That is a question posed in interreligious dialogue. To be authentic, dialogue requires much more than "tolerant conversation" in which participants are "nice" to each other. It is also more than a sincere conversation in which all parties seek to learn more *about* each other. Anyone who truly commits herself to real dialogue commits herself to the possibility and to the expectation of learning *from* the other. And insofar as one learns something new or different *from another*, one is also learning something new *about oneself*. The goal is not just *information* but also *transformation*. One might have to change not only one's ideas but also one's religious identity, one's way of being religious.

I'm going to write out of my own personal search for a spirituality that can be experientially meaningful, intellectually coherent, and ethically responsible. My reflections as a theologian will, in other words, be based on my spiritual practices and experience. I hope that these reflections will be an example of theology as *"fides quaerens intellectum"* – spiritual experience trying to make sense of itself. I will be following the age-old Christian directive that the *"lex credendi"* (how we believe) should flow from the *"lex orandi"* (how we pray). Doctrine should be grounded in and tested by spirituality.

I will begin with some of the difficulties or stumbling blocks that I and – from my experience as a teacher and a preacher – many Christians have with what they have been told to believe about Jesus the Christ. If Christians no longer believe that "outside the church there is no salvation," many now struggle with the related claim "outside of Jesus there is no salvation."

Many Christians sense a discomforting ambiguity when they ask themselves: "Just how does Jesus save me? How is he my savior?" There is increasing dissatisfaction with the *atonement theory* – that Jesus's death somehow paid the price that satisfied God's wrath or demand for justice after the "original sin."

But what is to take the place of atonement? I want to suggest that our conversation with Buddhism can provide some very welcome help.

I will be using the notion of "functional analogy" as it is developed by my co-author, Roger Haight, in our recent book *Jesus and Buddha: Friends in Conversation* (Haight and Knitter 2015). Functional analogies between two differing traditions would be those teachings or symbols that, despite their profound differences, serve similar purposes or respond to similar concerns and thus can offer possibilities of comparison that illumine and enrich each other.

The Tibetan Buddhist practice from which I would like to suggest some functional analogies with the saving role of Jesus is that of *Guru Yoga*, particularly as taught by my teacher, Lama John Makransky, as "benefactor practice."[1] Tibetan teachers recognize the need for embodiments or visual representations of the ultimate reality that is beyond conceptual comprehension. These are our "spiritual benefactors," who have embodied and so can reveal the nature of mind. For Buddhists, of course, the primary spiritual benefactor will be Buddha, or Tara, or one of the vast team of bodhisattvas. Makransky encourages Christians to welcome Jesus, as well as Mary, as their spiritual benefactors.

Crucial for this practice is to visualize and truly *feel* the presence of the spiritual benefactor. Visualizations of the benefactor are intense, particular, contextual, and set in the vivid colors of what St. Ignatius in the Jesuit Spiritual Exercises might call the *"compositio loci."* The practitioner is encouraged to feel the energy of the benefactor's love that embraces and holds her fully and penetrates, as Makransky puts it, into every cell of one's body. After having received the love of the benefactor into one's total being, the practitioner, in the second step of this practice, extends the love to all sentient beings.

The final phase is to let the images of the benefactor dissolve and allow oneself to merge nonconceptually into the Essence Love that was manifest and communicated through the benefactor. This is the "nonconceptual" goal of the practice. We grow in awareness that there is a nondual oneness between the spiritual benefactor and ourselves and also between the teacher and student, between benefactor and recipient, between savior and saved, within the vast cognizant, compassionate space that contains and animates us all.

When Christians visualize Jesus as their spiritual benefactor, they can discover deeper ways of understanding and experiencing Jesus. Seventy times St. Paul uses the phrase "en Christo einei" – to be in Christ Jesus. The Buddhist benefactor practice functions analogously for the Christian as a way of waking up to what it means or how it feels "to be in Christ Jesus," or to "put on the mind of Christ" (Phil 2:5), or to be the body of Christ (I Cor 12:27). Having gone through the visualization of Christ, having received of the love of Christ, having extended that love to all the others that make up his body, and finally having let the image go in order to fuse into the mystery of the risen Christ-Spirit, the Christian can pronounce, with clarity, "It is now no longer I who lives; it is Christ living in/as me" (Gal 2:20).

This is salvation – not as an atoning process that takes place outside of oneself but as a transformative unitive experience. Jesus saves in essentially the same way that the transcendent Buddha saves: not by constituting the nature of mind or God's saving love, but by revealing and so making it effectively present. With Christ, one is a recipient and a conduit of the Essence Love that Jesus called Abba. To be saved, therefore, is the nondual experience of being in Christ Jesus. In this experience, Jesus certainly plays a very unique role. But it is a uniqueness that is, by its very nature, larger than Jesus and so shareable with other unique embodiments of Essence Love or Spirit.

In another functional analogy, both Buddha and Jesus can be considered "liberators" – as bearers of a message that can enable humans to achieve the well-being of what Buddha called enlightenment and of what Jesus called the Reign of God. They shared a common starting point for their preaching: the sufferings that all humans (though some more than others) have to face: the inadequacies, the perplexities, the insufficiencies, the diminishments, the pains and disappointments that darken human existence. Both teachers began their missions out of a concern for the sufferings of their fellow human beings.

As indicated in the Second of the Four Noble Truths, for Buddhists, the fundamental cause of suffering is found in the *tanha*, or self-centered greed, that all humans have to deal with. This selfishness is caused by the ignorance that human beings are born into. Hence, the importance of *enlightening*, or transforming our sense of who and what we are. What we really are, according to the teachings of the Dharma, is *anatta – not-selves* – beings who exist as interbeings with others. Our own well-being consists in fostering the well-being of others. Enlightenment is to wake up to that truth, that reality.

At this point, liberationist Christians will remind Buddhists that the results of ignorance go beyond the individual. The actions that follow upon my lack of awareness of my nature as *anatta/not-self* are not only *my* actions; they become, slowly but inevitably, *society's* actions. My own ego-centered attitudes and acts become embodied in social forms; they incarnate themselves, as it were, in the way society works. If Buddhists understand *karma* to be the unavoidable results that follow every action or choice we make, Christians will point out that individual karma becomes *social karma*.

Sinful or greedy structures remain even after individuals have been enlightened. Liberationist Christians insist on the reality of *social sin*, which can remain even after individual sin has been removed. To transform the structures of one's awareness and thinking does not necessarily change the structures of society. One can be enlightened and full of compassion for all sentient beings without realizing that one remains a part of an economic system that continues to cause suffering to others.

So Christians remind Buddhists that transforming oneself is different from – and should not become a substitute for – transforming society. This implies that compassion, though necessary, is insufficient. Justice is also necessary. If compassion calls us to feed the hungry, justice urges us to ask why they are hungry. Mindfulness is necessary for living a life of inner peace, but we also need *social mindfulness* of how our reified, ego-centric thoughts and fears become reified social or political systems.

If Buddhists are to effectively extend their practice of personal mindfulness to include social mindfulness, they will also have to take seriously the Christian liberationists' call for a *"preferential option for the oppressed."* This preference calls upon all spiritual seekers to be sure that their quest includes, as an integral element, the effort to become aware of the experience of those who have been pushed aside, those who don't have a meaningful voice in the decisions of state or school or neighborhood. Our "mindfulness" must also include them, their experience, their reality.

This is what the liberation theologians mean by the *"hermeneutical privilege of the poor."* From their position of suffering and exploitation, the oppressed can see the world in ways that the powerful or the comfortable cannot. The mindfulness we practice on our cushions or in our pews must be balanced and expanded by the mindfulness gained on the streets.

If Christians remind Buddhists that personal transformation is *incomplete* without social transformation, Buddhists in turn will remind Christians that social transformation is *impossible* without personal transformation. For Buddhists, I believe, inner transformation of consciousness has a *certain priority* over social transformation.

One can carry out the task of being a bodhisattva only if one has experienced the wisdom that produces compassion. Prajna, or wisdom, is what one knows when one begins to wake up to the interconnectedness or the interbeing of all reality. Realizing that one's very being or self is not one's own but the being of all other selves, one will necessarily feel compassion for all sentient beings.

Buddhists are calling Christians to recognize (or reaffirm) the subtle, but real, *primacy of contemplation over action* and of *compassion over justice.*

The primacy of contemplation over action

There is a Buddhist conviction that we must undergo a profound personal transformation before we can "wisely" interact with the world around us. We are born into a fundamental ignorance that we must deal with before we can begin to truly know who and what we and the world really are. If we don't overcome this ignorance before fixing the world's problems, we're probably only going to cause more problems. Although Buddhists have much to learn from Christians about *what kind of action* must arise out of contemplation (that is, socially transformative action), Christians need to learn from Buddhists *why action without contemplation is unsustainable and dangerous.*

Buddhist contemplation aims at a nondual experience of our interbeing or reciprocal interdependence with what is ultimate (the nature of mind/spirit). This is what establishes in us an inner peace; it is also what sustains us in working for the Reign of God. No matter what happens, no matter how much failure or opposition, if we *are* peace, we will continue to try to *make* peace (Hanh 1992). Such inner peace and groundedness is a protector or an antidote to the danger of burnout that threatens all social and peace activists. Working for peace and justice is hard, often frustrating, work.

The primacy of compassion over justice

But contemplation manifests its priority not only by sustaining action but also by guiding it. Thich Nhat Hanh challenges the Christian insistence on the "preferential option for the oppressed." God, he declares, doesn't have preferences. God – or Essence Love – embraces all beings – poor and rich, oppressed and oppressor – *equally* (Hanh 1995).

Christians remind Buddhists that compassion without justice – that is, without reform of structural injustice – is not enough to relieve suffering; Buddhists remind Christians that, just as there can be no peace without justice, there can also be no justice without compassion.

This Buddhist challenge reminds us of what Jesus himself taught. People will know who Jesus's disciples are not by their work for justice, but by their love for each other. Jesus's "first commandment" is love, not justice (Jn 13: 35). And Jesus called on us to love our enemies as much as we love our friends, which means loving the oppressor as much as we love the oppressed. This doesn't mean we will not confront our enemies and oppressors. But our primary motivation for doing so will not be the demand of justice, but the demand of love. We will confront oppressors with what Makransky calls "a fierce compassion" (Makransky 2014).

Thich Nhat Hanh, in his little book on *Living Buddha, Living Christ*, informs Christians that, for a Buddhist, God doesn't have favorites. He is thus reminding Christians that just as there is a relationship of nonduality between emptiness and form, or between Abba-Mystery and us, so there is a nonduality between oppressed and oppressor. Both are expressions of interbeing and Abba-Mystery. The actions of oppressor or oppressed are clearly different. But their identities are the same. And that means that *my own* identity is linked to both oppressed and oppressors.

Therefore, we do not respond to the oppressed out of compassion and to the oppressor out of justice. No, we respond to *both* out of compassion! Compassion for both the oppressed and the oppressor. So, yes, we want to liberate the oppressed. But *just as much*, we want to liberate the oppressors. Compassion for the oppressor will be expressed differently than compassion for the oppressed. But *just as much*, we want to free the oppressors from the illusions that drive them to greed and to the exploitation of others. Such a nonpreferential option for compassion that extends equally and clearly to both oppressed and oppressors will be the foundation on which justice can be built, on which structures can be changed.

Some kind of a spiritual practice that will foster and sustain our inner transformation and resources is imperative. To have begun the process of awakening to oneness with Christ and to what Jesus experienced as the unconditional love of the Abba-Mystery can assure us that our efforts are not just our own efforts. Once we begin to wake up to the wisdom that reveals to us that all our efforts are grounded in and expressions of the Abba-Mystery that is active in and as us, once we begin to realize that in working for peace and justice we are doing what our Christ-nature necessarily calls us to do – then we will also realize that, as the *Bhagavad Gita* tells us, the value of our actions are not determined by their fruits. The value of our actions is in our actions themselves, for they are also the actions of Abba.

This deeper experience of the nonduality between the Abba-Mystery and the world, or between the future and the present Reign of God, assures Christians that even though their efforts to bring the world closer to the Reign of God fail, Abba and the Reign are still present and available. In both success and failure, the Reign of God is both already/not yet.

The Buddhist experience of "enlightenment," of waking up to what Mahayana Buddhists term our "Buddha-nature," is, I believe, a prompt for Christians to enter more profoundly into the unitive experience signaled in John's description of Jesus as "one with the Father" and "one with us" (Jn 14), or in Paul's description (I would dare say "definition") of a Christian as someone who exists "in Christ." I am suggesting that the nondual unity that Mahayana Buddhists affirm between emptiness and form, or between Nirvana and Samsara, or (in Thich Nhat Hanh's terminology) between interbeing and all finite beings, is analogous to, if not the same as, the unity between Jesus and Abba or between Christ and us. The divine and the finite, the creator and the created are, like emptiness and form, distinct but insepa-rable. They co-inhere. They "inter-are."

When we begin to "awaken" to our oneness with Christ in the Father, when we begin to feel that "it is no longer I who live but Christ who lives in me" (Gal 3: 21), we are awakening to what Buddhists call *prajna*, or *wisdom* – the awareness of the fundamental, all pervasive interconnected-ness of all reality. We are all truly "one in the Spirit." And this realization that we are interlinked in the Divine Mystery will naturally bring forth in us what Buddhists call *karuna*, *compassion*, for all our fellow human beings – indeed, for all sentient beings. To love our neighbor is not a commandment; it is a natural necessity.

Here Buddhists are offering us Christians an opportunity to clarify, per-haps reform, our soteriology – our doctrine on how Jesus brings about "sal-vation." The cross can save a world wracked by the sufferings caused by greed and hatred and violence by embodying and making clear the power of nonviolent love. Jesus died on the cross not because the Father willed it, but because he refused, as the Dhammapada counsels, to answer hatred with hatred. Rather than answering the violence of the colonizing Romans and their local collaborators with his own violence, rather than abandoning his mission of proclaiming the Reign of God, he responded with love and trust, and, as the Latin American martyrs express it, he was "disappeared."

And the power of this embodiment of nonviolent love was such that, after he died, his followers, gathered around the table to break bread and remember him, realized that he was still with them. His example of love confronting hatred, of nonviolence responding to violence, transformed their lives with the power to go and do likewise. To be so transformed is to be redeemed and saved. His followers share in his "Christ-nature," just as the followers of Buddha continue to realize their "Buddha-nature." And by realizing my Buddha-nature, I have been able to understand and to live my Christ-nature.

Note

1 This benefactor practice is laid out clearly and practically in Makransky's *Awakening through Love* (2007).

References

Haight, Roger, and Paul Knitter. 2015. *Jesus and Buddha: Friends in Conversation*. Maryknoll: Orbis Books. doi:10.1086/696274

Hanh, Thich N. 1992. *Peace Is Every Step: The Path of Mindfulness in Everyday Life*. New York: Bantam.

Hanh, Thich N. 1995. *Living Buddha, Living Christ*. New York: Riverhead Books.

Makransky, John. 2007. *Awakening Through Love*. Somerville, MA: Wisdom Publications.

Makransky, John. 2014. "A Buddhist Critique of, and Learning from, Christian Liberation Theology." *Theological Studies* 75 (3): 635–657. doi:10.1177/0040563914541028

Panikkar, Raimundo. 1979. "The Myth of Pluralism: The Tower of Babel – A Meditation on Non-Violence." *CrossCurrents* 29 (2): 197–230.

7 "Why not ten 60-foot wells?"[1]

Peter Savastano

Religious book knowledge and the heart's religious experiences

William C. Chittick, the scholar of Islamic philosophy and Sufism, distinguishes between two kinds of spiritual knowledge: "transmitted" and "intellectual." We acquire transmitted knowledge by studying theories about religion constructed by acknowledged experts such as theologians, religious scholars and the custodians of orthodoxy (Chittick 2007).[2] Transmitted knowledge, therefore, is that which we take for granted based on the claims of authority and expertise. Such received knowledge, religion based on theories, doctrines, and dogmas, has a venerable history, because the transmission of ancient traditions from master to student and from past communities to new generations is paramount in educating human beings. We learn the rules so as to conform our experiences to align with our received traditions that socialize us into the religious communities into which we are born. But this book knowledge and accumulation of theories is not enough. Inevitably, theories are never enough: theory eventually hits the wall of personal experiences. For those whose religious knowledge limits a genuine spiritual journey or quest, a breaking out of traditional and received forms, Chittick claims the acquisition of "intellectual knowledge" becomes crucial, although his term is counter to what Westerners would understand by this term as knowledge gained by reasoning and processes of abstraction. However, in the Islamic mystical tradition and in its particular emphases employed by the Sufis (Muslim mystics), intelligence is not acquired solely by the ratiocinative functions of the mind alone. "Intellectual knowledge" is learning by and through the heart (*qalb*), a knowledge formed in the crucible of one's experiences "on the ground" as opposed to the nonturbulent flights of personally untested theories. Grounding spiritual experiences are attained (hopefully) by practices through which we write our own books. In Islamic mysticism, the intellect is the "heart," the core of a person's religious and spiritual self where experiences override theories to produce deeper truths.

DOI: 10.4324/9780429000973-10

I am an academic, an anthropologist of religion and consciousness by training, forced by my guild to teach my students traditional concepts and theories rather than to transmit what I have learned about being human and religious through my life's actual experiences. I know how to write and speak about the Great Mystery (God) conventionally in ways all scholars in my field would approve. It has taken me years to realize that I teach my students best as I learned best. I help them to trust their own experiences so that they can confidently test for themselves the theories we discuss in class. They must not regurgitate for me what has been written and said. Instead, they learn best when they are free to explore the viability of theories within the context of their own lives and experiences. As the Quaker saying goes: "Jesus said this, Paul said that, George Fox says this, but what do you say?" In the light of these received traditions, who are you? Let your "heart" be critical. What's your perspective on these theories from where you actually stand? My students must learn, as I have struggled to learn, that in the face of religious traditions I must "hold my ground" and realize that, in the end, as Thomas Merton wrote, "only experience counts."

A foremost scholar of world religious traditions, Huston Smith, during an interview in the 1990s with NPR's Terry Gross, referred to the personal path he found and made through his encounter with various religious traditions. He learned he knew these traditions best when he practiced what they preached:

> Mine has been a rather peculiar history, and I don't want to leave the impression that one is in any way spiritually ahead because of this kind of incorporation. I liked what a teacher in India once said to me. If you are drilling for water, it's better to drill one 60-foot well than ten 6-foot wells. And generally speaking, I think a kind of smorgasbord cafeteria, choosing from here and there is not productive. So I would not at all put what's happened, I feel, to be feasible for me in any way ahead of where I might be if I had devoted my entire spiritual exercises to Christianity.

The authenticity of Smith's scholarship, however, is that he did dig ten 6-foot wells, metaphorically speaking, rather than one 60-foot well. The map he charted through his own spiritual journey was uniquely informative. We would not hold his career in such esteem had he not explored and been transformed by the many practices he utilized from religious traditions other than his received Christianity.

Over the course of my own 49-year spiritual journey, I, too, have heard exhortations similar to the one given to Smith by the Indian teacher. In my case the warnings to me that I should stick with one religious tradition only and not "dig ten 6-foot wells instead of one 60-foot well" has been suggested to me by a number of spiritual teachers from whom I have sought enlightenment. Over the course of my life, I have sat at the feet of teachers of my received traditions, Catholic and Eastern Orthodox, but I have also sat with the Quakers, with a Qalandar Sufi Shaykh from Kashmir, with a Zen Buddhist teacher, with a Tibetan Buddhist Lama, and with a Tibetan Bon Lama. At first, I tried to follow their instructions but, ultimately, another deeper urge took over. Their exhortations often contradicted my life's experiences. At the same time, I have always been aware that relying on personal experience risks delusion, so for over 20 years I have maintained a relationship with a spiritual director. My spiritual guide has helped me to discern and adhere to a personal spiritual path that can ground and critique all my "inner promptings." But like Huston Smith, my spiritual journey has plumbed heights and depths. My heart knowledge has been expanded through my immersion in religious traditions other than the Christian tradition into which I was baptized and first nurtured.

I self-identify as an Episcopalian Christian who is also an ordained Episcopal Clergyperson. But I acknowledge that my being grounded in my Episcopalian tradition has been given more solid ground by my practices in various religious traditions that include the Tibetan, Zen and Bon-Buddhist, the universal Sufi tradition, strands of Native American sacred healing traditions, and diverse forms of Western Esotericism.[3]

In choosing to follow my inner guide, I have found it beneficial to dig many 6-foot wells rather than only one 60-foot shaft. I have allowed "the Spirit" through my experiences with other religious traditions to disclose its presence to and within me. I have engaged "the Spirit" and have become more in touch with the Divine Presence within by going outside the circle of Christian concepts, symbols, and narratives that I still must acknowledge as my native tongue, religiously speaking.

The importance of practice

In my experience, spiritual exercises have been the agents of my spiritual transformation and growth. More than my studies of doctrine and dogmas, it is practice that facilitates actual spiritual experience. Yet I am also an academic, an anthropologist, and a scholar of religious studies. As an anthropologist I conduct research by doing fieldwork, learning a society's culture by participating in it as comprehensively as possible rather than observing it from afar. I consider spiritual exercises drawn from various religious traditions as a form of doing inner fieldwork. I have learned less about "the Spirit" alive in religious traditions by hearing and so much more by tasting and feeling.

I cannot name every practice from every spiritual tradition I have engaged in and found fruitful, but it might be illustrative to list at least a few.

Christian exercises

I have practiced Centering Prayer as developed by Fr. Thomas Keating, Cynthia Bourgeault, and others.[4] Within Eastern Orthodoxy, I pray with holy icons and practice "prayer of the heart" as inspired by the collection of texts from the early fourth century CE to the eighteenth century known as the *Philokalia*. The English translation of this Greek and Slavic compendium exposes the *hesychastic* practice of continually reciting "the Jesus prayer," its most complete form being "Jesus, Son of God, have mercy on me a sinner." The recitation of this prayer involves bodily postures, often in the form of prostrations that accompany the recitation of the prayer. One of the aims of this practice is to redirect one's consciousness away from its traditional Western orientation in the head and place one's awareness into the heart. The prayer is usually synchronized with the inhalation and exhalation of the breath while using a prayer rope to count the number of repetitions of the prayer (and also as a way of engaging the body). The greatest proponent of the *hesychastic* method of prayer is Gregory Palamas (1296–1359) in his classic *The Triads* (Palamas 1983).

From the Quaker tradition, I have incorporated the practice of sitting in silent, expectant waiting on The Inner Light of Christ, or The Light Within, as more universalist Quakers refer to the divine presence immanent in human beings.

Sufism

From the Sufi tradition, I have participated in the Dances of Universal Peace and by the "turning" of the Mevlevi lineage of Sufis, popularly known as "whirling dervishes." The Mevlevi regard Rumi as their primary *sheikh* (master) and founder. I have practiced the *Zikr* (Remembrance) of the Divine Names, of which there are traditionally 99, identified in the *Qur'an*. I have prayed the formula *La ill Allah illallahu* recited in synchronization with the breath, both in a group and individually.[5]

Buddhism

From the Vajrayana Buddhist tradition, I have practiced the *Tersar Ngondro*, translated as "Preliminary Practices." These meditations involve the body (postures), speech (recitation of mantras), and mind (visualizations), all of which are done simultaneously and draw on the various yogas (stages of development toward enlightenment) of the rich tantric repertoire of sadhanas (meditation practices).[6]

My involvement with Bon-Buddhism[7] also required the practice of a *Ngondro*. However, since my engagement with Bon-Buddhism was approximately five years, I did not do as much practice in that tradition as I did in Vajrayana Buddhism. In both lineages of Bon-Buddhism and Vajrayana Buddhism, I received many empowerments (*Wongs*), which are direct transmissions of the Buddha-mind of Enlightenment from the teacher to the student, and initiations (*Lungs*), which authorized me to engage in various meditation *sadhanas* beyond the preliminaries of the *Ngondro*.

My encounters with Zen Buddhism included sitting practice (*shikan taza*, which means "just sitting" in English) under the guidance of a Zen teacher. I received instructions during *sessiens* (intensive sitting and walking meditation retreats) and *koan* study, that is, meditation upon a series of paradoxical sayings and their commentaries, of which the most famous is "What is the sound of one hand clapping?" (Yuasa 1981).

Shamanism

I have engaged with "shamanism," a troubled term from the perspective of the many Indigenous peoples whose sacred ritual and healing traditions have been so labeled by Western scholars. I have taken workshops and various trainings in what I would term "neo-shamanic" techniques and rituals. From neo-shamanism I have similarly employed journeying techniques as I had been taught them to engage Jesus, the Virgin Mary, and many of the saints to whom I am devoted. In as much as Tibetan Buddhism has shamanistic components, I have used Vajrayana Buddhist "visualization" techniques to visualize Christian holy personages, like Jesus, the angels, or particular Christian saints to whom I am devoted.

There are also times when my experience of the divine surpasses all concepts and metaphors. This is an experience of the apophatic nature of The Great Mystery which I describe as "the scaffolding falling away."

To realize the divine in nonanthropomorphic terms and more as dynamic, verb-like qualities or attributes, such as "The Real" (*al-Haqq*) or as Mercy or Compassion (*ar-Rahman* or *ar-Rahim*), liberates me from thinking of God as a white male with long hair and a beard. This practice of visualizing the divine or ultimate reality as energies or qualities facilitates an experience of The Great Mystery that is vibrant and active rather than as static or nounlike. To switch modes of perception in this way facilitates an encounter with ultimate reality (holy wisdom) as a way of being that is greater than one limited by human characteristics. I am also able to plummet the depths of my being where I can encounter such divine attributes or qualities as bubbling up from deep within the recesses of my consciousness. These qualities are reflections to me of what Thomas Merton referred to as *Le Point Vierge*, that place in our consciousness which intimately unites us to the Divine Presence, making it difficult to make distinctions between the divine and the human.[8]

In describing the divine as the real, as ultimate reality, and as my personal favorite, The Great Mystery,[9] I am describing the personal, relational God of the Abrahamic traditions, but not anthropomorphically. It might seem that I am describing some impersonal force or entity much more in alignment with the nontheistic traditions such as Taoism or Buddhism, but that is not at all what I am doing. But by engaging in these non-Christian practices, I have expanded my understanding and experience of the Abrahamic God. On other levels, my engagement with Taoism and Buddhism has allowed a personal encounter with the Great Mystery informed by contemporary physics.[10]

Some years ago, I had a conversation with my spiritual director about whether or not God, ultimate reality, or The Great Mystery is personal or impersonal. We agreed that ultimate reality or God manifests in both personal and impersonal modes (or sometimes simultaneously as both), analogous to particle and wave theory in contemporary physics. We agreed that we humans do not control the mode in which the "divine" is disclosed to us; nor can we control how and when such disclosure happens. Manifesting in personal mode is analogous to particle mode in physics, while manifesting in impersonal mode is akin to wave mode. It is difficult to measure or prove a subjective experience of the Great Mystery, but at various times in my life I have experienced the divine both as a deeply personal and relational presence (I/Thou) and/or as an impersonal ground or force (I/It) that is animating my own consciousness and that of all of creation simultaneously.

The downward spiral

No doubt I leave the impression that I have engaged in a rather meandering assortment of traditions in one lifetime (the very cafeteria or smorgasbord experiences Huston Smith describes and cautions against). However, my practice of the contemplative traditions of many religions has not been superficial or casual. I have studied and practiced in these various traditions over extended periods, sometimes up to 15 or 20 years consecutively. Taking this approach has prepared me for doing Theology Without Walls.

The pattern that best illustrates my inclusive religious experiences and spiritual exercises is that of a downward spiral initiated in my life as a youth of 15. Each time I have engaged with one of these traditions, I have practiced their exercises for several years at a time before moving on to another tradition. However, re-engagement does not occur with a previously engaged tradition until I have received inner instructions to do so. Each time I have engaged in another spiritual practice, I have gone deeper into it, thus making the pattern downward spiral–like. As I have spiraled down through various practices from other traditions, I have also maintained my engagement with my original Christian tradition simultaneously and interspiritually.

My engagements with various spiritual exercises have always included the study of sacred texts by drawing on many different academic disciplines; an encounter with living teachers of these traditions with whom I have studied; and an adopting of the ritual, devotional, and meditative practices that each tradition offers to the spiritual seeker.

My interspiritual approach has allowed me to learn not only the transmitted knowledge of these religious traditions but also their devotional and ethical practices that are their beating heart. Interspirituality has provided the field site by which I test a religious tradition's transmitted knowledge through my personal experiences. I theorize and practice interspiritually so as to taste the intellectual knowledge that is rooted in my heart and not only in my books. I have touched the kernel beyond the shell of each tradition. Aided by my spiritual director, I have discerned what spiritual practices have worked for me by years of testing and experimentation.

The scaffolding falls away

I now explore one of the most important features of this downward spiral pattern of living interspiritually. It can be identified as the experience of having "the scaffolding fall away," where all structure momentarily disappears as one realizes one knows nothing of the divine. It is an utterly apophatic moment when one enters a "cloud of unknowing." This consciousness of a void surpasses and defies all symbols, concepts, and sacred narratives, all of the predetermined givens of any particular religious tradition.[11] Living under this "cloud of unknowing" is basically an inexpressible experience as one "free-falls" when all the structures fall away.

In *Participation in the Mystery, Transpersonal Essays in Psychology, Education and Religion*, Jorge N. Ferrer writes that "Participatory enaction entails a model of spiritual engagement that does not simply reproduce certain tropes according to a given historical *a priori*, but rather embarks upon the adventure of openness to the novelty and creativity of nature or the mystery" (Ferrer 2017, 15). By participatory enaction, I understand Ferrer to mean that the mystery is capable of unfolding in unpredictable ways. There are no predetermined maps for navigating the experience. One enters a seemingly vast wilderness of thick trees. As Sarah Coakley so astutely points out,

> A love affair with a blank, such as contemplation is, is a strange subversion of all certainties, a stripping, often painful, of what one previously took for granted [. . .] The act of contemplation involves a willed suspension of one's rational agendas, a silent waiting.
>
> (Coakley 2013, 342, emphasis added)

One becomes a co-creator (through participatory enaction) in the novelty of the mystery's unfolding. To be a co-creator, as I read Ferrer, means that I am not separate from The Great Mystery or the cosmos, but rather, I have participatory agency in the process of novel, revelatory unfoldings. As such, I bring to the process of this novel cosmic unfoldment my bodily, instinctive, sexual, emotional, intellectual, and intuitive intelligence, all of which become the media for the manifestation (and embodiment) of The Great Mystery in ways unique and particular to me.

Ferrer goes on to write:

> Hence, the participatory perspective does not contend that there are two, three, or any limited quantity of pre-given spiritual ultimates, but

rather that the radical openness, interrelatedness, and creativity of the mystery or the cosmos allows for the participatory co-creation of an indefinite number of ultimate self-disclosures of reality and corresponding religious worlds.

(Coakley 2013, 16–17)

Reading Ferrer helps me to name this experience of "the scaffolding falling away." I am momentarily lost in The Great Mystery. I am an active participant in the radiance of the Mystery's disclosure. I realize that I am a part of the unfolding, multiple possibilities of reality. I experience a world of possibilities in which I am, simultaneously, a co-creator and a total stranger. My task or "fate" is to explore the novelty of this experience in the hope that, as I assimilate it, I might be able to articulate it by making this "void" visible to myself and possibly for others.

When the epiphany of The Great Mystery within my consciousness reveals itself, I am stripped of all points of reference. In my experience, these periods of "the scaffolding falling away" coincides with the moment when my immersion in a particular religious tradition exhausts itself, when all elements of a tradition lose agency to help one's searching. As much as I might cling to it, warning myself that I must remain faithful to the tradition engaging me, the reality is that I have no agency that mediates my relationship with ultimate reality or the divine.

In trying to make sense of this experience on a theoretical level, John Caputo's exposition of Jacque Derrida's work has been most helpful: "The point of view of Derrida's work as an author is religious – but without religion and without religion's God – and no one understands a thing about this alliance," Caputo writes (Caputo 1997, xviii). I have been in the place Caputo describes here, especially in the last 15 to 20 years. I make no claims of being finished with this process. I am not in control when it happens.

This space/place/state with no scaffolding is both elating and troubling. I am elated because it is a life-enhancing adventure to lose the path of each religious tradition regarding prayer and meditation, with nothing to rely on or to guide me in the process. It is troubling because this loss of something to rely on leaves me having to face The Great Mystery alone and uncertain of the novelty which may emerge. In dealing with this uncertainty, not only have Caputo and Derrida provided guideposts along the way, but so have some Sufi traditions which acknowledge that there is a station in the spiritual quest when one transcends (or descends from) any religious structure as every crutch falls away.

Lessons from Thomas Merton and Sufism

The twentieth-century Catholic monk, mystic, poet, and social justice activist Thomas Merton, knew this too. Being very much aware of this part of the process by which the constructs of a religious tradition no longer provide support or succor, one must come face to face with The Great Mystery on its terms. Here, Merton presciently anticipated thinkers such as Derrida, Caputo, and Ferrer. He did not have the opportunity to do very much subsequent writing about his own experience of what I name as having the scaffolding fall away, due to his sudden death on December 10, 1968. He was, however, able to recognize his own experience when he read a book that matched his own experience, *Final Integration of the Adult Personality* by A. Reza Arasteh (1965a).

Arasteh was an Iranian American psychologist who explored, through a Sufi lens, the process by which certain human beings undergo final spiritual integration. As the penultimate step in this final stage of adult integration, Arasteh emphasizes a phase by which a person is stripped of all cultural references and constructs, but most specifically those cultural references and constructs that are provided by her or his religion. He presents his case studies of ordinary twentieth-century persons experiencing this process. He also names well-known historical figures whom he identifies as having experienced final integration, among whom are the twelfth-century Persian Sufi Rumi and the eighteenth-century German poet, naturalist, and mystic Goethe.

In *Final Integration of the Adult Personality* and his subsequent books (Arasteh 1965b, 1980), Arasteh proposes a series of necessary steps or "stations" in final integration by which one is stripped of one's religious conditioning and traditions. This results in what he calls an "anxious search." The result of this anxious searching is the ultimate experience of returning to the religious tradition of one's cultural heritage,[12] free of its doctrinal and dogmatic constraints. Now integrated, according to Arasteh, one's own inner guide engages with the divine. But in light of Ferrer's ideas briefly outlined earlier, there may, in fact, be no need to return to one's religious tradition, given the novel and pluralistic ways that "The Great Mystery" may choose to disclose itself. "*The future of religion*," writes Ferrer, "*will be shaped by spiritually individuated persons engaged in processes of cosmological hybridization in the context of a common spiritual family that honors a global order of respect and civility*" (Ferrer 2017, 37, original emphasis). Thomas Merton, quoting Arasteh, sums up this state of final integration:

> The man (sic) who has final integration is no longer limited by the culture in which he has grown up. "He has embraced *all of life*. . . . He has experienced qualities of every type of life": ordinary human existence, intellectual life, artistic creation, human love, religious life. He passes beyond all these limiting forms while retaining all that is best and most universal in them, "finally giving birth to a fully comprehensive self." He accepts not only his own society, his own community, his own friends, his own culture but all mankind (sic). He does not remain bound to one limited set of values in such a way that he opposes them

aggressively or defensively to others. He is fully "Catholic" in the best sense of the word. He has a unified vision and experience of the one truth shining out in all its various manifestations, some clearer than others. He does not set these partial views up in opposition to each other but unifies them in a dialectic or an insight of complementarity. With this view of life he is able to bring perspective, liberty and spontaneity into the lives of others. The finally integrated man (sic) is a peacemaker. That is why there is such a desperate need for our leaders to become such men of insight.

(Merton 1998, 207)[13]

Arasteh believed that such a final integration of the adult personality was achieved by only an exemplary few because of the suffering and anxiety required to attain this state. "Many are called, few chosen." I do not claim that my experiences of "the scaffolding falling away" is a prelude to my attaining final integration. About such possibilities, it is best to remain speechless. If the end all spiritual exercises is the revelation of one's ignorance, perhaps this is the only outcome to which I can authentically aspire. I realize I am no longer the teacher, only a novice always needing to begin again and again.

Notes

1 I am deeply grateful to my friend and colleague, Jonathan Montaldo, Thomas Merton scholar and of all things mystical extraordinaire, for his helpful suggestions in improving this chapter.
2 See especially Chapter 2.
3 About Native American sacred traditions, I have just finished editing a collection of essays on the Roman Catholic monk, mystic, social activist, and poet Thomas Merton's engagement with such traditions entitled *Merton & Indigenous Wisdom* (2019).
4 See especially, Keating (2012), Bourgeault (2016), and Frenette (2012).
5 See especially, Helminski (2000). *La illaha illallahu* is usually translated as "There is no God but God" with the addition of the *Hu*. Sufis often interpret *La illaha illallahu* as "There is nothing but God," and the *Hu* on the end of the formula suggests the vibratory or energetic nature of God's presence much in the same way that *Om* does in Hinduism.
6 Unfortunately, time and space constraints do not permit me to go into any greater detail about the nature of Tibetan Buddhist practices, nor does the promises one makes when being initiated into these practices to not reveal their details any more than I have. For those who are curious or would like to explore these practices for themselves, the internet offers a rich resource of possible connections to teachers and Dharma Centers.
7 The Bon tradition of Buddhism in Tibet claims to be an older, more ancient form of Buddhism than that brought from Nepal to Tibet by Padmasambhava in the eighth century CE. In fact, the lore is that the founder of Bon was a Buddha who lived at least 2,000 to 8,000 years before the historical Buddha that most of us are familiar with. It is also believed that Bon embodies much more the pre-Buddhist indigenous shamanism of Tibet.

8 For more on *Le Point Vierge*, see Shannon (2002, 363–364).
9 As previously noted, to refer to the sacred as The Great Mystery is the way that seems to best approximate my own first-hand personal experience. I should also note that I am indebted to the First Nation Indigenous peoples of the Americas sacred ritual and healing traditions for this way of addressing the sacred.
10 There is a vast literature on the intersection of religion, science, and physics – too much to elaborate on here. However, one deeply personal source by one of the leading thinkers of contemporary physics is Heisenberg (1971). Another much more current is Lightman (2018). For ways in which the Abrahamic traditions are enriched and expanded through engagement with the sacred ritual and healing traditions of the First Nation Indigenous peoples of the Americas, see Charleston (2015). Charleston is a citizen of the Choctaw Nation of Oklahoma and also a retired Bishop of the Episcopal Church.
11 Although there is a wealth of writings on the apophatic dimension of mystical experience, among the best, though not easy reading, is Sells (1994). One of the interesting aspects of Sells's book is that it addresses apophatic experience from within the context of many religious traditions rather than only the Christian tradition. Another is Keller (2015).
12 And, by extension I would add, to any religious tradition in which one has immersed oneself.
13 See especially Essay XIII.

References

Arasteh, Reza A. 1965a. *Final Integration of the Adult Personality*. Netherlands: E. J. Brill.

Arasteh, Reza A. 1965b. *Rumi the Persian*. New York and London: Routledge & Kegan Paul.

Arasteh, Reza A. 1980. *Growth to Selfhood*. New York and London: Routledge & Kegan Paul.

Bourgeault, Cynthia. 2016. *The Heart of Centering Prayer, Nondual Christianity in Theory and Practice*. Boulder, CO: Shambhala.

Caputo, John D. 1997. *The Prayers and Tear of Jacques Derrida, Religion Without Religion*. Bloomington and Indianapolis: Indiana University Press. doi:10.1177/004057369905600126

Charleston, Steven. 2015. *The Four Vision Quests of Jesus*. New York: Morehouse Publishing.

Chittick, William C. 2007. *Science of the Cosmos, Science of the Soul: The Persistence of Islamic Cosmology in the Modern World*. London: Oneworld Publications.

Coakley, Sarah. 2013. *God, Sexuality and the Self, An Essay 'On the Trinity.'* Cambridge, England: Cambridge University Press. doi:10.1017/s003181911300079x

Ferrer, Jorge N. 2017. *Participation in the Mystery, Transpersonal Essays in Psychology, Education, and Religion*. Albany: State University of New York.

Frenette, David. 2012. *The Path of Centering Prayer, Deepening Your Experience of God*. Boulder, CO: Sounds True.

Heisenberg, Werner. 1971. *Physics and Beyond, Encounters and Conversations*, edited by Ruth Nanda Anshen. New York, Evanston and London: Harper & Row.

Helminski, Camille, trans. 2000. *The Mevlevi Wird*. Soquel, CA: The Threshold Society.

Keating, Thomas. 2012. *Invitation to Love, The Way of Christian Contemplation*. Twentieth Anniversary ed. London & New York: Bloomsbury.

Keller, Catherine. 2015. *Cloud of the Impossible, Negative Theology and Planetary Entanglement*. New York: Columbia University Press. doi:10.1111/rsr.12229

Lightman, Alan. 2018. *Searching for Stars on an Island in Maine*. New York: Pantheon Books.

Merton, Thomas. 1998. *Contemplation in a World of Action*. Notre Dame, IN: University of Notre Dame Press.

Merton, Thomas. 2019. *Merton & Indigenous Wisdom*. Louisville, KY: FonsVitae Press.

Palamas, Gregory. 1983. *The Triads, the Classics of Western Spirituality*. Mahwah, NJ: Paulist Press.

Sells, Michael A. 1994. *Mystical Languages of Unsaying*. Chicago and London: The University of Chicago Press.

Shannon, William, Christine M. Bochen, and Patrick F. O'Connell. 2002. *The Thomas Merton Encyclopedia*. Maryknoll, NY: Orbis Books. doi:10.1017/s0360966900000876

Yuasa, Nobuyuki. 1981. *The Zen Poems of Ryokan*. Princeton, NJ: Princeton University Press.

8   Theology Without Walls

An interspiritual approach

Rory McEntee

[C]ommunity cannot feed for long on itself; it can only flourish where always
the boundaries are giving way to the coming of others from beyond them –
unknown and undiscovered brothers [and sisters].

– Howard Thurman, *The Search for Common
Ground* (Thurman 1986)[1]

Introduction: embodying TWW, the Snowmass Dialogues

In 1984, Father Thomas Keating, a Roman Catholic monk in the Order of
Cistercians of the Strict Observance (also known as "Trappists"), convened
a group of advanced contemplatives from differing religious traditions,
including Buddhist, Hindu, Jewish, Islamic, Native American, Russian
Orthodox, Protestant, and Roman Catholic participants. The idea was to
engage one another in intimate dialogue over five days in a private retreat
setting. Its primary purpose was not "interreligious" dialogue, in the sense
of learning about the doctrines and practices of religious traditions other
than one's own. Rather, as Keating describes it, he invited the participants to
"meditate together in silence, and to share our personal spiritual journeys,
especially those elements in our respective traditions that have proved most
helpful to us along the way" (Miles-Yepez 2006, xvii). Participants were
not meant to speak *for* their tradition – as representatives – but first and
foremost as human beings engaged in spiritually transformative processes,
processes informed and inflected by religious and cultural traditions.

Keating, who has been my most formative spiritual mentor and who
passed away just a few months ago (at the ripe old age of 95), was a powerful figure in the renewal of the Christian contemplative tradition. He
helped develop the now widespread silent meditation technique of Centering Prayer and pioneered experiments in interreligious exchange as abbot
of St. Joseph's monastery in Spencer, Massachusetts. Over decades of participating in interreligious dialogues, Keating began to realize that the most
interesting "dialogue" always seemed to happen at the margins of events, in
private during meals, for instance, or in car rides to and from the airport.

DOI: 10.4324/9780429000973-11

Once participants found themselves on stage, however, a different dynamic ensued. They spoke to the audience, not to each other, and often felt they had to represent their religious tradition, limiting what they felt comfortable saying. What would happen, Keating wondered, if we simply shared our spiritual journeys as human beings, learning from one another, and discovering together our experiences of ultimacy?

Keating's insight was an auspicious one. The group he convened in 1984 continued to meet once a year for five-day retreats over the next 30+ years, ending in 2015. For the first 20 years the group kept no records and published no reports. They decided on complete privacy so they could speak freely about their experiences of spiritual transformation – without worrying that some "heresy" might get back to their religious communities where many were leaders. It was not a static group, as members came and went throughout the years, but a handful also remained for all 31 years. Eventually, a book was published recounting the first 20 years of their work, and later a documentary was produced (Miles-Yepez 2006; Olsson 2013). The group became known as "The Snowmass Interreligious Conference," often referred to simply as "The Snowmass Conference," since they held the majority of their yearly retreats at Keating's monastery in Snowmass, Colorado. During the final ten years, as members began inviting "mentees" to guide and pass on their accumulated wisdom, the name changed to the "Snowmass InterSpiritual Dialogue Fellowship" (SISD).

I personally participated in SISD as Keating's mentee in 2010, and subsequently became its administrator and a participant for the final five years. I now carry forward the work they began through a new dialogue series, known as "The Future of Religion & Interspirituality (1986)."[2] I introduce this because I intend to use it as a fulcrum for a broader exploration of the Theology Without Walls (TWW) project. The experience of intimate dialogue among diverse and committed spiritual practitioners yields insights, as we will see later, that can be difficult to discern through textual analysis or philosophical reflection. Such "interspiritual" dialogues are imbued with a humanizing ambience, where TWW is pursued as an embodied, existentially potent affair – one with germane consequences for a new generation of spiritual seekers.

An interspiritual approach to TWW

Wayne Teasdale introduced the term "interspiritual" in his 1999 book *The Mystic Heart* (Teasdale 1999). He used the word to denote a new type of spiritual search emerging from the increasing phenomena of religious traditions sharing with one another from the depths of their experiences of ultimacy (Teasdale 1999, 10, 26). Teasdale spoke of a new interspiritual paradigm for the religious quest, one "that permits people from various traditions, or from no tradition, to explore the spiritual dimensions of any religion" (Teasdale 2002, 173). Two elements were essential to his understanding of interspirituality: 1) *experiences* of ultimacy, especially experiences occurring within the context of long-term commitments to contemplative practice; and 2) the *sharing* of such experiences in collaborative ways, where the revelatory experiences of others affect our own religious quest.

Teasdale believed interspirituality could pave the way for an enlightened global culture by helping to create a "continuing community among the religions that is substantial, vital, and creative." Interspirituality was not meant to subsume or surpass the world's religious and spiritual traditions or to form a "homogenous superspirituality," but rather to "make available to everyone all the forms the spiritual journey assumes." What makes interspirituality possible is the "openness of people who have a viable spiritual life" and who develop a "determination, capacity, and commitment to the inner search across traditions." Teasdale envisioned the world's religious traditions as spiritually interdependent, "because an essential interconnectedness in being and reality exists" (Teasdale 1999, 26, 27). Such an interdependence of life is often proclaimed by traditions themselves.

The context for an interspiritual approach, then, is one in which ultimacy is explored from multiple perspectives within a collaborative mode of inquiry, with an emphasis on potential transformative possibilities of a spiritual or religious nature. This makes an interspiritual approach an inherently *contemplative* endeavor that includes both personal experience and the teachings of traditions, and highlights a dialogical methodology as a vital aspect of its repertoire. An interspiritual approach to TWW therefore embraces "the religious quest as transformative journey" (see later). Of course, religion is many things and can be studied just as any other human endeavor might. These include sociological, historical, economic, psychological, and scientific perspectives, to name just a few. TWW, I would argue, should include these perspectives in its endeavor. However, TWW is first and foremost *theology* – the *logos* of *theos*, "to know and articulate" what we can of ultimate reality.

Theology must ultimately be concerned with that which is irreducibly "religious" in human life. Elsewhere I have argued that this irreducible component involves "the religious quest as transformative journey" (McEntee 2017, 618). That is, religion, for everything else that it is, is in essence concerned with a transformative journey that aligns, transmutes, awakens, and orients one in various degrees of harmony with God, Buddha-nature, Dao, Allah, Yahweh, Great Spirit, Heaven, Brahman, "the axiological depths of nature," etc.[3] I use the term "ultimate reality" for all this as a vague comparative category of family resemblances, without equating any of them. My aim here is to show some of the consequences and possibilities of this trajectory as a locus of reflection.

For instance, from this perspective one might regard sacred texts as only secondarily concerned with dogmatic or metaphysical formulations of a confessional nature. The primary context of sacred texts would be interpreted with respect to the ways in which particular orientations, practices, metaphysical frameworks, narrative stories, and commitments function so as to affect varying textures of transformative possibilities hidden in humanity's entanglement with ultimacy.

As an example, consider the Four Noble Truths of Buddhism. John Thatamanil makes a distinction between understanding the Four Noble Truths and an experience of satori, or enlightenment. An intellectual understanding of the Four Noble Truths Thatamanil calls "second-order knowledge," while experiencing satori gives "first-order knowledge" of ultimacy (which Thatamanil also refers to as "practical knowledge of ultimate reality"). Without denying the importance of a confessional stance towards the Four Noble Truths – after all, being Buddhist assumes one takes "refuge" in the Three Jewels of the Buddha, the Dharma, and the Sangha, at least *until* one reaches enlightenment – we may nevertheless proclaim that the finger pointing to the moon is not the moon. It is an embodied, existential experience of satori that ultimately brings about the "comprehensive transformation" hinted at and articulated by the Four Noble Truths (Thatamanil 2016, 357). Thus, the Four Noble Truths might be interpreted not only on a dogmatic level of their metaphysical agreement or incommensurability with other theological frameworks but also as a functional means of transformative possibility. That is, one might ask what underlying orientations are contained within the Four Noble Truths that serve to prepare and initiate one into transformative processes that are undergirded by ultimacy.

Incommensurability or homeomorphic equivalent?

Let me offer an example from our aforementioned Snowmass Conference. In the dialogues, a Tibetan Buddhist posed the following question to a Christian contemplative (paraphrasing): "If there remains a concept of the self, how does one deal with the problem of egotism that emerges from progressing along one's spiritual path?"

The question alludes to an apparent "incommensurability" between the Buddhist doctrines of *anātman* ("no-self," or literally, "no ātman," ātman being the "self" or "soul" within various schools of Hinduism) and the Christian doctrine of a personal soul. The answer, from a Christian perspective, is that all progress happens only through grace. One is never "good," only blessed. When someone referred to Jesus as "good," he admonished them: "Why do you call me good? No one is good – except God alone."[4]

At a level of doctrine we find (perhaps) incommensurable "accounts of reality." However, I would suggest that in considering "the religious quest as transformative journey," we have found what Raimon Panikkar referred to as a "*homeomorphic* equivalence."[5] Viewed from a functional level of contemplative transformation, we might rephrase the question as, "How does one deal with the problem of human selfishness and ego aggrandizement, especially concerning so-called 'progress' along a contemplative path, which is meant to transform and transmute, rather than aggregate, this quality within human beings?"

For Buddhists, an account of (perhaps even "an experience of") reality that emphasizes the illusionary nature of any substantial sense of self and that includes numerous practices that aim to deconstruct such a concretized notion of self function to combat ego aggrandizement as one progresses on a path, leaving no foothold whatsoever for an ego (or sense of self) to grasp onto. For Christians, an account of (and "experiences of") reality that sees human nature as utterly and completely dependent upon God for its own process of sanctification and that ultimately lays all "good" not in the hands of one's self but to God alone functions in a similar way.

In terms of how each of these conceptualizations and/or experiences operate at the level of "transformative journey," within their respective soteriological and theological frameworks, one can see that both work to induce a humble state of mind and to uproot the temptation to attribute to oneself fruits that may arise from walking a contemplative path. Although this may not be the only thing (or even the most important thing) that these concepts work to achieve within their respective frameworks, it can be acknowledged that, whatever else they do, they serve to accomplish in particular ways certain similar functions in the interiority of practitioners.

What once appeared incommensurable now finds consonance, at least in certain respects.

A tale of difference

One of the long-term participants in the Snowmass Dialogues was a highly respected senior monk in the Ramakrishna Order. I'll call him Swami. The Ramakrishna Order is a Hindu monastic order established by Swami Vivekananda, a famous disciple of the Indian sage Sri Ramakrishna (Vivekananda took the first Parliament of World's Religions in Chicago in 1893 by storm, leading to an influx of Hindu thought and teachings in the West). The Ramakrishna Order generally follows the teachings of Vedanta Hinduism, and its branches in the West are often known as "Vedanta Societies." If you were to walk into Swami's monastery you would find four pictures of venerated teachers on the wall (a scene repeated in many Ramakrishna monasteries throughout the United States), which include Ramakrishna, Sarada Devi (Ramakrishna's wife and spiritual counterpart, often referred to as the "Holy Mother"), Jesus, and the Buddha. According to the teachings of the Ramakrishna Order, at various periods throughout cosmic ages the divine reality appears as a human being in order to guide and teach others. Such human beings are called "avatars," which means "descent of the divine." Jesus, the Buddha, Ramakrishna, and Sarada Devi are all considered avatars, or divine incarnations, within the Ramakrishna Order. Each avatar is seen to carry specific messages for humanity appropriate to the time and place in which they appear, yet each is believed to have "discovered the same truth" and have come to "reestablish the one eternal religion" (Vedanta Society of Southern California 2019). Because Swami accepted and experienced Jesus as a divine incarnation, and venerated him as such, he felt that he mostly understood the Christian contemplative path and shared their experience of Jesus.

Swami brought this outlook with him as he began to participate in the Snowmass Dialogues. Over the years, however, he began to realize that his experience of Jesus as a divine avatar from the perspective of Vedanta Hinduism was *not* the same experience of Jesus that Christians seemed to be having in the depths of their contemplative life. This forced Swami to reconsider his position on both Jesus and Christianity. The differences Swami was registering were not the obvious ones on a doctrinal level or ones that might be proposed as the result of immaturity on a spiritual path. Christian practitioners who Swami considered very advanced in the spiritual life simply did not encounter Jesus in the same way as one among many avatars. There was a type of phenomenological variance in the experience of Jesus that affected the transformative journeys of those who experienced him in this way, opening up the possibility that perhaps the revelation of Jesus could not be circumscribed within a Hindu doctrine of avatars.

This was a joyous discovery for Swami, as he now realized he had much to learn and discover about the experience of Jesus that was not present in his own tradition. These kinds of nuanced differences are often better discovered in person, *dialogically*, where one can triangulate around another's experience – and others can triangulate around one's own experience. A dialogical methodology enhances the ability to home in on both differences and similarities that might be extremely difficult (or even impossible) to discover through the reading of texts or the lens of theological frameworks abstracted from the religious quest as transformative journey. Differences such as these speak to the need for a discerning openness to the experience of others and to a willingness to discover unrealized aspects of our own journey, as well as undiscovered possibilities in the journeys of others.

An interspiritual approach to TWW insists that we remain open to these differences. There are an abundance of reasons for such humble openness, including to more fully discover aspects of ultimacy; to contextualize our own spiritual journeys and experiences of ultimacy in ever more nuanced ways; to discover unknown transformative possibilities for our own religious or spiritual path; to develop reverence for the transformative possibilities we discern in others; to know that there exist transformative possibilities undergirded by ultimacy that are not, and perhaps never will be, part of our path, and that is okay; and finally to help incarnate an ever-growing solidarity that thickens *through* difference. The participants of the Snowmass Dialogues report they bonded more through discussing their disagreements than they had in discovering their points of agreement. As differences were discussed, people became franker about what they believed. Without trying to convince others, they simply offered their understanding as "a gift to the group" (Miles-Yepez 2006, xix).

The importance of contemplative traditions for TWW

What does it mean to "know" or "articulate" ultimate reality? For some, this may refer to an interpretive meaning of a sacred text. However, for contemplative traditions, to "know" ultimate reality has always meant in some sense to *embody* it. To "articulate" ultimate reality is to live it, to manifest it in some way, to harmoniously align one's self with it, or even in some sense to identify with it. Knowing and articulating ultimate reality, for these traditions, is always correlated with a transformation of one's being-in-the-world, a transformative journey of the "head, heart, and hands," as Teasdale put it.

From an interspiritual perspective, a transformative journey of the head includes a sculpting of the intellect through the active shaping of the theological frameworks we construct ("interpretive schemes" in Thatamanil's language), as well as a "striving to understand the specific, subtle meanings of religious concepts and how the traditions relate to each other" (Teasdale 1999, 29). A transformative journey of the heart occurs in the depths of spiritual practice and the applications of spiritual teachings to daily life (this is similar to Thatamanil's "therapeutic regimes"). The journey of the heart reflects an *embodiment* of one's spirituality and serves as both the offspring of one's commitments and a reciprocal source of information that informs them (that is, transformations of the heart do more than "install" interpretive schemes into the "body, mind, and heart," as Thatamanil describes, but also, from an interspiritual perspective, change and inform such schemes in a reciprocal manner; Thatamanil 2016, 357). Finally, a transformative journey of the hands involves the collaborative projects we engage in with others of differing beliefs and practices for the common good, especially with regard to issues of social and environmental justice (Teasdale 1999, 29).

Louis Komjathy, a leading scholar in the field of contemplative studies, has taken care to emphasize that contemplative traditions are unique; are rooted in particular cultures, practices, and soteriological frameworks; and can appear incommensurable in certain respects (for instance, Komjathy finds that diverse religious and contemplative traditions offer "mutually exclusive, equally convincing accounts of 'reality'"; Komjathy 2015, 39). At the same time, one tends to find "recurring patterns and parallel practices across traditions" (Komjathy 2018, 137). These include sustained commitment to contemplative practices and "recognition of the value of interiority, presence, seclusion, silence, stillness, and so forth" (Komjathy 2018, 142). Komjathy goes on to describe contemplative traditions as ultimately about "transformed existential and ontological modes," utilizing what he calls "psychologies of realization" to achieve such transformations (Komjathy

2018, 108). Of particular interest for TWW is Komjathy's suggestion that contemplative traditions are engaged in the mapping of "more 'advanced' ontological conditions" through "committed and prolonged contemplative practice" (Komjathy 2015, 54), which must be distinguished from "meditative dilettantism" (Komjathy 2018, 128). From this point of view, we might come to appreciate advanced contemplatives as "professionals," in a sense of religiously inflected ontological exploration. It is important to note that these transformed modes of being can, and often do, include sociopolitical concerns, as seen, for instance, in the life and writings of Thomas Merton, Dorothy Soelle, Abraham Heschel, Mahatma Gandhi, Dorothy Day, Martin Luther King, Jr., Thich Nhat Hahn, and Howard Thurman.

Advanced contemplatives, thus, can be valued as professionals with expertise, as it were, of experimentation with the practices and modes of being-in-the-world that accomplish transformative possibilities undergirded by ultimacy to varying degrees. A contemplative tradition, then, is a community of inquiry that forms around such experimentation and accomplishments, and includes the collected magisteria of the community – the sacred texts, stories, theologies, practices, and practitioners. Different traditions define transformative processes in various ways, giving birth to potentials hidden in the human heart. One experience does not necessarily equate to another. A Christian experience of mystical union with God or Jesus may be different from a Buddhist experience of the "fundamental nature of the mind." I say "may be" because I do not wish to prejudge these matters and do not believe that inquiry into them has progressed to a point where we can be sure of the differences and overlap in experiences of ultimacy. Such questions rather compose an existentially significant and potent field of exploration into matters of ultimate importance and should be approached with an open mind – and an open heart.

Contemplative life, then, can (and should) be seen in some sense as *a* professional area of expertise of human encounter with ultimate reality (not necessarily *the* professional area). It is not that other forms of encounter with ultimate reality need be circumscribed or considered more or less important. Rather, it is to note the uniqueness of contemplative experience and the shared "family resemblances" of contemplative traditions, and hence their importance for TWW. Another way to think of contemplative traditions is as communities of inquiry into ultimate reality that tend to manifest predictable, embodied divine "traits," to use a term from the academic field of contemplative studies, or what I have called elsewhere "divine adornments."[6] Such traits, such as *bodhichitta* in the Buddhist tradition or *caritas* in the Christian tradition, need not be equated and can be seen as uniquely embodied results attained to varying degrees within particular contemplative traditions.

From this perspective, the importance of contemplative life for TWW becomes radiantly apparent. If TWW wishes to consider all relevant "revelations, enlightenments, and insights" into ultimate reality, then seriously consulting those for whom this is an area of expertise, mainly advanced contemplatives, would seem to be a *sine qua non* of such an undertaking. Given the uniqueness of individual contemplative traditions, it becomes equally important for TWW to consider the *particularities* of varying contemplative traditions, including possible differences in resulting "divine adornments" or "traits," without a trenchant need for simplification or generalization.

TWW as theological milieu for the "spiritual but not religious"

The interspiritual approach to TWW explored here would be of benefit to the growing, but inchoate, spirituality of the "spiritual but not religious" (SBNR). For instance, TWW can help provide a locus of thought for SBNRs to consider as they survey an ever-growing, and perhaps confusing, landscape of potential spiritual practices they might adopt. TWW does this by engaging a discursive community to reflect upon traditional contemplative practices, the possible transformative effects of such practices, and the strengths and weaknesses of various practices. These analyses should include sociological, religious, and political perspectives, as well as address what it might mean to extract such practices from their cultural and theological frameworks. It is not hard to see how such a discourse might be of immense benefit to SBNRs as they attempt to navigate their own unique, individualized paths amidst a smorgasbord of spiritual practices and religious frameworks, some of which are authentic, others which are commercialized, and still others which are downright dangerous.[7] Knowing some of the pitfalls and dangers, as well as how to cultivate discernment among such diverse spiritualities, would contribute to the efficacy of an SBNR's spiritual quest.

TWW can help as well to provide various conceptions of ultimacy that transgress confessional boundaries. This serves SBNRs in developing more sophisticated frameworks for understanding their own spiritual paths. TWW also provides a discursive community for SBNRs to hone and shape their understandings through academic exchange. One might imagine future scholars working on theological frameworks and philosophical or political theologies from ever-deepening interspiritual perspectives. Such a development would also be of benefit to those in religious traditions as well as to the SBNR movement, as it would naturally continue to deepen reflection on questions of difference and individuality, discernment of spiritual maturity, the relationship of religious traditions to one another and to their own institutionalized forms, and the very concept of what it means to be "religious."

Who is to say that SBNRs will not eventually be regarded as forerunners of a new religious spirit, a religious spirit that sees the religious quest as a transformative journey, embraces democratization of the spiritual life, and in this sense, may be particularly apt for our times?

Interspirituality as a religious path

Over the first few years of the Snowmass Conference participants worked through difficulties in trying to formulate some common points of agreement. They eventually produced a document, which became known as "The Points of Agreement" (yet remained out of the public eye for decades). Choosing "ultimate reality" as their reference word for ultimacy, the points consist of eight statements about ultimate reality and the human condition, such as a recognition that the world religions "bear witness to the experience of ultimate reality"; that ultimate reality cannot be limited by names or concepts; that it is the ground of actuality and potentiality; that all human beings have a potential for transformation, wholeness, enlightenment, transcendence; etc.; that "disciplined practice is essential to the spiritual life," yet nevertheless all spiritual attainment is, in the end. "not the result of one's efforts" but instead dependent upon ultimacy itself; and that ultimacy may be experienced outside of religious practices, such as "through nature, art, human relationships, and service to others" (Miles-Yepez 2006, xvii).[8]

One point of agreement in particular, however, interests me here. It reads, "Faith is opening, accepting, and responding to Ultimate Reality. *Faith in this sense precedes every belief system*" (Miles-Yepez 2006, xvii, emphasis mine).

To see faith as something that exists prior to every belief system is to turn on its head a more widespread, pedestrian understanding of faith, where "faith" exhibits a "belief" in something that perhaps cannot be proven, like the trinitarian nature of God, for instance. If, on the other hand, faith *precedes* any belief system, then it stems not from assent to some humanly constructed religious framework, but rather exists as an intrinsic aspect of humanity's entanglement with ultimacy. *Faith*, in this sense, is inherent to the human condition. One might choose not to explore it or to refuse its quiet, constant nudging. Or one may nurture it, and this would seem to be the purpose of belonging to a religious tradition. However, if one's faith exists before one's tradition does, then the tradition itself becomes a vehicle for the nurturing of an intrinsic human capacity. Distinctive "nurturings" of this capacity contribute to differing substantiations of ultimacy. It is worth noting again that committed practitioners from different religious traditions were able to affirm this statement on faith.

All human beings have a capacity for transformative growth that aligns them in increasing degrees with ultimacy. This capacity exists outside of any religious tradition. An interspiritual approach further affirms the diversity of such approaches and entertains the possibility that diversity in manifestation is at the heart of ultimacy, and that therefore the many ways of nurturing our "faith" is a consequence, or reflection, of such multiplicity. Each particular way will inevitably have strengths and weaknesses, bringing unique insights into the nature of ultimacy and the transformative possibilities of human beings to align and orient themselves towards ultimacy. These are not preordained ways, mapped out prior to their manifestation, but rather are birthed within spontaneous and creative impulses at the heart of manifestation. *These differences are but a flowering of life itself and compose a reflection of ultimacy.*

Given this, spiritual impulses that look to give rise to new types of religiosity, such as we see today in the West among multiple religious belongers, SBNR, and interspiritual folks, need not be seen as disconnected from ultimacy just because they are not embedded in traditional religious forms. A better question would be: Are they responding to their "faith" in the sense given earlier? One might consider the possibility that, for these individuals, nurturing their faith – that is opening and responding to ultimacy – creatively manifests in nontraditional religious ways. Certainly it is not hard to see some of the qualities we often associate with these nontraditional spiritualities as undergirded by ultimacy, such as a spiritual longing for transformation; questioning unhealthy institutional and hierarchical religious structures; naming and addressing problems of embedded patriarchies, colonialisms, and racism that exist in *all* of our religious traditions; emphases on issues of social and ecological justice; democratic sensibilities in exploring differences among spiritual orientations; and the freedom to follow and embody one's sense of the sacred – that is, to nurture one's "faith."

To nurture one's faith requires commitments. Such commitments lie at the root of an interspiritual path, which is where I delineate between an ambiguous use of the term "spiritual" and what it means to be "religious." Spirituality is not a mere component of our lives. The spiritual is a kind of intrinsic quality to life itself, part of the ground of actuality and potentiality and the ever-present possibility of opening and responding to ultimacy. The spiritual overflows into all of life, its ambiguity pointing towards its ever-present nature as ground. To be "religious" involves an *active* cultivation of this spiritually transformative capacity, which opens up a vast territory for discernment. This in turn implies a need for theological reflection and practical experimentation regarding concepts of spiritual maturity and the efficacies of various spiritual practices and orientations. It is a *religious* practice to bring one's religious and spiritual commitments into the reflective light of the intellect and to make oneself aware of one's orientations towards ultimacy so that they may continually be (re)evaluated and evolve as one's journey proceeds.

Further, as religious denotes, in the terms of this chapter, commitments to a transformative journey – that is, a spiritual path that attempts to continually orient and reorient one towards ultimacy in ever clearer and more transparent ways with greater faith, hope, love, service, compassion, and wisdom, and confidence in the ameliorating potency of one's quest – then an interspiritual religious path would be one where one's religious *identity* is primarily predicated upon such commitments. This could obviously occur both within and without religious traditions. That is, an interspiritual religious path may be journeyed on within a traditional religious identity or walked in such a way that is not embedded in any singular religious tradition. Interspirituality imparts a sense of solidarity with all those who walk committed paths of a spiritually efficacious nature.

I'd like to conclude on a personal note, with a closing story from the last day of the final Snowmass Dialogue. As practitioners from many of the world's different religious traditions sat in a circle in the meditation hall at St. Benedict's monastery, looking out onto the vast landscape of the Rocky Mountains through the wall-length, cathedral-like windows surrounding us, we began to go around the circle, offering thoughts on our experience and what we might take back to our religious traditions and communities as a result. As various responses were given and one after another told of insights – some difficult, others joyous – that they would endeavor to offer back to their communities, I was overcome with the coalescence of an incipient, but growing, awareness. As it happened, I was the last to speak, and when I did my voice stammered with emotion.

"It is wonderful to hear about all of the myriad things you will be bringing back to your home traditions," I told them.

> It brings me joy, but I would be lying if I did not admit to a hint of sadness. I do not have a tradition to "return" to, for it exists here, *among you. This is my tradition.* My spiritual (and religious) home is to be found amidst the spaces you have created, in that which has come into being through your willingness to open yourselves, and your traditions, to one another, without defensiveness and in love. It exists within the interchange and synergy of spiritual energies that entwine when you come together. And amidst the silence we share. And the personal, intimate testimonies of those who have dedicated themselves – in endearing, instructive, and inspirational ways, to their own transformative journeys.

This tradition, my tradition, is what I have called "interspiritual." I have come to know, through friends, colleagues, and mentors across the globe, that I am far from alone in claiming it. I have no doubts that though youthful, it is also undergirded by ultimacy, as all authentic religious traditions are. Its story has only begun to be told.

Notes

1 Citation refers to Friends United edition.
2 The new dialogue series, known as FRIS for short, is an invitation-only dialogue held at contemplative centers around the country, run by The Foundation for New Monasticism & Interspirituality, of which I am a founding member. For more, see Foundation for New Monasticism & InterSpirituality, founded in 2015.
3 For "axiological depths of nature," see Wildman (2016), in reference to a religious naturalist perspective.
4 *The Bible.* New International Version. Grand Rapids: Zondervan House, 1984. Lk 18:19.

5 See Panikkar (1981) and Panikkar (2014), among other Panikkar books as well.
6 For "traits," see Komjathy (2018); for "divine adornments," see McEntee (2017).
7 "Authenticity" here is a matter of discernment, often practiced within discursive communities of practitioners. These communities can, and perhaps should, exceed the boundaries of one's own tradition and/or spiritual commitments. TWW, broadly understood, would constitute one such diverse community.
8 An interesting tidbit here I know from personal knowledge is the difficulty the participants had in even choosing a term for ultimacy. For example, the Christians preferred "ultimate mystery," but Buddhists could not assent to "mystery," as they felt this disputed their viewpoint that ultimacy can be directly awakened to.

References

Foundation for New Monasticism & InterSpirituality. Founded 2015. www.new-monastics.com (accessed September 5, 2019).

Komjathy, Louis. 2015. *Contemplative Literature: A Comparative Sourcebook on Meditation and Contemplative Prayer*. Albany, NY: SUNY Press. doi:10.1353/scs.2018.0017

Komjathy, Louis. 2018. *Introducing Contemplative Studies*. Hoboken, NJ: John Wiley & Sons.

McEntee, Rory. 2017. "The Religious Quest as Transformative Journey: Interspiritual Religious Belonging and the Problem of Religious Depth." *Open Theology* 3 (1): 613–629. doi:10.1515/opth-2017–0048

Miles-Yepez, Netanel, ed. 2006. *Common Heart: An Experience of Interreligious Dialogue*. xix. New York, NY: Lantern Books.

Olsson, Stephen. 2013. *An Inter-Spiritual Dialogue with Father Thomas Keating*. Sausalito, CA: CEM Productions, DVD.

Panikkar, Raimon. 2014. *Mysticism and Spirituality, Part One: Mysticism, Fullness of Life (Opera Omnia, Vol. I)*. Maryknoll: Orbis Books. doi:10.1017/hor.2015.89

Panikkar, Raimundo. 1981. *The Unknown Christ of Hinduism: Towards an Ecumenical Christophany*. Maryknoll: Orbis Books.

Teasdale, Wayne. 1999. *The Mystic Heart: Discovering a Universal Spirituality in the World's Religions*. Novato, CA: New World Library.

Teasdale, Wayne. 2002. *A Monk in the World: Cultivating a Spiritual Life*. Novato, CA: New World Library.

Thatamanil, John J. 2016. "Transreligious Theology as the Quest for Interreligious Wisdom." *Open Theology* 2 (1): 354–362. doi:10.1515/opth-2016–0029

Thurman, Howard. 1986. *The Search for Common Ground: An Inquiry into the Basis of Man's Experience of Community*. Richmond: Friends United Press.

Vedanta Society of Southern California. 2019. https://vedanta.org/what-is-vedanta/the-avatar-god-in-human-form/ (accessed January 23, 2019).

Wildman, Wesley J. 2016. *Science and Religious Anthropology: A Spiritually Evocative Naturalist Interpretation of Human Life*. London, England: Routledge. doi:10.4324/9781315607757

9 With open doors and windows

Doing theology in the spirit of William James

Jonathan Weidenbaum

Introduction: concrete experience

In a last essay published just before his death, William James concedes that the early work of Benjamin Paul Blood, a self-styled philosopher and fellow experimenter in nitrous oxide, manages to "charm the monist in me unreservedly" (James 1978). Despite this brief confession of sympathy for a picture of the universe as constituting a single unity, the article is largely a celebration of an eccentric and unsung thinker's turn away from monism and a confirmation, by way of direct religious experience, of James's own metaphysical pluralism.

Titled "A Pluralistic Mystic," James's final essay encapsulates much of the distinctive spirit of his approach toward different philosophical and theological frameworks. This includes, first, a search after rich and pronounced experiences wherever and whenever they may be found. Intuitions that are pathological, paranormal, and even drug-induced join religious experiences in possessing revelatory value for James and are presented as disclosing truths otherwise obscured from our more routine and ordinary forms of being. While never eschewing the importance of rational reflection upon our first-hand perceptions, a receptivity toward the freshness and immediacy of concrete experience is front and central for James. "Philosophy, like life," he affirms in *Some Problems of Philosophy*, "must keep the doors and windows open" (James 1996b, Ch. 4). Indeed, the analogy of open doors and windows as our proper orientation toward the world is found in numerous places throughout James's authorship.[1]

Second, James's exhibition of Blood demonstrates his almost uncanny ability to grasp the vital core of any religious or philosophical point of view and from what always seems like an insider's perspective. Continually arguing that beneath even the most rarefied theoretical constructs is a preconceptual feel for the way things are, James's capacity for entering into and articulating the living kernel beneath different worldviews is very likely connected with the beauty of his prose. It is one reason why a careful analysis of lived human experience is such a central preoccupation of his.

DOI: 10.4324/9780429000973-12

Third, James is a seminal contributor to the philosophy of religion, one whose ruminations are often focused on the justification of the spiritual life. "I feel now," James writes triumphantly in his article on Blood, "as if my own pluralism were not without the kind of support which mystical corroboration may confer" (James 1978). Whether championing the right to believe ahead of all evidence or assessing the extent to which mystical experience may validate our philosophical convictions, the thought of James possesses endless resources for assessing theological positions in the face of what is arguably the single, most far-reaching development of the modern world: namely the ascendancy of the empirical attitude and the natural sciences.

But James's essay on Blood reveals one more tendency of his orientation toward different philosophies and religions. Even while keeping his doors and windows wide open to the full spectrum of human experience, James was never shy of making evaluative judgements with regard to different visions of the real. With regard to the contest between accepting a universe in which salvation is assured for all and one in which it isn't, James asks: "Is all 'yes, yes' in the universe?" Doesn't the fact of 'no' stand at the very core of life?" (James 1975a, 141). No matter how much his inner monist may reverberate when reading the earlier writing of Blood, a support for a more baroque and pluralistic cosmos over the pristine One of the idealists so predominate in his time remains an implacable theme of James's philosophical work. "A Pluralistic Mystic" is his last affirmation of such a commitment.

James's thoughts on religion are sufficiently abundant to allow for multiple voyages beyond the barriers of denomination. What follows is merely one creative attempt to articulate the relevance of his thought for just such an adventure. Our main strategy is to press a few of James's most essential themes into a two-storied methodology. While our first step argues for the necessity of opening our windows and doors as broadly as possible to the depth of experiences that animate different theological sensibilities, the second digs further into the thought of James in order to ascertain one of the standards we may use to evaluate between religious philosophies. Both sections begin with episodes weaned from my involvement with Theology Without Walls, debates in which Jamesean themes have proven their relevance.

Because Theology Without Walls is in its infancy, it is the perspective of the author that a concentration on methodology is more essential at this early stage than any finished or even tentative theological picture. And yet James's theological positions – his "over-beliefs" as he calls them in the *Varieties* – are not without their place.[2] A penultimate section therefore introduces us to James's mature theological statement – mainly as a demonstration of our methodological principles at work. Our brief conclusion will ride the spirit of James beyond the assumptions underlying his method and will point the way toward a few topics well worth exploring in the future of a Theology Without Walls.

Varieties

In more than one discussion with my colleagues in Theology Without Walls I have met with disapproval for speaking against philosophies in which the *summum bonum* of the spiritual life is the understanding of all things, sentient beings and galaxies alike, as manifestations of a single and perfect divine ground. One well-known philosophy of religion that sees this realization as the common goal of every authentic spiritual tradition – despite the outer doctrinal and ritual differences between faith communities – is the "perennial philosophy." Popularized by Aldous Huxley in *The Perennial Philosophy*, and defended by a number of authors known as the Traditionalists, the identification of our deepest selves with a formless and all-inclusive ultimate reality is here deemed as a higher plane of awareness than that of a relationship to a transcendent and personal deity. As this unitary insight is often provided by the contemplative and meditative traditions of the world East and West, monistic systems of thought like *Advaita Vedanta* and Neo-Platonist mystics like Meister Eckhart are therefore favorites among perennialist writers.

Skimming through portions of the chapter of mysticism in *The Varieties of Religious Experience*, proponents of such a perennialist-type theology would find much to delight in James's well-known study of the topic. Among the defining feature of mystical experiences for James are their seemingly *noetic*, or knowledge-bearing, quality, for they are felt "as states of insight into depths of truth unplumbed by the discursive intellect" (James 2004, 329). In one section, James quotes and refers to a myriad of contemplative authors – Eckhart, Silesius, Boehme, the Upanishads, and many others – and declares that the "overcoming of all the usual barriers between the individual and the Absolute is the great mystic achievement" (James 2004, 362).

But even here, within James's survey of mysticism, we are made aware of the radically different theological perspectives surrounding mystical experience. The precise reason why mystical experiences are *not* binding upon those who haven't undergone them is the sheer range of their interpretation: "It is dualistic in Sankhya, and monistic in Vedanta philosophy. I called it pantheistic; but the great Spanish mystics are anything but pantheists" (James 2004, 368). And stepping back to view *The Varieties of Religious Experience* as a whole, we see how it truly earns the beginning of its title as a *varieties*. For in it we are treated to testimonies ranging from those of grounded inner peace to moments of near-hallucinatory horror; from the spiritually inspired overcoming of addiction to God-intoxicated flights of ecstasy; from the confident joy and optimism of the "healthy-minded" for whom dwelling on evil is but a vice, to a concentration on the problems of existence which is the "sick soul." One of James's lengthiest descriptions is his account of the sudden reconfiguring of the self after its own inner tensions and divisions have brought it to its lowest point (James 2004, lectures

VIII–IX). Although James later asserts that "the faith-state and mystic state are practically convertible terms," this is a religious experience more akin to what is found at a Protestant tent revival than the full self-transcendence of a Sufi dervish or contemplative, a sensibility articulated theologically by Luther, Kierkegaard, and the Neo-Orthodox theologians of the twentieth century (James 2004, 367).[3]

Doing Theology Without Walls in the spirit of James means being receptive to religious experiences of all kinds. It also means perceiving the meaning within *all* forms of experience, even those not explicitly religious. In "On a Certain Blindness in Human Beings," James writes of the manner in which our encounters with people unlike ourselves may serve as a kind of epiphany, as not only a necessary shattering of our prejudices and assumptions but also as a complete re-centering of our inner lives.[4] We let our guard down before the other, and "then the whole scheme of our customary values gets confounded, then our self is riven and its narrow interests fly to pieces, then a new centre and a new perspective must be found." This is an insight akin to the I–Thou relationships of Martin Buber or our heeding of the face of our neighbor as described by Emmanuel Levinas – philosophies focused not a mystical descent within our consciousness at all, but in our active and moral comportment towards others.[5]

Finding nondual spiritual experiences within and across different traditions, the adherents of perennialist-type theologies interpret such experiences as more fundamental than other forms of intuition, religious and otherwise. But this comes with the cost of either ignoring or trivializing equally transformative experiences, including those which speak of an unbridgeable distance felt between the self and the other and I and a Thou. For the Jamesean involved in Theology Without Walls, a compelling reason must be found to justify prioritizing one form of intuition over another. Moreover, because nondual religious philosophies tend to lean toward a monism or quasi-pantheism in which the divine is understood as the sole or most basic reality, negative and tragic sorts of experiences are often deemed by them as either derivative or illusory. There are philosophical problems with this kind of denial, but this is a theme to which we must return later.

Moral strenuousness

Keeping our doors and windows open does not guarantee that every idea is of equal value in navigating what drafts may come through. This point is not always well taken. I recall a meeting of Theology Without Walls in which the very idea of using principles to discern the worth of different theological positions was seen as arrogant and arbitrary – the imposition of our inherited prejudices and assumptions. Isn't this a betrayal of the very *purpose* of a Theology Without Walls, it was asked. For isn't the practice of discriminating between theological visions just a placing up of more walls? To which one may respond that employing some kind of principle of evaluation is implied by the *very title* of a Theology Without Walls: namely, to not have walls. We do not, for instance, ignore a religious tradition because it rejects theism (i.e., Jainism and Buddhism).

But the other side of the argument is not without a few important concerns. We certainly must not shun thinkers or insights, for instance, that do not fit our *a priori* religious convictions. In a private letter to his fellow perennialist Huston Smith, Frithjof Schuon lambasts the thought of Kierkegaard for, among other things, its nonconformity to several of the more official and acceptable metaphysical systems as seen from a Traditionalist perspective. The religious thinker who pitted the risk-filled commitments of faith against the abstract certainties of reason and flouted the theological orthodoxies of his time must, in Schuon's recommendation, "be rejected without pity, I will even say: with horror" (Schuon 1975). No attitude can be more anathema to those who heed James's contention that in demanding conformity between different religious figures and directions of the spirit, "the total human consciousness of the divine would suffer" (James 2004, 420).

To explore theological perspectives in the spirit of William James is to employ principles of evaluation that are neither arbitrary nor smuggled in by way of our prior theological commitments. Early on in the *Varieties* James argues that the veridicality, or truth-bearing status, of a religious experience must be judged using the same standards as *any* form of experience: the sheer force by which it grips us, how well it fits in with our other beliefs, and finally its influence upon our ethical life (James 2004, 28).[6] It is the last of these criteria that take us to the very heart of James's philosophical anthropology – his take on human nature.

In an early and key essay, James offers a description of rationality as the felt transition from a state of puzzle and unrest to one of contentment, ease, and sense of normal mental functioning. Philosophies that help to bring about this feeling of rationality must meet a number of conditions, one of which is to not disappoint or fail to engage our "active propensities," or "to give them no object whatsoever to press against" (James 2004, 82). Time and again in his writings, James argues in favor of those worldviews that speak not only to our spiritual intuitions but also our practical and ethical ones – those that draw upon the morally "strenuous mood" (James 2004, 211). The yearning for the unique satisfactions and rigors of the ethical life are, for James, built into our very makeup as human beings.

In another of his early essays, our cognitive and intellectual faculty is depicted as a kind of second department – one which, following our immediate sensory experience, exists primarily for the purpose of guiding our behaviors (James 2004, 113–114). For James, we are not minds in isolation, subjects cleaved off from a separate realm of objects, but whole and embodied organisms existing in and through an environment. Judging between worldviews with a concern for how they link with a few of "our deepest desires and most cherished powers," the moral life chief among them, is therefore no arbitrary move for James but follows from his observations as a pragmatist and consummate phenomenologist (James 2004, 82).

In his letter to Smith, Schuon complains that Kierkegaard has no conception of the *intellect* – what for the Traditionalists is not our faculty for discursive reasoning but our organ of direct illumination from the divine, even a spark of the Absolute within (Schuon 1975). To do theology in the spirit of William James is to be receptive to this feature common to many of the most refined spiritual philosophies, as James has done in his chapter on mysticism in *The Varieties*. But it is not to remain there, for we are practical and moral creatures as well as contemplative ones. Returning to his triadic picture of the human being, James diagnoses the *gnostical* urge to realize the completeness of our identity with the divine as an illegitimate swallowing up of our active and practical nature into our contemplative one, a disappearance of the third department of our being into the second (James 1956, 138–140). It is for these reasons that James writes sympathetically of the ascetic tendencies of the saint in the *Varieties*, what for him is only a more extreme representation of those for whom "passive happiness is slack and insipid, and soon grows mawkish and intolerable" (James 2004, 263).

In short, one standard employed by a Jamesean in order to discern between theological positions – a principle found directly within our experience rather than invoked arbitrarily – is to favor those perspectives that cultivate the morally strenuous life in addition to our yearning for communion with an ultimate reality.

A finite god

To summarize a Jamesean approach toward a Theology Without Walls, we should, first, be open not only to the deeper intuitions which fuel and motivate other theological positions but equally to experiences of all kinds – even those that don't sit so easily within our prior and cherished philosophical and religious assumptions. And second, we have the right to accede value to those theological positions that draw upon, and enhance, our moral energies over those that do not.

For the project of a Theology Without Walls, James's own theological conclusions are of ancillary importance to his methods. And yet James's mature speculations are a good demonstration of these principles at work.

To do philosophy and theology in the spirit of James means to acknowledge what so many monistic- and pantheistic-type perspectives so often trivialize or even deny: the unrefined edges of life, the phenomena of pain and suffering, the gaping holes which beset the universe. It is in the interest of being inclusive that in the *Varieties* James prefers the more complex universe of the sick soul rather than the simpler and happier metaphysics of the healthy minded. As "a rectilinear or one-storied affair," what the latter ignores "may after all be the best key to life's significance, and possibly the only openers of our eyes to the deepest levels of truth" (James 2004,

148, 151). Moreover, and as we saw in the previous section, philosophies which claim that all is undergirded by a transcendental perfection too easily allow our propensities for worldly activity to atrophy, and are therefore inadequate. James's approach toward assessing different theologies leans toward the recognition of a partly precarious cosmos, a *melioristic* universe, as James labels it in *Pragmatism*, in which our efforts may play a role (James 1975b, lecture VIII).

We should recognize even how self-defeating the denial or trivializing of evil is when analyzed more carefully. For as James points out toward the end of his first lecture in *A Pluralistic Universe* (what is partly an expansion of his over-beliefs in the *Varieties*), to push for an acosmistic universe in which all pain and finitude are understood as a kind of primal ignorance, a veil blocking us from a nondual state of awareness or ultimate reality, is only to land ourselves within yet another duality. This is between the perspective of the Absolute in which all such limitations are overcome and the grittier vantage point of our own existence – one seemingly hemmed in by limitations of all kinds. In this way, to envision a perfect and all-inclusive ultimate reality would be every bit as alienating as looking upward from our lowly plane toward an all-powerful creator deity (James 1996a, 38–40). This theological picture is not only an insult to the human condition, but it deflates all motivation to rely upon our own efforts to help make the cosmos a better place.

For these reasons, the god defended by James is finite, a being limited "in power or in knowledge, or in both at once" (James 1996a, conclusions or lecture VIII). This notion of a finite deity, a god for whom we are partners with the gradual perfecting of the world rather than as passive subjects, can appeal to the ethicist in us.[7] And yet because his deity is also a greater consciousness in which our smaller selves are a part, this model can appeal somewhat to the mystic's sense of union with a greater and more expansive divine reality.[8]

Conclusion: many doors and windows

Throughout the preceding pages we have unpacked the relevance of William James for the project of a Theology Without Walls. In no small part, this is the method of including as much of the full range of human experience, particularly religious experience, as we can. Even the standard of promoting the morally strenuous life is a principle found within our living engagement with things and is not imposed from without. Or so I have argued.

Since James's time, however, there has been some fruitful reflection on the nature and character of religious experiences. Although James's Protestant upbringing and influence may have helped bias his investigations toward the experiences of gifted individuals and against the role and mediation of institutions, the social nature of the spiritual life should never be left out of our focus. We may not go as far as James's colleague and sparring partner,

Josiah Royce, that authentic religious experience, at least for Christianity, *must* be social (Royce 2001, 40–41). But social it may be. Charles Taylor offers an example of how his exultation at watching the victory of his hockey team is heightened by the fact that he rejoices with an entire city (Taylor 2003, 28). There are also some who argue for the necessity of recognizing how background beliefs and inherited dogmas infiltrate even the most ecstatic and rarefied of our experiences. Hence, it may not be just the interpretation or felt intensity of our intuitions that are shaped through culture and historical context, but their very content.[9]

A Jamesean approach to a Theology Without Walls is always ready to draw upon the unique experiential insights of individuals as they have surfaced in different places and times – whether such heights of awareness are achieved through meditation, discovered in the throngs of a personal crisis, or even induced through chemicals. But a contemporary Jamesean methodology must equally be attentive to experiences forged through entire communities, as well as the shared social and theological tenets in which the most defining of our spiritual intuitions have been fermented and cultivated. This may be a bit of a departure from James's own preoccupations, particularly in the *Varieties*. And yet peering out upon the world's divergent theological visions, it is keeping well within his spirit to open as many of our doors and windows as possible.

Notes

1 Richard Gale provides a list of James's references to open windows and doors in the introduction to *The Divided Self of William James* (Gale 1999, 4).

2 See the conclusion for his discussion on over-beliefs.

3 D.S. Browning affirms that "the Niebuhrs, Tillichs, and Bultmanns of the neo-orthodox period could have turned to James as easily as to Kierkegaard or Heidegger" (Browning 1980).

4 Found in *Talks to Teachers* (James 1962).

5 For Buber's (1970) and Levinas's (1969) most definite and well-known statements on our relationships to others, see *I and Thou* and *Totality and Infinity* (Buber 1970), respectively.

6 After refuting the idea that religious experiences can be dismissed as mere products of physical disorder, what he labels "medical materialism," James suggests that "*Immediate luminousness*, in short, *philosophical reasonableness*, and *moral helpfulness* are the only available criteria."

7 Some may appreciate the similarity of this idea with several notions found in Lurianic Kabbalah, including the mission of human beings to enact *tikkun olam*, or the reparation of the cosmos. See the seventh lecture in Gershom Scholem's *Major Trends in Jewish Mysticism*, the landmark introduction to this topic.

8 Whether or not James has completely resolved all of the tensions between the ethical and the mystical facets within his own work, let alone for theology in general, is too large a topic for this chapter. See Gale (1999) and Weidenbaum (2013).

9 The idea that our background beliefs at least partly constitute our experiences is called *constructivism*. One scholar who draws our attention to James's overlooking of the manner in which historical context may inform religious experience is Proudfoot (2004).

References

Browning, Don S. 1980. *Pluralism and Personality: William James and Some Contemporary Cultures of Psychology.* Lewisburg: Bucknell University Press.

Buber, Martin. 1970. *I and Thou*, trans. Walter Kaufmann. New York: Simon & Schuster.

Gale, Richard. 1999. *The Divided Self of William James.* Cambridge: Cambridge University Press.

James, William. 1956. *The Will to Believe and Other Essays in Popular Philosophy.* New York: Dover.

James, William. 1962. *Talks to Teachers on Psychology; and to Students on Some of Life's Ideals.* Mineola: Dover Publications, Inc.

James, William, ed. 1975a. "Pragmatism." In *Pragmatism and the Meaning of Truth.* Cambridge: Harvard University Press.

James, William. 1978. "A Pluralistic Mystic." In *Essays in Philosophy*, edited by Frederick Burkhardt, Fredson Bowers, and Ignas K. Skrupskelis. Cambridge: Harvard University Press.

James, William. 1996a. *A Pluralistic Universe.* Lincoln: University of Nebraska Press.

James, William. 1996b. *Some Problems of Philosophy.* Lincoln: University of Nebraska Press.

James, William. 2004. *The Varieties of Religious Experience.* New York: Sterling Publishing.

Levinas, Emmanuel. 1969. *Totality and Infinity: An Essay on Exteriority*, trans. Alphonso Lingis. Pittsburgh: Duquesne University Press.

Proudfoot, Wayne. 2004. *"Introduction" to the Varieties of Religious Experience.* New York: Sterling Publishing.

Royce, Josiah. 2001. *The Problem of Christianity.* Washington, DC: The Catholic University of America Press.

Scholem, Gershom. 1946. *Major Trends in Jewish Mysticism.* New York: Schocken Books.

Schuon, Frithjof. 1975. "Letter on Existentialism." www.studiesincomparativereligion. com/public/articles/Letter_on_Existentialism-by_Frithjof_Schuon.aspx (accessed November 12, 2018).

Taylor, Charles. 2003. *Varieties of Religion Today: William James Revisited.* Cambridge: Harvard University Press.

Weidenbaum, Jonathan. 2013. "William James's Argument for a Finite Theism." In *Models of God and Alternative Ultimate Realities*, edited by Jeanine Diller and Asa Kasher, 323–331. Heidelberg: Springer. doi:10.1007/978-94-007-5219-1_27

Part III

Challenges and possibilities

Introduction

Jerry L. Martin

Sympathetic critics are invaluable, because they articulate the challenges a new way of thinking must face. Peter Feldmeier explores the potential of Theology Without Walls (TWW). He begins with the Vatican's evolution toward inclusivism. He shows how seeing the parable of the Pharisee and the tax collector through Buddhist eyes can temper our own judgmentalism, and how Taoist attitudes could prevent a pastor's manipulative behavior. In this mode, TWW is a kind of comparative theology. The alternative is simply "to think theologically utilizing the vast array of insights from the world's great depositories of wisdom and insight." Ask "what is love or compassion?" and "draw insights from the widest net possible."

On the other hand, Feldmeier sees a danger in a kind of "theological free-for-all" that ignores consistency. Christianity and Daoism, for example, each has its own metaphysics. Religious insights are "tied to structures of thought that can be incommensurable." Perhaps there can be no "meta-narrative" that accounts for everything. Moreover, any theology must reflect a "living faith." Feldmeier concludes by asking what TWW would look like "in its most robust expression."

One approach to method is offered by Wesley J. Wildman and Jerry L. Martin. The transreligious theologian faces choices between "theological possibilities that cut across the religions." Three of the most plausible models of ultimate reality are an agential being, the ground of being, and a subordinate god within a more fundamental ultimate reality. Each has its own appeal. Agential being models are best fitted to "the human tendency to see intentionality in events." "Reality as a whole is invested with personality and purpose, meaning and intelligibility, goodness and beauty." Subordinate god models have a "two-tiered" view, with God having the appealing properties of an agential being, without the difficulties posed by trying to have a personal being account for the whole of reality. Ground-of-being models avoid anthropomorphism and best express the limits to human cognition that point toward apophaticism.

The models can be tested against what we know from "cognitive science, evolutionary psychology, comparative religion and other sources." Each model will have to meet such "explanatory standards" as "applicability,

DOI: 10.4324/9780429000973-13

adequacy, coherence, consistency, and pragmatic considerations such as ethical consequences, aesthetic quality, social potency, and spiritual appeal." Choices that fit well with one criterion may fit poorly with another. Hence, there are "conceptual stresses" within each model. "Fortunately, comparative religion and comparative theology have prepared an array of fruitful cross-cultural concepts, issues to be addressed, and theological options to consider."

Among the resources that can now be brought to bear on theology is the cognitive science of religions (CSR). Johan De Smedt and Helen De Cruz ask "what theologians can learn" from CSR and "what it identifies as commonalities across religions." They connect their approach to "Hick's religious pluralism, Ramakrishna's realization of God through multiple spiritual paths, and Gellman's exhaustible plentitude." The authors begin with a wide-ranging survey of accounts, religious and nonreligious, of the "origins of religious belief." Those views that begin with a natural or innate knowledge of God have had the challenge of explaining religious ignorance and religious diversity. Here, "CSR can shed new light." "A unifying theme throughout this literature" is that "religion is natural" and that religious beliefs result from cognitive processes that "operate in everyday life, such as discerning teleology, detecting agency, and thinking about other people's minds." The authors explore CSR research with regard to "belief in supernatural agents and its connection to cooperation, teleological thinking, and afterlife beliefs." They argue that "the dispositions outlined by CSR do give us some insight into the divine" and that insight is pluralistic.

Wesley J. Wildman draws on cognitive science, evolutionary psychology, and biology to explore the theologically salient topic of love and desire. He wants to understand "why these concepts, and the corresponding experiences, are so powerful for us, and why we feel they take us so deeply into the nature of the reality we receive, create, and inhabit." For him, as a religious naturalist, divine love does not refer to the thoughts, feelings, intentions, or actions of a divine being, but to "the valuational depth structures and dynamic possibilities of the natural world."

The story of human love begins with the "neutral-behavioral love systems" of the primates evolving into humans. "There are at least four relatively distinct brain and behavioral love-and-desire systems, three of which are directly related to what we human beings call romantic love."

These systems need not be taken as normative. "Just as it is tempting to derive moral norms from descriptive information about nature (the naturalistic fallacy), so it is all too easy to impute to the depths of nature what we find emerging in human moral worlds (the projection fallacy)." For the religious naturalist, "love and desire have cosmic significance," not because they were "always there," but because they emerge within the biocultural realm as "a sign and an instance of the potent axiological possibilities in the very depths of nature" as "we choose what love and desire will mean for us."

10 Is Theology Without Walls workable?

Yes, no, maybe

Peter Feldmeier

Yes

The concept of Theology Without Walls is not only an intriguing project, it's one that already aligns with my theological tendencies. I write as a Roman Catholic theologian who has been fascinated by other religions and the potential value they have in informing my own religious sensibilities. As a religious studies major in college (almost four decades ago), I gained an appreciation for other ways of being religious that were quite different from my own. I allowed myself to be open to the religious other, enough so that I subsequently utilized non-Christian classical texts for spiritual reading, including the Upanishads, the Dao De Jing, and classic Zen texts. Much later, in doctoral studies, I wrote my dissertation on comparing the teachings of the Catholic John of the Cross to the Buddhist Buddhaghosa for the purpose of seeing how Buddhist practices might be incorporated into the Christian life without compromising Christian theology; no small project there.

Since the Second Vatican Council (1962–1965), Catholicism has taken a respectful stance toward the religious other, even proclaiming that, through the grace of God, God's saving presence was active in other religious traditions. In no way was this imagined to be some version of relativism. The Church was clear: although God was present and active in other traditions, nonetheless "she proclaims and is in duty bound to proclaim without fail, Christ who is the way, the truth and the life. In him, in whom God reconciled all things to himself, men find the fullness of their religious life" (*Nostra Aetate*, #2).

In the theological discipline of theology of religions, this position became known as *inclusivism*. Here one's home religion is believed to be absolutely true, even while recognizing God's presence in the religious other. There is a kind of imperialism in inclusivism, as other religions are not imagined to be on par with one's own. Vatican II saw the truths articulated in others as "a preparation for the Gospel" (*Lumen Gentium*, #16). One of the great liabilities in the inclusivism position is that it tends to look for and affirm those qualities in other religious traditions that look like one's own. If one

DOI: 10.4324/9780429000973-14

has the fullness of truth, then the religious other could only have partial truths, something that reflects one's own whole truth. It is difficult for the inclusivist to see any unique quality in the religious other, something valuable in its own right.

Since Vatican II, the Catholic Church has added something of a wrinkle in its promotion to dialogue with other religions. In 1984, the Vatican's Pontifical Council for Interreligious Dialogue published a document titled *The Attitude of the Church toward Other Religions*. Here it outlined various forms of dialogue. These were 1) Dialogue of Life, focusing on common humanity; 2) Dialogue of Collaboration, focusing on humanitarian issues; 3) Theological Dialogue, seeking greater mutual understanding; and 4) Dialogue of Religious Experience, including sharing one's spiritual life and religious practices. Dialogue here is described as "not only discussion, but also includes all positive and constructive relations with individuals and communities of other faiths which are directed at mutual understanding and enrichment" (#3). The religious other is presumed to have spiritual truths or insights that the Church can learn from. The document goes on to say that "a person discovers that he does not possess the truth in a perfect and total way but can walk together with others toward that goal. Mutual affirmation, reciprocal correction, and fraternal exchange lead the partners in dialogue to a greater maturity." It is an engagement with other religious faiths for "mutual enrichment" (#21). The text concludes that there may be great differences between various religions, but "[t]he sometimes profound differences between faiths do not prevent this dialogue. Those differences, rather, must be referred back in humility and confidence to God who 'is greater than our heart' (1 Jn 3:20)" (#35).

This document became for some Catholic theologians a game-changer. It seems to argue that both the non-Christian tradition *and* Christianity can be reciprocally corrected, that non-Christian insights can lead the Christian toward a greater maturity, and that both traditions can be mutually enriched by his encounter. Thus, the non-Christian tradition has religious goods the Church does not. Further, where there are differences, the document appeals to God who transcends what our hearts (or minds) can imagine.

While secure in one's primary faith commitments, seeking insights through mutual learning is nothing new to some expressions of Catholicism, even at the formal level. Already in 1974 the Federation of Asian Bishops' Conference in Taiwan declared,

> How then can we not give them [the other religions] reverence and honor? And how can we not acknowledge that God has drawn all peoples to Himself through them? . . . The great religions of Asia with their respective creeds, cults and codes reveal to us diverse ways of responding to God whose Spirit is active in all peoples and cultures.[1]

Theologians have taken up this call as well. The renowned David Tracy announced three decades ago that "[w]e are fast approaching the day when it will not be possible to attempt a Christian systematic theology except in serious conversation with the other great ways" (Tracy 1990, xi). Tracy's insight has borne fruit in what is known as comparative theology. Comparative theologians attempt to do systematic theology in light of dialogue with other religious traditions. Here one engages the texts, theologies, practices, and religious imagination of another religious tradition. This encounter gives one insight from a broader religious context to do Christian theology. Not only does such a procedure widen one's theological imagination, it also facilitates a more authentic sympathy for the religious other. What is attempted by comparative theology is not a syncretistic unification of all religions, but rather a fresh set of eyes and resources to rethink one's own tradition in new ways.

Let me provide a couple of examples of how this might work. Consider Jesus's parable in Luke 18 of two men who went to the temple to pray. One was a Pharisee and the other a tax collector.

> The Pharisee, standing by himself, was praying thus, "God, I thank you that I am not like other people: thieves, rogues, adulterers, or even like this tax collector. I fast twice a week; I give a tenth of all my income." But the tax collector, standing far off, would not even look up to heaven, but was beating his breast and saying, "God, be merciful to me, a sinner!" I tell you, this man went down to his home justified rather than the other; for all who exalt themselves will be humbled, but all who humble themselves will be exalted.

Jesus's point is obvious: do not be self-righteous or judgmental but humble, as this is the truly authentic religious posture before God and others. Let us, however, consider this parable through the lens of Buddhism. According to Buddhism, all unskillful thinking, particularly that which inflates the ego, is an expression of delusion and suffering. And the fact that the Pharisee does not see this demonstrates just how unaware he is of the situation. He is suffering but does not know it. Let us take this a further step: almost certainly most readers (you and I) have found ourselves in disdain of the Pharisee (I hate people like that!). Ironically, we are tempted to judge the judgmental Pharisee and take on his same toxic mental state. Buddhist wisdom guides us away from such tendencies with its incisive assessment of how a *conditioned* mind works and how to become free from such unskillful, conditioned reactivity. One last step: Buddhist wisdom neither condemns the Pharisee nor us, but instead invites us to see how delusion and suffering work in the psyche. Buddhist wisdom allows one to embrace the parable more fully and to cultivate compassion toward all who suffer – the Pharisee, the tax collector, and oneself alike. In short, listening to Buddhism can help us understand our own religious predicament more clearly, and this without compromising our own religious faith.

Let us consider an additional example. In Daoism, there is something known as the *Wu-forms. Wu* is a Chinese negative that is often used as a prefix. *Wu-wei* (no-action) refers to the value of nonimposing activity. One does not force something, but instead learns to work with the possibilities at hand. *Wu-zhi* (no-knowing) refers to letting go of any artificial constructs that would blind one from the uniqueness of the new moment. *Wu-yu* (no-desire) refers to letting go of one's neurotic need to be attached to some static agenda. In Daoism, the universe is an evolving mystery unfolding before one. The best experience is to participate in it as it is. The *wu-forms* dispose the soul to embrace life as art and optimize creative possibilities without trying to manipulate one's experience. The *wu-forms* can teach one to cultivate an open, spacious mind and heart, respectful of the reality unfolding before one.

A great temptation in pastoral ministry is to impose an agenda on others. Perhaps the congregation is not vibrant at, say, a wedding. The pastor might want to pump up the energy. But all this guarantees is that the minister and congregation are out of sync. *Wu-wei* suggests entering the energy that exists and working skillfully with it, not against it. Or perhaps the pastor meets a parishioner in crisis. He or she may be uncomfortable with the pain or ambiguity of the situation. The principle of *wu-yu* can help the pastor to stop seeking a personal agenda and to be present as the suffering person needs one to be present. For the minister, this does not mean that "I must get rid of this pain." One does not come to the situation imagining that its conclusion ought to be joy, surety, or healing. Although these are laudable goals, they are imposed goals. Indeed, someone may need to grieve or be in doubt a long time. One ought not to force anything. In both these cases, insights from religious others can actually help one's own religious sensibilities and even pastoral presence (Feldmeier 2013, 192–197).

Theology Without Walls seems to me the kind of project that can draw on the uniqueness of various traditions and show how, in dialogue, new insights might emerge. If utilized in the earlier sense, Theology Without Walls would take on a kind of post–Vatican II inclusivistic perspective. Here one would have a starting point with a home tradition that seeks to invigorate itself with the myriad of insights available from other religious traditions. They could provide complementary insights that might create a more robust version of one's own tradition or stretch one's traditional boundaries. I see it as potentially a version of comparative theology.

This is not the only way Theology Without Walls might work. It could take on the presuppositions that belong to a more pluralist camp. Some theologians imagine the great religious traditions as proceeding along the same trajectory, fundamentally doing the same thing. These are broadly known as pluralists. Typically, pluralists rely on several reasonable principles. The first is that God *as* God transcends all conceptuality. Concepts, they argue, are what humans do, how humans think. They exist to help us negotiate the created world. But God radically transcends the world. Thus, any God talk can only correspond to human ways of imagining or making sense of God *for us*. Pluralists, such as John Hick, Wilfred Cantwell Smith, and Paul Knitter, ask, "What's in a name?" If there is one Transcendent Absolute, and if that Absolute transcends conceptuality, then it matters little whether we call that Absolute God, Brahman, Eternal Dao, and so on. Of course, religions do have their uniqueness, they concede. Still, all authentic religions are dealing with the same reality in different ways.

Pluralists also tend to see religions as not only pointing to the same divine Reality, but also looking much like each other. They share many of the same ethical perspectives, and it is uncanny how similar they are in terms of the kinds of transformation they describe, and even what union with God is like according to their various exemplars. In many traditions, the ordinary self seems to get discarded, while the true self finds a kind of oneness or even quasi-identity with the divine. One literally re-centers oneself in God. As Marianne Moyaert notes,

> Pluralists are determined to promote real openness, real reciprocity, and real transformation. They argue for a paradigm shift that would enable Christians to move away from their millennia-long insistence on the superiority and finality of their way, whether in its exclusivist or inclusivist version, and to recognize the independent validity of other religions.
>
> (Moyaert 2014, 120)

That other religions are fundamentally doing the same thing allows for a kind of sharing of resources and insights that seem to go far beyond what any other theology of religions could offer, and it is the most likely perspective one would hold for a Theology Without Walls project. If most or all religions are *not* fundamentally doing the same thing, then one wonders from where one would start, that is, which first principles would ground one's theology and how one might negotiate competing perspectives? Thus, I think that Theology Without Walls could proceed as some form of pluralism.

One must recognize, however, that so far my framing of Theology Without Walls has been contextualized through some form of a theology of religions. Jerry L. Martin, both privately and in conference forums, insists that this is utterly unnecessary. He argues: Why not simply proceed to think theologically, utilizing the vast array of insights from the world's great depositories of wisdom and insight? What is love or compassion? How does one become holy? How ought the Divine Absolute be understood? To attempt to answer such questions, why not draw insights with the widest net possible? Surely, we might want to start with our own natural operating paradigm, be that Christianity or Hinduism, etc., but Theology Without Walls does not need a theology of religions to do this. While acknowledging that everyone comes to texts or teachings with what Gadamer calls *pre-understanding*,[2] one could attempt a kind of *tabla rasa* (clean slate). What is compassion? Let's see what Christians say, what Buddhists say, what Muslims say, and so on to come up with a larger and more holistic view of it, informed by its many expressions in various traditions. What is holiness? Again, let's consult broadly.

In affirming the possibilities of Theology Without Walls we might also recognize that it commends itself to a larger public. Young and middle-age adults in the United States are increasingly identifying with being a "none," that is, not identifying with a given religious tradition but refusing to self-identify as either agnostic or atheist. Progressively, Americans are skeptical about exclusive religious claims, decidedly rejecting fundamentalist religious framings and imagining religions as about the same agenda. They also eschew what they think is the typical politicization of religion.[3] Thus, Theology Without Walls seems to fit the zeitgeist or spirit of the time. Responding to such a spirit, Julius-Kei Kato calls for a "*hybridity* that makes us members of multiple *worlds* and citizens of a global world" (Kato 2016, 271).

No

So far in this chapter, it looks as though Theology Without Walls is not only commendable but perhaps even indispensable if one is going to do credible theology in this globalized and multiple-religious world. But like most things, the issue is far more complicated. Inclusivist theologians recognize that their home religion really does take priority. The point of interreligious dialogue from an inclusivist framework is to appreciate and revere the religious other and in small ways to allow one's own tradition to be challenged. But here all religions are assuredly not equal. In responding to what was considered overreach by some theologians, the Vatican's Congregation for the Doctrine of the Faith reacted strongly with its publication of *Dominus Iesus: On the Unicity and Salvific Universality of Jesus Christ and the Church*. Written by Cardinal Joseph Ratzinger, who later became Pope Benedict XVI, *Dominus Iesus* insisted:

> What hinders understanding and acceptance of the revealed truth: the conviction of the elusiveness and inexpressibility of divine truth . . . relativistic attitudes toward truth itself . . . the metaphysical emptying of the historical incarnation of the Eternal Logos, reduced to a mere appearing of God in history; the eclecticism of those who, in theological research, uncritically absorb ideas from a variety of philosophical and theological contexts without regard for consistency, systematic connection, or compatibility with truth.
>
> (#4)

Dominus Iesus concedes that there may be some elements of truth in other religions, but "[i]t is also certain that *objectively speaking*, they are in a gravely deficient situation in comparison with those who, in the Church, have the fullness of the means of salvation" (#22).

The great concern that Ratzinger had was a kind of theological free-for-all that neither recognized the priority of the Christian gospel, nor respected the complexity of trying to incorporate insights from other traditions without concern for philosophical or theological consistency. I hope that my example of Daoist insights was helpful to see how comparative work can yield fruitful results. I am also aware, however, that there are massive complexities in making any theological claims that include Daoism. Daoism has its own particular metaphysics that contrasts strongly with Western notions of God. Daoism is virtually *acosmic*, with no sense that there is an absolute, eternal Reality undergirding created reality. The Dao is not God in any sense; there is no God exactly, but only the ceaseless flow of life. There is no Transcendent Absolute, and thus to draw on its metaphysics is to risk violating the principle of noncontradiction – they can't be both true. And where a Daoist concept depends on such a metaphysic, there will be serious problems incorporating such a concept into a theistic view.

This is one of the biggest concerns I have for Theology Without Walls: its scope seems to be simply too large. What the most responsible comparative theologians do is relatively small and discrete. Francis Clooney, the foremost authority in comparative theology, is a good example. He has spent his career comparing Hindu insights with Christian ones. In every attempt, his scope is highly circumscribed. Clooney writes,

> [T]he opportunities present in the interreligious situation are most fruitfully appropriated slowly and by way of small and specific examples taken seriously and argued through in their details. . . . Interreligious theology is not the domain of generalists but rather of those willing to engage in detailed study, tentatively and over time.
>
> (Clooney 2001, 164)

Further, his work is intended to both stretch and be faithful to his own faith (i.e., Christianity). In commenting on comparative theologians, Michael Barnes notes that they favor "*experiments*, focused micro-studies that acknowledge the freedom of the Spirit while at the same time driving the faithful thinker deeper into the mystery of the divine encounter as it is inscribed in . . . the *home* tradition" (Barnes 2016, 241).

Pluralism is not without its own method problems. Critics have observed that pluralists tend to home in on what appears similar in different religions without taking seriously the differences. They tend to look for evidence from an already predetermined pluralist assumption, something of a conclusion looking for supportive data. I noted earlier that witnesses of mystical union look very much alike among various religions. But others have argued that if you looked carefully, the similarities fade in light of the particularities of each religion. A scholar of mysticism, Stephen Katz, has argued that the past two decades of research have now rejected the earlier assumptions that mystics were having the same experiences. These assumptions, he states, are "simplistic and untrue to the data at hand" (Katz 2013, 5). According to Katz and others, Muslims have Islamic mystical experiences, Jews have Jewish experiences, Buddhists have Buddhist experiences, and so on (Katz 2013, 5–6).

Not only have pluralists potentially overshot their mark on any unifying qualities in the world's religions, they can tend to undermine their own home religion in striving for universal claims. In a friendly debate between myself and Paul Knitter, we discussed whether Buddhism and Christianity were commensurable, that is, able to be aligned. I charged Knitter with downgrading God (from a Christian point of view) and eternalizing creation. I also charged him with misappropriating classic Buddhist texts. Whether my position succeeded is for the scholarly audience to decide. Regardless, the danger lurks large when striving to see a unified religious world that may not be so unified after all.[4]

This same problem occurs without a theology of religions informing one's assumptions. The quasi–*tabla rasa* position, discussed earlier, has yet to deal in a satisfying way with the problems of uniting insights from various religions without recognizing that those very insights are tied to structures of thought that can be incommensurable with other structures of thought. Many scholars argue that religions simply cannot be well compared or mutually drawn on. In George Lindbeck's influential book, *The Nature of Doctrine*, he argues that religions resemble languages that are intrinsically unique and inseparable from their respective cultures. Lindbeck writes,

> Adherents of different religions do not diversely thematize the same experience, rather they have different experiences. Buddhist compassion, Christian love and . . . French revolutionary *fraternité* are not diverse modifications of a single human awareness, emotion, attitude, or sentiment, but are radically (i.e., from the root) distinct ways of experiencing and being oriented toward self, neighbor, and cosmos.
>
> (Lindbeck 1984, 40, as cited in
> Moyaert 2014, 131)

Moyaert notes that "according to Lindbeck, there is still a second reason why religions are untranslatable. Religions are all-encompassing interpretive schemas." Thus, citing Lindbeck, "nothing can be translated out of the idiom into some supposedly independent communicative system without perversion, diminution or incoherence of meaning" (Moyaert 2014, 131). In short, trying to incorporate Nirvana into some Christian interpretive scheme is certain to undermine what Buddhists really mean by Nirvana, as well as to compromise Christianity, which simply has no message regarding Nirvana or interest in it. We might call Lindbeck the herald of a new kind of theology of religions, that is, the postliberal or postmodern position. In short, it proclaims that there can be no *meta-narrative*, no absolute vision or paradigm that could absorb or account for everything.

A final potential problem with a Theology Without Walls has to do with its readership. I noted earlier that this is the kind of project that would appeal particularly to the *nones*, those who reject particular or exclusive claims from religion but are open to larger universal claims. The problem is that this is less a community than it is an audience. Centuries ago, the great Christian theologian Anselm of Canterbury famously defined theology as *fides quaerens intellectum* – faith seeking understanding. What any theology requires, including Theology Without Walls, is a living faith. Faith is the condition of possibility for theology to make sense, to be valuable. I wonder if Theology Without Walls would actually help this audience or if it would encourage its readership away from a particular faith. I see religions as forums for spiritual transformation. I also see religions as having their own particularities and unique expressions of this transformation. Religions operate as paradigms or lenses of interpretation of experience. Their respective dogmas act like fences within which its members live. Such fences could be permeable, even climbable, but they seem to be necessary. They give religion form. Could Theology Without Walls be ultimately formless?

Conclusion: maybe

Some scholars, including me, believe that all the earlier positions and those of their critics can be overstated. Inclusivism rightly insists that if one thinks one's religion is true – really true – then this has consequences as to what one thinks of alternative faiths. But inclusivism cannot account for authentic and very different religious expressions that do not fit well into its own religious tradition. If the Catholic Church, for example, takes on the inclusivist model, it does so without consistency. If one can really learn from the religious other, then one's tradition cannot have all the goods. Pluralism rightly sees universal tendencies that make interreligious sharing possible. I am not at all convinced that other religions are so incommensurable as Lindbeck insists. There really are massive similarities that make interreligious sharing possible. On the other hand, pluralism does underestimate religious differences. And although the postmodern position is right to warn against colonizing the religious other, it overstates its own position. If religions are different languages, we can learn these languages and see cognates in our own. Further, there is no *pure religion* that has not been influenced by forces outside itself. For example, early Christianity was decidedly influenced by Neoplatonism. Thomas Aquinas, the great medieval synthesizer, unabashedly drew on Aristotle, Plato, and Islamic and Jewish sources such as Avicenna and Maimonides.

Thus, I see Theology Without Walls as valuable and in some ways already being done fruitfully. But I must ask, what would it look like in its most robust expression? By what method? Would it have a theological foundation, say, Christianity, and then extend this to include insights from the world's religions? Or would it start from scratch and attempt a unified theory of religion? How would it address philosophical positions that have very different and even colliding first principles? These are the questions that would have to be answered. If successfully addressed and defended, then – maybe!

Notes

1 Cited in Chia (2016, 49).
2 See Gadamer (1975, 274–289).
3 See Putman and Campbell (2010), *passim.*
4 This debate initially took place at the Catholic Theological Society of America in 2015 and subsequently published as Knitter and Feldmeier (2016).

References

Barnes, Michael. 2016. "The Promise of Comparative Theology: Reading between the Lines." In *Interfaith Dialogue: Pathways for Ecumenical and Interreligious Dialogue,* edited by Edmund Kee-Fook Chia, 237–250. New York: Palgrave Macmillan.

Chia, Edmund Kee-Fook. 2016. "Response of the Asian Church to Nostra Aetate." In *Interfaith Dialogue: Pathways for Ecumenical and Interreligious Dialogue,* edited by Edmund Kee-Fook Chia, 45–56. New York: Palgrave. doi:10.1057/978-1-137-59698-7_4

Clooney, Francis X. 2001. *Hindu God, Christian God: How Reason Helps Break Down the Boundaries between Religions.* Oxford: Oxford University Press. doi:10.1086/382319

Feldmeier, Peter. 2013. "Christian Transformation and the Encounter with the World's Holy Canons." *Horizons* 40 (2): 192–197. doi:10.1017/hor.2013.72

Gadamer, Hans-Georg. 1975. *Truth and Method.* Trans. Garrett Barden and John Cummings. New York: Seabury Press.

Kato, Julius-Kei. 2016. "Epistemic Confidence, Humility, and Kenosis in Interfaith Dialogue." In *Interfaith Dialogue: Pathways for Ecumenical and Interreligious Dialogue,* edited by Edmund Kee-Fook Chia, 265–276. New York: Palgrave Macmillan. doi:10.1057/978-1-137-59698-7_20

Katz, Steven. 2013. "Introduction." In *Comparative Mysticism: An Anthology of Original Sources,* edited by Steven Katz, 3–22. Oxford: Oxford University Press.

Knitter, Paul, and Peter Feldmeier. 2016. "Are Buddhism and Christianity Commensurable? A Debate/Dialogue Between Paul Knitter and Peter Feldmeier." *Journal of Buddhist-Christian Studies* 36 (1): 165–184. doi:10.1353/bcs.2016.0015

Lindbeck, George. 1984. *The Nature of Doctrine: Religion and Theology in a Postliberal Age.* Philadelphia: Westminster Press. doi:10.1177/004057368504200214

Moyaert, Marianne. 2014. *In Response to the Religious Other: Ricoeur and the Fragility of Interreligious Encounters.* Lanham: Lexington Books.

Putman, Robert, and David Campbell. 2010. *American Grace: How Religion Divides and Unites Us.* New York: Simon & Schuster. doi:10.1017/s0022381612000771

Tracy, David. 1990. *Dialogue with the Other: The Inter-Religious Dialogue.* Louvain: Peeters.

11 Daunting choices in transreligious theology

A case study

Wesley J. Wildman with Jerry L. Martin

The transreligious theologian faces daunting choices. These choices are not *between* religions – because for transreligious theologians the relevant data, concepts, and methods are not restricted to those of a single tradition – but rather between theological possibilities that cut across the religions. Understanding this is a critical part of the answer to the appealingly practical question about how we might go about the difficult task of transreligious theology. To the end of such understanding, this chapter presents a case study to illustrate the way theological options cut across traditions, inviting us along a pathway into the territory of transreligious theology oriented more by conceptual affinities and tensions than by religious identifications.[1]

Consider the category of ultimate reality, which fits postaxial religious traditions reasonably comfortably, and even many nonaxial traditions with tolerable awkwardness. This is a classic example of a vague comparative category: it has been specified with a variety of mutually incompatible models that exist side by side within traditions and recur in various modalities across traditions.[2] Three of the most plausible, highly developed models of ultimate reality are an agential being (personal theism, or not-less-than-personal theism, where this divine being is the ultimate reality), the ground of being (beyond the categories of existence and nonbeing, and thus not a being but a principle that resists comprehensive understanding), and a subordinate god (a personal or not-less-than-personal God or gods within a more fundamental ultimate reality). Each ultimacy model boasts a long heritage, impressive explanatory power, significant cross-cultural visibility, and considerable internal diversity.

The agential being model supposes that, whatever else it may be, ultimate reality is a being aware of reality, responsive to events, and active within the world. Reality as whole is invested with personality and purpose, meaning and intelligibility, goodness and beauty. Every aspect of reality is rendered as coherent as the narrative of a focally aware and purposefully active personal life. No theory of ultimate reality is better fitted to the human tendency to see intentionality in events and to give group identity an authoritative focus.

Subordinate god models assert that there is at least one God, who is a being with determinate characteristics existing within a more fundamental

DOI: 10.4324/9780429000973-15

reality. In this two-tiered view, God has the personal characteristics that make agential being models so appealing – providing existential meaning and a focus for community bonding – but the challenging task of providing an understanding of reality as a whole is addressed at a more abstract, impersonal level. Subordinate god models offer a way to avoid some of the conceptual stresses that beset agential being models.

Ground-of-being models make an ontological shift from God as a being to God as the ground or source of reality. This God is typically conceived as the source of being and nonbeing, and thus beyond those categories, which makes talk of existence or nonexistence unintelligible. To the extent that we can identify patterns and fundamental structures within the reality in which we live and move and have our being, we generate insights into the character of the ground of being but a full understanding always necessarily retreats from the grasping cognition of human beings, or indeed of any being whatsoever. This is why ground-of-being models are often expressed using apophatic strategies of indirection.

Consider a couple of examples of diversity internal to traditions. First, in the South Asian context, the theology of Rāmānuja (from the dvaita Vedānta tradition of Hindu philosophy) expresses personal theism. Rāmānuja's theology was formulated in explicit opposition to the advaita, or nondual Vedānta tradition, which belongs to the ground-of-being class of ultimacy models. Here we see a fundamental conflict internalized within the vague category of ultimate reality and persistently debated within the rich Vedānta tradition. Meanwhile, next door in Persia, Zoroastrianism presented two non-ultimate Gods, one good and one evil, who jointly constitute ultimate reality. This subordinate-gods cosmological vision eliminates the moral paradoxes of a personal ultimate and the moral neutrality of a nonpersonal ultimate and with striking clarity calls upon each human being to choose a moral side.

Second, in the Western context, the ancient tradition of the Israelite religion, as it transformed into Judaism and early Christianity, gave powerful articulation to a subordinate-being model of ultimate reality. Here God is not ultimate reality, but rather a force for goodness and justice within a wider chaotic reality. Creation was understood as this God taming chaos to fashion an intelligible moral order. Within three centuries of its origins, Christianity had produced a new understanding of creation in which God creates from nothing, thereby making a personal being the ultimate reality, with all of the attendant theodicy problems. In the same environment, early Stoicism was propounding a ground-of-being model that also influenced Christianity as it sought to articulate the radical transcendence associated with its emerging view of God as ultimate reality itself, rather than as the religiously relevant component of ultimate reality.

These models are live options for the transreligous theologian, once their cross-cultural character is recognized, but only if the theologian is prepared to leave the complex beauty of a single familiar religious continent to sail the oceans seeking conceptual affinities and tensions among the world's religious ideas and practices. Even within the domain of comparative theology, not all theologians find that journey appealing and would rather root themselves in one religious continent and learn from one or more other traditions how to root themselves ever more deeply. Fair enough; there is room for many theological temperaments within comparative theology. But transreligious theology takes a different journey, tackling fundamental theological questions as they arise within the human species, in all of its cultural and religious diversity and biological and bodily givenness. That conception of transreligious theology guides this chapter's exploration of ultimate-reality models that cut across religious traditions and co-exist within each tradition.

Identifying the presence of the three models cutting across religious traditions helps to shape the choices before the transreligious theologian. Comparing those models is a critical component in making rational choices. One line of comparative analysis begins with the observation that the three models exemplify different approaches to managing the human reality of anthropomorphic cognition, whereby we make use of what we think we know best (human beings) to understand what we surely know least (ultimate reality). For at least the following three reasons, comparing ultimacy models in terms of the ways they embrace or resist anthropomorphism may be a good place for the transreligious theologian to focus inquiry.

First, anthropomorphism is prominent in theological traditions and widespread in popular devotion, so it is difficult to avoid. The world of religious symbolism is replete with anthropomorphic imagery that promotes spiritual engagement, and there need not be anything naive or excessive about it. Moreover, some philosophic models ascribe to ultimate reality characteristics that are derived from human experience, such as awareness, feelings, intentions, plans, and agency. Yet intellectuals also critique anthropomorphic conceptions of ultimate reality as profoundly misleading, so there is a rich array of material here for the transreligious theologian to engage and process. Second, a tradition rich in anthropomorphic images and stories may well be the departure point of a theologian raised in or attached to a theistic tradition. This makes anthropomorphic models of ultimate reality of immediate interest to many comparative and transreligious theologians. Third, from cognitive psychology and evolutionary biology, we have learned that anthropomorphic cognition appears to be something like a cognitive default, in the sense of the most natural, ready-to-hand way of thinking available for making sense of the world around us, including difficult-to-interpret aspects of that world. Unfortunately, cognitive defaults of all kinds, including this one, are prone to error. Human beings routinely project consciousness, agency, and purpose where there is none. Our tendency to misapply anthropomorphic cognition does not refute anthropomorphism, but it does raise a red flag that transreligious theologians should evaluate carefully.

Anthropomorphism isn't a simple continuum, ranging from extreme to none. There are three relatively independent dimensions of theological anthropomorphism: intentionality, practicality, and narrativity. Intentionality is the degree to which the model attributes intentional action, consciousness, and purposes to an invisible being such as a deity. Practicality is the degree to which a model of ultimate reality has existential grip and relevance to the immediate concerns of people's lives. Narrativity is the degree to which the model supports rich traditions of story, legend, and miracles that provide meaning to people's lives and shared referents for a community.

Anthropomorphism can be stronger or weaker in relation to each of these three dimensions, and theologians have adopted a variety of positions – opposing anthropomorphism here, employing it there. The variety of configurations possible seems to offer the theologian considerable freedom, but the choice is meaningfully constrained. Each dimension can be tested against relevant information from cognitive science, evolutionary psychology, comparative religion, and other sources. The theologian may have to balance what best reflects the scientific data against what most effectively provides existential orientation and a sense of religious community. Then a complex theological hypothesis will have to be tested against explanatory standards, including applicability, adequacy, coherence, consistency, and pragmatic considerations such as ethical consequences, aesthetic quality, social potency, and spiritual appeal. Framing and ranking the relevant criteria are themselves theological choices.

Because choices that fit well with one criterion may fit poorly with another, the theologian should expect difficult decisions and conceptual stresses. For example, the ground-of-being model may be appealing to those who give great weight to evolutionary psychology and cognitive science, but may be found to be spiritually disappointing to those who sense that only a personal deity could be spiritually satisfying. The agential-being model may provide accessible spiritual understanding but struggle with scientific information about the ways human minds work. If the theologian finds the notion of providential action compelling, then God simply has to be an agent, but then the agential-being model must confront the problem of theodicy – which arises from the equation of the personal God, who contains no evil, with comprehensive reality, which does. Theodicy can be a problem also for those ground-of-being models that regard God as unambiguously good. Theodicy is not a problem for subordinate-deity models, such as process theology or Zoroastrianism, which can divorce God from the moral flaws of reality as a whole and thereby protect God's moral perfection.

The theologian will also face anthropomorphically inflected metaphysical questions about the ultimate conditions for reality. These include the problem of the One and the Many, the problem of evil, the problem of ontological dependence, the problem of causal closure, the problem of the intelligibility of reality, and so on. For example, suppose the theologian faces a choice between 1) the hypothesis of God as omnipotent creator (this could be either an agential-being or a ground-of-being position, depending on the details) and 2) the hypothesis of cosmic moral dualism famous from classical Manichaeism and Zoroastrianism (this belongs to the class of subordinate-deity models). How might the theologian reason about such a choice?

It would be relevant to consider how well each handles such theological issues as the problem of evil and the problem of the One and the Many. The theologian will find that absolute moral dualisms handle the problem of evil spectacularly well, at least in one obvious sense: the origin of both good and evil is cosmological, there is no perplexing question of one deriving from the other, and there is no possibility of eschatological consummation in favor of one or the other. By contrast, omnipotent creator theism offers a famously contorted solution to the problem of evil, with evil explained either as a mere privation of good in a good world created by a good God, or as spontaneously derived from the good and tolerated by a good God for a good reason, or as deliberately created by a good God for a good reason (which eschatology may reveal), or as rooted in God's own morally ambivalent nature.

In regard to the problem of the One and the Many, the strengths and weakness of the two models are reversed. Absolute moral dualisms attribute everything in reality to two co-primordial creative forces locked in eternal battle, but don't explain why things are determined in that dualistic cosmological way, essentially dodging the problem of the One and the Many. Meanwhile, omnipotent creator theism traces all of determinate reality to the divine nature and its creative act. One famous solution to the problem of the One and the Many describes this divine creative act not as a taming of chaos or the forming of pre-existent material but as creation from nothing (*ex nihilo*), which implies that everything is ontologically dependent on this divine creator. The only limitation to this splendid solution to the problem of the One and the Many is explaining the determinate nature of God – why should God be that way rather than some other way? Most *ex nihilo* creation traditions simply refuse to entertain that question, treating God as self-existent, and thus as the metaphysical backstop for all origins questions.

Thus, the model that solves one problem well does relatively poorly on the other. The transreligious theologian must ask: Is it more important to have an intelligible solution to the problem of evil or a compelling resolution of the problem of the One and the Many? Among those who would prefer to solve the problem of evil are Zoroaster, Confucius, and Alfred North Whitehead. Those who would prefer to solve the problem of the One and the Many include Plotinus, Śaṅkara, and Robert Neville. Still others, with competing metaphysical intuitions (such as the later Augustine), regard the two problems as equally important.

How does one decide which problem is more pressing? Here the dimension of anthropomorphism we call practicality – the ready applicability of ideas to the immediate concerns of life – becomes a vital consideration. Prioritizing a solution to the problem of evil underwrites a way to think about one of the great problems of human life, in which we are often preoccupied with the pain and frustration of finitude and the outrage and needless suffering associated with moral evil. The more anthropomorphic position does not bother about completeness of rational intelligibility when it is not immediately relevant (which it rarely is in ordinary life). The less anthropomorphic position maximizes the completeness of rational intelligibility. Agential-being models rate high on the practicality dimension of anthropomorphism, responding to existential needs and spiritual yearnings, but they do little to resist error-prone cognitive defaults. An overemphasis on stories, myths, legends, and miracles may impair theological richness, complexity, sophistication, and validity. By contrast, the less anthropomorphic position prioritizes the completeness of rational intelligibility even if the result is a theological vision of ultimate reality that regular religious people find difficult to digest.

Several strategies are available to mitigate anthropomorphism. Consider the role of time and change within the life of an agential God. The more highly anthropomorphic models take their conceptual clues from narratives of God as an agent, which are amply present in the Vedas, the Hebrew Bible, the New Testament, and the Qur'an. In these narratives, God is a being who communicates, makes decisions, and acts at particular times. These characteristics require the divine version of a temporal consciousness and the metaphysical capacity to change, develop, and feel. On the other hand, the theologian may come to regard a temporal, changing being as either unsuitable for a deity or impossible for an omnipotent creator. These reservations struck Aquinas, Avicenna, and Maimonides for Abrahamic theisms, and Udayana for South Asian theism.

The attribution of eternity, immutability, and impassibility to God mitigates the intentionality dimension of anthropomorphism and draws the less highly anthropomorphic agential-being models close to the ground-of-being models. These attributions may help provide a rational account of comprehensive reality, but they may weaken the notion of a loving, benign, acting God vital to some religious understandings. Similarly, a God standing outside time may imply divine foreknowledge incompatible with human freedom and natural divine responsiveness. Here again, subordinate-deity models, which do not use God to explain ultimate reality, may be able to avoid these difficulties.

Like theologians rooted within a single tradition, the transreligious theologian may feel forced toward some balancing of the personal aspects of divinity and the impersonal aspects of ultimate reality. The medieval synthesis of classical theism combines personal (Biblical) and nonpersonal (philosophical) elements to define key doctrines such as the Trinity and the hypostatic union (the unity of humanity and divinity in Christ). In these formulations, the theologian grants the philosophers' point that ultimate reality is not a being, but construes this as "not a being like created beings," and then continues to insist with the Bible that the divine being is personal, intentional, and active. Where some analysts saw only contradictions in this synthesis, others saw hard-won harmony.

The clearest way to save the idea of God as agential being is to dispense with the claim that this God is the ultimate reality, which is to shift from the agential-being class to the subordinate-deity class. Process theologians have made exactly that move. The clearest way to save the idea of God as ultimate reality is to drop the claim that ultimate reality is an agential being, which is to shift from the agential-being class to the ground-of-being class of models. Some theologians, such as Paul Tillich and many Jewish post-Holocaust thinkers, have done just that.

The transreligious theologian will also face the question of ontological dependence. The problem arises in classical theism when it asks how God can be truly omnipotent if there is something external to God with reference to which God's moral or ontological standing can be assessed? The doctrine of aseity or self-subsistence asserts that divine reality exists in, of, for, and from itself. This implies that all things – even the transcendental ideals of goodness, truth, and beauty – are ontologically dependent on God, derive from God, and are what they are because of God. The most austere form of aseity implies occasionalism, which is influential in Muslim theology: nothing occurs that God does not do, nothing is created that God does not create, and there is no causal continuity apart from the action of God to make causal patterns and regularities appear. Jewish, Christian, and Hindu theology tend to affirm aseity in a moderate form. The *ex nihilo* constraint ensures that nothing already exists alongside God when God creates, which is the constraint that process models of ultimate reality abandon. Thus, for the creation *ex nihilo* view, everything is ontologically dependent on God, and yet God is free to create as God sees fit, perhaps giving creation the power to sustain its own causal regularities.

A question that looms over all theological reasoning is: To what extent is ultimate reality to be regarded as generally fitting human modes of understanding? To what extent does ultimacy, by its very nature, exceed the grasp of finite knowers? If it exceeds too much, no knowledge and perhaps no relationship – at least no articulate relationship – to the divine is possible, as Aquinas argues in his discussion of analogy. If it fits too closely, the concept of God threatens to shrink to disturbingly human size. These issues are closely related to questions about religious language. To what degree are characteristics attributed to God literally and univocally? To what extent analogically or metaphorically or symbolically?

Symbolic interpretations shift reference away from the literal sense to some other meaning. Aquinas's doctrine of analogy offers an in-between view: God loves in a way that is analogous to the way human beings love – similar in respects sufficient to deserve the same word but different in respects appropriate to the difference between divine being and human being. Suitably reframed, divine agency can be retained even by ground-of-being models. Tillich rejects virtually all literal statements about God, but compensates for the loss of concrete meaning with a vibrant theory of symbolism.

Ground-of-being models tend to rank relatively low on all three dimensions of anthropomorphism – significantly lower than the least anthropomorphic agential-being models – but versions differ in how they handle each of the three dimensions. For example, subordinate-deity models are an intriguing combination of high intentionality and high narrativity at the level of the depiction of the subordinate deity – higher than many agential-being models – and low intentionality and low narrativity at the level of ultimate reality as a whole, which is not religiously relevant for these models. Of course, what qualities to attribute to the God or gods operating under the dome of ultimate reality presents further decisions for the theologian, as well as how precisely to conceive the nature and structure of ultimate reality. However, the transreligious theologian may decide to resist all forms of anthropomorphism. This choice would lead to religious naturalism, with ultimate reality conceived as the relatively characterless God Beyond God.

Comparative religion gives rise to another criterion the transreligious theologian may find useful: deferring to the most sophisticated philosophical understandings in the various traditions as offering a kind of religious "expertise." Ground-of-being models fit well with the expertise criterion. They can accommodate a symbolic account of diverse religious ideas and frame a metaphysics in which every viewpoint finds a natural place, even if they are not all of equal value. The expertise criterion causes trouble for agential-being models, whose insistence on a personal highest being as ultimate reality tends to lock theology into the single religion focused on this particular God and to block the rich theological possibilities that take in the truths from multiple faiths, including the venerable nontheistic traditions.

The expertise criterion, giving emphasis to the rich diversity of religious ideas and practices, may point the transreligious theologian toward some form of pluralism. The presence of plural religious practices and multiple divinities probably inspired the Upaniṣads, with their affirmation that Brahman is One – behind, between, and beyond all, both identical with the human spirit and utterly transcending it, grounding and uniting everything that is. The same vision powers the perennial philosophy's attempt to coordinate all models of ultimate reality into a hierarchy perfectly suited to accommodate the vast range of spiritual personalities and inclinations, with each soul driving toward the loftier, transpersonal models as it commutes through the saṃsāric cycle of lives.[3] A similar sensitivity to the perceived limits of religious images and ideas (images in conceptual form) inspires the apophatic declaration that ultimate reality is beyond all imagery and best met in linguistic indirection or even silence. Apophaticism is a strategy for speaking of ultimate reality by turning away from conceptual modeling, and indeed away from every kind of ultimacy speech – but all of this in such a way as to convey something indirectly about ultimate reality. There is a great deal to say, and much theoretical intricacy to negotiate, prior to lapsing into silence.

Whereas classical theism was always subject to conceptual stresses, the supposedly personal and nonpersonal elements of ultimate reality were more easily combined in past eras than they are now. The natural and social sciences have increased suspicions of the highly anthropomorphic default for human cognition. The sciences are most easily reconciled with naturalism, which either rejects all theological models as superstitions or invites new models based on the overflowing resources of nature itself, within which all human strivings, religious and otherwise, arise and find expression. Or, also compatible with the sciences, the response can be apophaticism, which finds the truest response to the divine, not in models, but in patterns of linguistic indirection that yield to a profound silence.

One of the challenges of transreligious theology is how to think theologically beyond a single tradition. What are one's materials, concepts, and guidelines? Fortunately, comparative religion and comparative theology have prepared an array of fruitful cross-cultural concepts, issues to be addressed, and theological options to consider. Theologians working beyond the walls now have ample resources for moving religious understanding forward.

Notes

1 With the help of Martin, this chapter reframes conceptual content from Wildman (2017) in a way designed to be helpful to transreligious theologians.
2 A properly vague comparative category is a key concept within the Cross-Cultural Comparative Religious Ideas project, the results of which are presented in three volumes edited by Robert Cummings Neville (2001).
3 For example, see Smith (1992).

References

Neville, Robert C. 2001. *The Human Condition, Ultimate Realities, and Religious Truth*. Albany, NY: SUNY Press.
Smith, Huston. 1992. *Forgotten Truth: The Common Vision of the World's Religions*. 2nd ed. San Francisco, CA: HarperOne.
Wildman, Wesley J. 2017. *In Our Own Image: Anthropomorphism, Apophaticism, and Ultimacy*. Oxford: Oxford University Press. doi:10.1093/oso/978019881 5990.003.0002

12 Cognitive science of religion and the nature of the divine

A pluralist, nonconfessional approach

Johan De Smedt and Helen De Cruz

Introduction

Cognitive science of religion (CSR) indicates that people naturally veer toward beliefs that are quite divergent from Anselmian monotheism or Christian theism. Some authors (e.g., Shook 2017) have taken this view as a starting point for a debunking argument against religion, whereas others (e.g., Barrett 2009) have tried to vindicate Christian theism by appealing to the noetic effects of sin, or the Fall.

In this chapter, we use a different approach: we ask what theologians can learn from CSR about the nature of the divine by looking at the CSR literature and what it identifies as commonalities across religions. We use a pluralist, nonconfessional approach to outline properties of the divine with reference to the CSR literature. We connect our approach to Hick's religious pluralism, Ramakrishna's realization of God through multiple spiritual paths, and Gellman's inexhaustible plenitude.

The origins of religious beliefs and their justification

What can the origins of religious beliefs tell us about their justification? From the eighteenth century onward, philosophers and scientists have considered this question by outlining natural histories of religion. These accounts not only examine the origins of religious beliefs but also ask whether those beliefs could be rationally maintained in light of their origins. Typically, eighteenth-century natural histories of religion (e.g., De Fontenelle 1728; Hume 1757) emphasized the diversity of religious beliefs and expressed skepticism about their rationality. For example, Hume (1757, 2) stated that religious beliefs were so diverse that "no two nations, and scarce any two men, have ever agreed precisely in the same sentiments."

By contrast, other authors since the early modern period, such as John Calvin and Pierre Gassendi, emphasized the universality of religion and took this as a starting point for the truth of religious claims. For example, Calvin (1559/1960, 43–46), following Cicero, made the empirical claim that there is "no nation so barbarous, no people so savage, that they have

DOI: 10.4324/9780429000973-16

not a deep-seated conviction that there is a God" and concluded "it is not a doctrine that must be first learned in school, but one of which each of us is master from his mother's womb and which nature itself permits no one to forget." Calvin appealed to an innate sense of the divine, a *sensus divinitatis*, which instills religious beliefs in us. An influential updated version of this argument is Plantinga's (2000) extended Aquinas/Calvin model, which argues that Christian belief can have warrant, even in the absence of rational argument, because it is produced by a properly working *sensus divinitatis* that God implanted in us.

However, religious diversity threatens to undermine any straightforward claim from universality to truth. If religious belief is universal, why do people across religious traditions hold mutually incompatible religious beliefs? The Medieval Muslim theologian Al-Ghazālī worried about this question, as he mused that children of Muslims tend to turn out Muslims, children of Jews tend to grow up as Jews, and children of Christians tend to become Christians. He proposed that everyone is born with the *fiṭrah*, a basic moral sense and natural belief in God, which can give rise to authentic religion or be perverted into false religions: "Every infant is born endowed with the *fiṭrah*: then his parents make him Jew or Christian or Magian [Zoroastrian]" (Al-Ghazālī, 1100/2006, 19–20). In this way, cultural influences can either help properly cultivate certain religious beliefs or have a distorting influence and give rise to false (in Al-Ghazālī's view, non-Muslim) ones. Similarly, Christian authors such as Calvin (1559/1960) and, more recently, Plantinga (2000, 184) appeal to the Fall as an explanation for why people's "natural knowledge of God has been compromised, weakened, reduced, smothered, overlaid, or impeded." As a result of our sinful condition, we are not only damaged in our cognitive structures, which hampers our knowledge of God, but also in our affection, which fails to orient itself to God.

Any argument that takes the prevalence of religious beliefs as a starting point to make claims about the existence and nature of the divine stumbles on the problem of religious diversity. In order to address this problem, authors from monotheistic traditions appeal to a sense of the divine combined with auxiliary principles such as the noetic effects of sin (Calvin and Plantinga) or to cultural transmission (Al-Ghazālī) to explain why religious beliefs are so divergent. For these authors, religious diversity is a problem. But, as we will show later, religious pluralism celebrates the diversity of religious beliefs, while at the same allowing for something akin to a sense of the divine.

The cognitive science of religion

CSR can shed new light on why religious beliefs are widespread and diverse. CSR is an interdisciplinary research program that uses findings from, among others, developmental psychology, cognitive science, and anthropology. A unifying theme throughout this literature is the commitment of

CSR authors to the idea that religion is natural. This does not necessarily mean religious beliefs are innate (although a few authors, e.g., Bering (2011) have made this stronger claim), but that such beliefs come relatively easily, with little formal instruction, as part of ordinary human development and socialization (McCauley 2011). CSR also holds that religious beliefs are the result of several cognitive processes, which are not exceptional but operate in everyday life, such as discerning teleology, detecting agency, and thinking about other people's minds. Within different cultures, these cognitive building blocks give rise to a wide range of religious beliefs. We will here briefly review three lines of research in CSR scholarship: belief in supernatural agents and its connection to cooperation, teleological thinking, and afterlife beliefs.

Across cultures, people believe in a variety of supernatural agents that are concerned with moral or ritual violations. Such agents include powerful gods such as Zeus or Kālī, the Hindu goddess who destroys evil, bestows liberation, and protects her people. But they also include supernatural agents with more limited capacities, such as the ancestors, place spirits, and the Chinese Kitchen God, who reports to the Jade Emperor about how families behaved during the past year. There is increasing evidence that belief in such supernatural agents enhances cooperation among members of the same religion by providing a sense of social control: people are less likely to behave antisocially (e.g., steal, cheat) if they believe they are being watched. Social control is particularly effective if the agents who are watching have the capacity to punish transgressions.

Initially, CSR authors believed that only very powerful creator gods, termed *high gods*, could foster cooperation in this way, because only high gods would care about moral transgressions. For example, Norenzayan (2013) speculates that belief in high gods decreased antisocial behavior, thereby enabling people to live in larger groups. However, more recently, there is increasing evidence that belief in a broader range of supernatural agents can motivate people to cooperate. For example, Purzycki et al. (2016) investigated whether people who believe in supernatural agents would be more generous toward others who have the same religion as themselves but who live far away. They let participants of a variety of supernatural faiths, including belief in garden spirits (horticulturalists from Tanna, Vanuatu), ancestor spirits (Yasawa, Fiji), and spirit masters, local spirits who have dominion over a small part of the landscape (Tyva, Siberia), play a game where they could allocate money either to themselves or to a distant or close person with the same religion. People were more generous to distant co-religionists if the supernatural beings they believed in were more knowledgeable and more able to punish moral transgressions. This supports broad supernatural punishment theory, which holds that a wide range of supernatural beings, not just supreme creators, can instill cooperation (Watts et al. 2015).

Cultural evolution, or potentially gene-culture co-evolution, is hypothesized as the driving factor in the cultural spread of the belief in specific supernatural beings. If belief in supernatural agents who are morally concerned and able to punish ritual or moral transgressions increases cooperation among people who hold the same beliefs, we can predict that such beliefs confer a fitness advantage (Norenzayan and Shariff 2008). In groups where belief in supernatural punishment by gods, spirits, or other supernatural beings is common, one could thus expect higher degrees of cooperation. This would provide selective pressure at a cultural level for the maintenance and spread of belief in supernatural punishment, and perhaps also help foster biological adaptations that make us prone to believing in such agents (Bering and Johnson 2005).

Teleological thinking is intimately tied to religion across cultures. Children and adults prefer teleological explanations for the origin of natural beings, including biological and nonbiological natural kinds, such as giraffes, tiger paws, and mountains. In a typical experiment, participants are offered the choice between two kinds of explanation for why a given object exists. Does it rain so that animals and plants can drink (a teleological explanation) or because water condenses into droplets (a mechanistic explanation)? There is robust empirical evidence that young children up to the age of ten prefer teleological over mechanistic explanations (Kelemen 1999). Moreover, when adults are put under time pressure, they are also more likely to endorse false teleological explanations, for example, "the Sun radiates heat because warmth nurtures life" (Kelemen and Rosset 2009). PhD holders in the sciences and humanities are also liable to endorse false teleological explanations under time pressure, albeit to a lesser extent than the general population (Kelemen, Rottman, and Seston 2013).

There is a link between teleological thinking and religiosity. Kelemen (2004) initially argued that children are intuitive theists because they attribute teleological features of the world to an intelligent designer. But later experiments cast doubt on this interpretation and indicate a broader connection between teleological thinking and supernatural beliefs and practices. For example, Kelemen, Rottman, and Seston (2013) found that scientists who tend to think of the Earth as having agency and caring for creatures (so-called Gaia beliefs), as well as theist scientists, think more teleologically than scientists who don't believe in the Earth as an agent or in God. Similarly, ordinary adults from the United States and Finland who endorse either Gaia beliefs or classical theist beliefs are more likely to think that objects (e.g., a maple leaf, a mountain) were made purposively by some being (Järnefelt, Canfield, and Kelemen 2015). Järnefelt et al. (2019) studied teleological beliefs in China, in a group of participants who mostly self-identify as atheists. However, all participants engaged at least in some religious practices, including revering ancestors, feng shui, and using lucky charms. They found that the more participants engaged in such religious practices, the more likely they were to endorse teleological explanations for nonbiological natural kinds. The Finnish and Chinese studies tentatively suggest that teleological thinking might also lie at the basis of nontheistic religious beliefs and practices. Indeed, research on teleology and life events suggests that teleological thinking persists in atheists and agnostics (e.g., Heywood and Bering 2014): when spontaneously reflecting on significant life events, atheists offer fewer teleological explanations than theists, but still suggest that things happen to them for a reason, for example, claiming that the universe wanted to give them a sign or send them a message.

CSR has also shown that afterlife beliefs are robust and cross-culturally widespread. Belief in the afterlife probably is rooted in social thinking, in our ordinary attributions of mental states to other agents in everyday life. As Merleau-Ponty (1945/2002, 250) already suggested, it is hard to imagine ourselves as no longer existing – it becomes intuitive and plausible to imagine ourselves in an afterlife, and any cultural scripts that propose an afterlife (e.g., reincarnation) can easily spread. Moreover, we find it difficult to imagine that others, especially those we interact with frequently, no longer exist. We continue to attribute mental states to them, even if they are not in physical proximity or if they are dead. Bloom (2004) characterizes humans as intuitive dualists: young children already make an intuitive distinction between people, using intuitive psychology to reason about them, and physical objects, using intuitive physics to interact with them. However, Hodge (2011) argues that our thinking about dead agents is not easily captured in mind/body dualistic terms. Watson-Jones et al. (2017) found that Christians in the United States think our psychology (personality, preferences, desires) will survive after death, but not necessarily our bodies, whereas Christians from Vanuatu (Melanesia) believe that our biological properties (bodies and bodily functions) will survive into the afterlife, but not necessarily our psychology. This indicates that within cultures and even within the same religion, different belief scripts about postmortem survival may develop and that Bloom's (2004) intuitive dualism may be too simplistic.

What does CSR mean for knowledge of the divine?

CSR shows that religious beliefs are the result of universal cognitive dispositions. Because these dispositions are underdetermined, religious diversity becomes inevitable. As we have seen, humans are naturally inclined to believe in supernatural agents, but these are not necessarily monotheistic gods. We are inclined to ascribe teleology, but this is linked to a broad notion of supernatural agency, including Mother Earth and ancestral spirits. We tend to believe in an afterlife, but that afterlife takes a number of different forms.

What, if any, conclusions about our knowledge of the divine can we draw from CSR? Shook (2017) takes CSR to claim that religious beliefs are innate, a position most CSR authors do not endorse (but see Bering 2011), and then subsequently takes the diversity of religious beliefs to spell bad news for their justification. Teehan (2016) argues that CSR puts pressure on theological views, such as that God would be omnibenevolent: religions encourage in-group favoritism and out-group derogation, which would entail that social evils such as racism and xenophobia would be part of God's plan. This would lower our belief that an omnibenevolent God exists, and theodicies that appeal to the Fall do not solve this problem.

By contrast, Barrett (2009) appeals to the Fall and sinfulness to explain religious diversity. If the cognitive dispositions we discussed earlier are God's way of instilling religious beliefs, why would they allow so much diversity?

> One possible answer is that a perfectly adequate concept of God does come as part of our biological heritage but that living in a sinful, fallen world this concept grows corrupt as we grow. If not for broken relationships, corrupt social structures, flawed religious communities, and the suffering that people inflict upon each other, perhaps children would inevitably form a perfectly acceptable concept of God. The diversity in god concepts we see is a consequence of human error and not divine design.
>
> (Barrett 2009, 97–98)

This approach, like Calvin's and Plantinga's appeal to the noetic effects of sin, comes at a cost: on the one hand, there is an inference from religious belief to the truth of those beliefs, but on the other hand, any religious beliefs that do not fit the preconceptions of these authors are dismissed as results of defective cognition. How can Barrett be sure what a "perfectly acceptable concept of God" is, and how can he prevent those human errors from bleeding out and casting doubt on *all* religious beliefs? This is a problem he does not address.

We want to suggest an alternative approach: the dispositions outlined by CSR do give us some insight into the divine, and religious diversity is not the result of sinfulness or error. Such a proposal fits within religious pluralism, the view that different religious beliefs provide knowledge (of some sort) of God or a supernatural reality. Religious pluralism has been defended by authors from different religious traditions, for example, the Christian John Hick (2006), the Hindu Sri Ramakrishna (Maharaj 2017), and the Jew Jerome Gellman (1997). A common starting point for proponents of religious pluralism is the parable of the blind men and the elephant, according to which several blind men approach the pachyderm. One feels the trunk and concludes an elephant is long and soft, another feels the tusks and concludes it is smooth and hard, yet another a leg and surmises it is broad and firm. Each blind man captures something of the reality of the elephant, but it would be a mistake for each to assume that their testimony is the best description of the animal and to ignore the contradictions in the others' depictions. Each blind man mistakes a part for the whole – rashly assuming his knowledge of the elephant is the only and whole truth about it. In the parable, it does not seem to occur to the blind men to talk to one another or to move around the elephant to feel its other body parts in order to gain a fuller understanding. Likewise, in real life adherents to different religions rarely take each other's views of the supernatural into consideration. Proponents of pluralism have provided divergent ways to flesh out how we come to knowledge of supernatural reality.

Hick (2006) postulates an ultimate reality that is conceived of in different ways within various cultural traditions. This ultimate reality is real (not a mere cultural construct), and religious practices and mystical perception grasp something genuine about it. At the same time, Hick avers that the supernatural remains ultimately unknowable. This Kantian perspective draws a distinction between a noumenal transcendent reality and the objects of devotion and religious practices that are mere phenomenal manifestations that believers construct. Hick's pluralism is not analogous to the situation of the blind men and the elephant: the elephant is not an unknowable noumenon, as much about the elephant is known by the individual blind men. In the light of CSR, Hick's account is unsatisfying, as it does not explain the common threads across religious traditions, such as belief in supernatural agents who care about what we do, belief that things occur for a reason, and belief in an afterlife. These commonalities would have to be dismissed because ultimate reality is unknowable. In Hick's Kantian picture, it does not matter whether religious beliefs are convergent to some extent (as CSR suggests) or diverge without clear bounds, as they grasp at an unknowable transcendent reality.

Ramakrishna was a Bengali Hindu mystic, originally a priest of the goddess Kālī (see Maharaj 2017 for a comprehensive overview). After researching and mystically engaging with a host of other traditions, he advocated the position that all religions are spiritual paths to the same divine reality, which he called God. To explain apparent tensions between religions – for example, that some see God as impersonal and others as personal, some see God as immanent, and others as transcendent, some see God as having some (anthropomorphic) form and others as formless – Ramakrishna argued that God is infinite and illimitable: God is both personal and impersonal, God is like a mother, but also like a father, a lover, a friend. Divergent paths of devotion lead to the same divine reality. As such, Ramakrishna's view aligns closer to the parable of the elephant and the blind men than does Hick's, as it accepts that different religious traditions capture aspects of divine reality. A similar concept is employed by Gellman (1997), who sees God as having an inexhaustible plenitude. God presents himself to mystics in different aspects, including his nonpersonal aspects to nontheistic mystics. There are some differences between Gellman's and Ramakrishna's proposals: Gellman offers this as a speculative hypothesis, rather than as an experienced state of affairs, and his account is focused on mystics rather than on religious believers more generally.

CSR does not privilege a specific religion, but indicates that there are common threads among religious traditions. This scientific claim is in line with Ramakrishna's pluralism. Why would God present himself in such varying ways? CSR indicates that religious beliefs arise as the result of an interaction between cultural context and ordinary cognitive processes. Because these cognitive processes allow for a wide range of religious beliefs, religious diversity becomes inevitable. At the same time, CSR also predicts robust cross-cultural similarities in religious beliefs and practices. Ramakrishna's views on religious diversity fit well with these predictions, as he saw different religions as multiple paths leading to the same supernatural reality. Contrary to Christian exclusivist thinkers, he saw religious diversity as a result of a deliberate divine plan, and not an unfortunate accident, because people from different religious communities have different cultural backgrounds, which make some religious views more palatable or plausible given their worldview. Ramakrishna used the parable of a mother who prepares several dishes to suit the different tastes of her children.

> Suppose a mother has five children and a fish is bought for the family. She doesn't cook pilau or kalia for all of them. All have not the same power of digestion; so she prepares a simple stew for some. But she loves all her children equally [. . .] God has made different religions to suit different aspirants, times, and countries. All doctrines are so many paths; but a path is by no means God Himself. [. . .] Indeed, one can reach God if one follows any of the paths with whole-hearted devotion.
>
> (Ramakrishna, cited in Maharaj 2017, 188)

Concluding thoughts

CSR shows that religions have substantial similarities. As we reviewed here, CSR indicates that people across cultures believe in supernatural agents who are concerned with what we do. They may be watchful garden spirits, or ancestors, or powerful gods, but they care about ritual and moral violations and thus discourage antisocial behavior. Moreover, those religious agents have goals: they make things happen or create natural kinds for some purpose or reason. Religious traditions suggest that humans will continue to exist in some form after death, in a distinctive afterlife as revered ancestors, souls in Heaven or Hell, or through reincarnation. This recurring set of beliefs accords better with Ramakrishna's religious pluralism that acknowledges such beliefs as different ways of tracking supernatural reality than with Hick's religious pluralism, which regards ultimate reality as unknowable. The findings of CSR do not allow one to infer which theological position is correct, but they can be put to use by empirically engaged theologians as they convey relevant information about the supernatural. This chapter provides initial groundwork for such an empirically informed natural theology.

References

Al-Ghazālī. 1100/2006. *Deliverance from Error*, trans. Richard J. McCarthy. Louisville, KY: Fons Vitae.

Barrett, Justin L. 2009. "Cognitive Science, Religion, and Theology." In *The Believing Primate. Scientific, Philosophical, and Theological Reflections on the Origin of Religion*, edited by Jeffrey Schloss and Michael J. Murray, 76–99. Oxford: Oxford University Press. doi:10.1093/mind/fzq080

Bering, Jesse M. 2011. *The God Instinct. The Psychology of Souls, Destiny and the Meaning of Life*. London: Nicholas Brealy. doi:10.24204/ejpr.v5i3.229

Bering, Jesse M., and Dominic Johnson. 2005. "'O Lord You Perceive My Thoughts from Afar': Recursiveness and the Evolution of Supernatural Agency." *Journal of Cognition and Culture* 5 (1–2): 118–142. doi:10.1163/1568537054068679

Bloom, Paul. 2004. *Descartes' Baby: How Child Development Explains What Makes Us Human*. London: Arrow Books.

Calvin, John. 1559/1960. *Institutes of the Christian Religion*, trans. Ford Lewis Battles. Philadelphia: Westminster Press.

de Fontenelle, Bernard L.B. 1728. *Histoire des Oracles*. La Haye: Gosse & Neaulme.

Gellman, Jerome I. 1997. *Experience of God and the Rationality of Theistic Belief*. Ithaca, NY: Cornell University Press.

Heywood, Bethany T., and Jesse M. Bering. 2014. "'Meant to Be': How Religious Beliefs and Cultural Religiosity Affect the Implicit Bias to Think Teleologically." *Religion, Brain & Behavior* 4 (3): 183–201. doi:10.1080/2153599x.2013.782888

Hick, John. 2006. *The New Frontier of Religion and Science: Religious Experience, Neuroscience and the Transcendent*. Basingstoke: Palgrave Macmillan.

Hodge, Mitch K. 2011. "On Imagining the Afterlife." *Journal of Cognition and Culture* 11 (3): 367–389.

Hume, David. 1757. "The Natural History of Religion." In *Four Dissertations*, 1–117. London: A Millar.

Järnefelt, Elisa, Caitlin F. Canfield, and Deborah Kelemen. 2015. "The Divided Mind of a Disbeliever: Intuitive Beliefs About Nature as Purposefully Created Among Different Groups of Non-Religious Adults." *Cognition* 140: 72–88. doi:10.1016/j.cognition.2015.02.005

Järnefelt, Elisa, Liqi Zhu, Caitlin F. Canfield, Marian Chen, and Deborah Kelemen. 2019. "Reasoning About Nature's Agency and Design in the Cultural Context of China." *Religion, Brain & Behavior* 9 (2): 156–178. doi:10.1080/2153599x.2018.1449137

Kelemen, Deborah. 1999. "Why Are Rocks Pointy? Children's Preference for Teleological Explanations of the Natural World." *Developmental Psychology* 35 (6): 1440–1452. doi:10.1037//0012-1649.35.6.1440

Kelemen, Deborah. 2004. "Are Children 'Intuitive Theists'? Reasoning About Purpose and Design in Nature." *Psychological Science* 15 (5): 295–301. doi:10.1111/j.0956-7976.2004.00672.x

Kelemen, Deborah, and Evelyn Rosset. 2009. "The Human Function Compunction: Teleological Explanation in Adults." *Cognition* 111 (1): 138–143. doi:10.1016/j.cognition.2009.01.001

Kelemen, Deborah, Joshua Rottman, and Rebecca Seston. 2013. "Professional Physical Scientists Display Tenacious Teleological Tendencies: Purpose-Based Reasoning as a Cognitive Default." *Journal of Experimental Psychology: General* 142 (4): 1074–1083. doi:10.1037/a0030399

Maharaj, Ayon. 2017. " 'God Is Infinite, and the Paths to God Are Infinite': A Reconstruction and Defense of Sri Ramakrishna's Vijñāna-Based Model of Religious Pluralism." *Journal of Religion* 97 (2): 181–213. doi:10.1086/690478

McCauley, Robert N. 2011. *Why Religion Is Natural and Science Is Not.* Oxford: Oxford University Press.

Merleau-Ponty, Maurice. 1945/2002. *Phenomenology of Perception*, trans. Colin Smith. London & New York: Routledge.

Norenzayan, Ara, and Azim Shariff. 2008. "The Origin and Evolution of Religious Prosociality." *Science* 322 (5898): 58–62. doi:10.1126/science.1158757

Norenzayan, Ara. 2013. *Big Gods. How Religion Transformed Cooperation and Conflict.* Princeton, NJ: Princeton University Press. doi:10.1111/heyj.12678

Plantinga, Alvin. 2000. *Warranted Christian Belief.* New York: Oxford University Press.

Purzycki, Benjamin G., Coren Apicella, Quentin D. Atkinson, Emma Cohen, Rita A. McNamara, Aiyana K. Willard, et al. 2016. "Moralistic Gods, Supernatural Punishment and the Expansion of Human Sociality." *Nature* 530: 327–330. doi:10.1038/nature16980

Shook, John R. 2017. "Are People Born to Be Believers, or Are Gods Born to Be Believed?" *Method & Theory in the Study of Religion* 29 (4–5): 353–373. doi:10.1163/15700682–12341389

Teehan, John. 2016. "Cognitive Science, Evil and God." In *Advances in Religion, Cognitive Science, and Experimental Philosophy*, edited by Helen De Cruz and Ryan Nichols. 39–60. London: Bloomsbury Academic. doi:10.1558/jcsr.36383

Watson-Jones, Rachel, Justin T. Busch, Paul L. Harris, and Cristine H. Legare. 2017. "Does the Body Survive Death? Cultural Variation in Beliefs About Life Everlasting." *Cognitive Science* 41: 455–476. doi:10.1111/cogs.12430

Watts, Joseph, Simon J. Greenhill, Quentin D. Atkinson, Thomas E. Currie, Joseph Bulbulia, and Russell D. Gray. 2015. "Broad Supernatural Punishment but Not Moralizing High Gods Precede the Evolution of Political Complexity in Austronesia." *Proceedings of the Royal Society of London B: Biological Sciences* 282 (1804): 20142556. doi:10.1098/rspb.2014.2556

13 Love and desire, human and divine

A transreligious naturalist account

Wesley J. Wildman

Introduction

Love and desire are profound realities of the very greatest importance to human beings and are critical to narratives defining the meaning of life for our species. Science fiction has imagined self-aware, moral species without love or desire, but they leave me cold. I prefer the passion and energy of love and desire, even allowing for the accompanying problems. Why are these concepts, and the corresponding experiences, so powerful for us, and why do we feel they take us so deeply into the nature of the reality we receive, create, and inhabit? It's a fair question. After all, the cosmos doesn't display a lot of desire until biological complexity reaches a high order, and even in the biological realm desire is a lot more widespread than love, which is as rare in the big scheme of things as it is valuable. Why, therefore, do we human beings sense that love and desire tell us something profound about reality as a whole, rather than merely something profound about ourselves? If there were a divine agent who deliberately created the world out of desire and love, then there would be a basis for inferring something about ultimate reality from human experiences of love and desire. But that line of thinking is for other people to pursue. I'm interested in a transreligious, *naturalist* account of love and desire, human and divine.

The divine part of such a story refers not to the thoughts, feelings, intentions, or actions of a divine being – not a possibility for the religious naturalist – but to the valuational depth structures and dynamic possibilities of the natural world. Not all naturalists are interested in the axiological (i.e., valuational) depths and flows of natural reality. Yet specifically *religious* naturalists see in those depths the very ground of being, which they understand to be the correct logical referent of claims that theists make about gods (see Wildman 2017). It follows that peering into those depths for an account of love and desire makes sense as an activity of transreligious theological inquiry. There are touchpoints across the world's religions for such an enterprise, from shamanism of many types to varieties of African traditional religion, from the mystical and philosophical strands within the large religious traditions with sacred canonical literatures, to the formally naturalist or atheist traditions of philosophical reflection.

DOI: 10.4324/9780429000973-17

The human part of this story, of this transreligious-naturalist account of love and desire, does not refer to the many abstract characterizations of the human person and its destiny or purpose offered within the supernatural worldviews of religions and other wisdom traditions. Rather, the reference is to fully embodied human beings in social worlds realizing some possibilities and foreclosing others in every moment of their fleeting lives, driven by potent desire and its equally insistent companion, aversion. The one universal language we have for communicating across the differences of human bodies, for discussing shared human character under and within human individual and cultural differences, is – no, not the language of love, but the language of science (see Wildman 2009). That's where I'll start this brief meditation, eventually working my way down to divine love and desire in the depths of nature.

Human love and desire

For centuries, love has been the domain of poets, novelists, and musicians, and in many respects it remains the domain of luminaries within the humanities. But in the last few decades, scientists have taught us a lot about love – not only about the intricacies of the outworkings and failures of love in individual lives but also about the brain and behavioral systems that support the expression of love in the vast majority of human beings across cultures, apparently in much the same way for the last 50,000 years or so (Fisher 2004). These neural-behavioral love systems evolved in other species first, and we see them active in many primate species, though very differently than in human life. There are at least four relatively distinct brain and behavioral love-and-desire systems, three of which are directly related to what we human beings call romantic love (Fisher et al. 2002). Behaviors corresponding to these systems have been discerned in all human cultures, in some cases, and the vast majority of cultures, in other cases, with the exceptions being accounted for by explicit cultural suppression. Never underestimate the capacity of culture to fashion something novel from the givens of biology! It is fair to assume we are talking about biologically universal aspects of human bodies, despite the varied ways that cultures regulate and give expression to them (the key anthropological study is Jankowiak and Fischer 1992). On top of those powerful love-and-desire systems ride intentions that we employ to guide our behavior in accordance with, or possibly in spite of, or even in resistance to, surrounding social norms for regulating this intense domain of human life.

Probably the most fundamental love-and-desire system is maternal love, which is nearly universal across half of each mammalian species. It is critical for mammalian flourishing and, in human beings especially, it has significant overlaps with two of the three types of romantic love and desire to be discussed in what follows (Zeki 2007). Maternal love and sexual attraction are probably the most evolutionarily primal of the four love-and-desire neural-behavioral love systems – one erotic in nature and the other not. Because maternal love is (obviously) not universal in the human species, and because it is fractionated and marshaled by the more romantic and sexual forces of love and desire, I'll set it to one side. In what follows, I focus on the other three love-and-desire systems.

The first of these three love-and-desire systems is sexual attraction. The sexual-attraction system is realized through a mesolimbic neural pathway for which dopamine is the key neurotransmitter, but the sex hormones testosterone and estrogen (and others) are key to activating and regulating this system (Fisher, Aron, and Brown 2006). Love and desire as sexual attraction has no fixed lifespan, but it peaks in late adolescence for males and in the mid-30s for females, waxes and wanes during relationships, and gradually abates through the aging process after the peak is passed. Testosterone levels in human males spike when trying to mate and take a big hit when becoming a father for the first time, so the system reflexively adjusts to some life circumstances. Love and desire in this case refer especially to pleasure seeking and pleasure giving through copulation. The opportunity to mate spurs competition among males, and also among females when sex seems to be on offer, and it spills over into other circumstances as well. In fact, the sexual-attraction love-and-desire system is a specialized application of a more general testosterone system that figures in many parts of life, particularly when people are young, and particularly among males, who have less developed self-regulation capabilities than females until their mid-to-late 20s. The testosterone system unleashes a potent set of drives and underwrites a lot of human aggression; indeed, the part of it we call the sexual-attraction system can also cross the line into violence. Unregulated, the sexual-attraction system has the potential to cause social chaos through aggressive rivalries and pregnancies for which people are not ready. Unsurprisingly, this love system is carefully regulated in all human cultures, though in very diverse ways.

The second love-and-desire system is infatuation. Although the tapestry of mate choice is relevant to all sexually reproducing animal species, the infatuation love-and-desire system appears to be a distinctively human thread within that tapestry. The neurochemistry of infatuation within human beings has several dimensions. The feel-good neurotransmitter dopamine plays a critical role, giving us the feeling of intoxication. So does cortisol, which produces anxiety and stress, at least for the first year or two, when we tend to try hardest in new relationships. Higher dopamine is coupled with lower levels of another neurotransmitter, which pushes serotonin down to levels associated with people suffering from obsessive-compulsive disorder and helps to explain why infatuation feels so much like an all-consuming obsession. This neurochemical cocktail also deactivates regions in the frontal cortex that are responsible for being critically minded and able to evaluate evidence fairly, which accounts for the fact that "love is blind" very often and can lead to poor judgment (Zeki 2007). Love and desire as infatuation, once activated in a relationship, has a lifespan of about seven to ten years. A plausible evolutionary explanation for this timeline is that it is just long enough to get a couple of children more or less independent and able to help their mother gather protein and carbohydrates for survival. At the most general level, dopamine neural circuits recruit our capacities for valuation, for deciding what is important and directing the focus of our attention. The infatuation love-and-desire system involves distorted valuation in a cloud of longing, whereby we truly only see what we want and need to see in our beloved. A friend could point out our error of judgment, even backed up by solid evidence, and often enough we won't believe it, saying that "you don't know my lover like I do" or some other gloriously and ecstatically self-deluded rationalization for ignoring a lover's well-established patterns of behavior. In Western culture, this is what we mean by being *in love* – immersed in feelings so overwhelming that we experience the desire to possess and to be possessed comprehensively, knowing with certainty that this state of bliss will fulfill all our longings. Of course, we are mistaken in this intoxicated certainty, yet even the mistake bespeaks the depth of longing in life to realize infinite possibilities within the inescapable limitations and ambiguity of the finite.

The third love-and-desire system is bonding. The key neurotransmitters in this case are oxytocin, the so-called "cuddle chemical," and vasopressin; both are powerfully involved in romantic love and maternal love. They are released in large quantities in orgasm and during breastfeeding, triggering potent feelings of closeness, and they are also released in romantic love (Zeki 2007). The bonding system has no lifespan and can actually strengthen as we age, under the right circumstances. We can also destroy progressive bonding with a partner through actions that undermine trust, which is a critical element in maintaining close bonds. In application to love and desire, the bonding love-and-desire system functions in a specialized way to make two, or very few, people extremely tight-knit and loyal. The same system has less specialized applications to groups, where crises or rituals or other processes trigger intensified belonging and loyalty, while underlining the distinction between the in-group, where investment of precious resources in relationships is appropriate, and the out-group, where such investment is inappropriate (Choi 2011; De Dreu et al. 2011). That is, in solidifying closeness and loyalty, the bonding love-and-desire system also solidifies in-group identification against outsiders and amplifies both sensitivity to betrayal perpetrated by in-group members and suspicion toward strangers.

The fact that we human beings bear in our very bodies three biologically distinct love-and-desire systems is extremely important in many domains of human life, including the following four.

First, psychologically, these love-and-desire neurobehavioral systems are emotionally powerful and directly relevant to our everyday worlds. For example, it is critical to realize that the inevitable waning of infatuation need not be the end of romantic love in the other two senses. Plenty of couples experience incredibly potent feelings of shattered dreams, unmet longings, and associated resentment and grief a few years into a relationship. Indeed, across cultures permitting divorce, the peak divorce rate occurs four to five years into marriage, which is about seven to nine years into the relationship, as the last trace of infatuation evaporates (Fisher 1992). Instead of blaming one another for not living up to the ridiculous expectations we built in a haze of infatuation, it'd be smarter and kinder to recognize the inevitability of this process, to reset expectations, and to focus on strengthening the bonding system and nurturing sexual attraction.

Second, socially, the very same systems that underwrite love also reinforce in-group identities and support energetic monitoring of group boundaries to protect in-groups from outsiders. That is, the flip side of the biochemistry of bonding is xenophobia and racism. Both are biochemically spontaneous processes within human social environments. We do not have to be slaves to such emotional reactions because we can exercise determination and empathy to behave differently. But we certainly are biologically predisposed toward tight bonding with conspecifics and suspicion of strangers.

Third, politically, many of these dynamics operate silently, in nonromantic situations, including just below the surface of political conflict. For instance, they render us vulnerable to lazy acceptance of the incomprehensibility of our political opponents – "we'll just never understand how they could think that way, so there's no point in even talking about it." The result can be the collapse of civility in our public discourse and the damaging of our corporate problem-solving capacities. But some degree of awareness of how these neurobehavioral systems work could mitigate such problems.

Fourth, religiously, there are many ways of regulating or adapting these potent biobehavioral forces. For example, some conservative communities seem terrified of human bodies when it comes to managing the sexual-attraction love-and-desire system, excoriating young people for making out or masturbating, while simultaneously successfully activating the bonding love-and-desire system to strengthen suspicion of outsiders and sparking the infatuation system to apply to the many invisible beings of religious devotion. Meanwhile, some liberal religious communities delusionally pronounce their unlimited openness to all people, proclaiming universal acceptance, while remaining utterly oblivious to the very real social and psychological conditions for bonding and completely failing to see how exclusionary their behavior seems to those who are more realistic about the conditions for forming group identity, as many conservatives are. I'm pretty sure the conservative religious grip on the human love systems does more damage, if only because they're the ones who bring the most people into the world of their religious stories through activating bonding and infatuation circuitry for religious ends. Meanwhile, liberal religious communities are uncomfortable with too much emotionality and rightly suspicious of the dangers of in-group–out-group boundaries, so they refuse to avail themselves of the biochemical pathways to congregational flourishing that conservative communities employ. In our time, those liberal communities are withering on the vine.

Those four applications of the human love-and-desire systems are sufficient to make the point that knowing about our three neurobehavioral love systems matters. In particular, we need to understand that they are *portable*, in the sense that they are applicable not only proximally to love but also distally to out-group suspicion, religious devotion, purchasing patterns, voting tendencies, and many other domains of life. They are *multiply realizable*, in the sense that they are differently inflected by varied cultures, which take the biologically given constraints and interpret and regulate them in diverse ways. They are also *socially potent*, with huge economic and political implications – just consider the extent to which the contemporary music industry, the fashion and cosmetics industries, commercial films, and politics depend on testosterone-powered aggression, dopamine-fueled infatuation, and oxytocin-driven bonding and suspicion. It is no wonder that religious worldviews have always attempted to regulate love and desire and narrate them in pro-social ways.

When cultural, often religious, narratives of love and desire work well, people young and old cultivate virtuous patterns of behavior that support group well-being. People internalize ideals that direct their intentions and their powers of agency to loving and desiring in specific ways, typically ways that match community expectations. To love otherwise than this is to embrace pain and confusion and either triggers reversion to the norm or else flight in search of a community with more compatible norms. The emotional potency of these love-and-desire systems is such that, when activated, they help us detect the socially constructed character of the social norms we employ to regulate love and desire. For instance, in a monogamous culture, the man who is unfaithful to his wife soon confronts, privately or publicly, the cultural norm that regulates sexual behavior, and he must decide whether to reject the norm or return to conformity with it. The woman who loves another woman in a social environment inhospitable to homosexuality sees the heterosexual norm as a looming, oppressive reality and will be forced to reject the norm secretly, reject the norm and relocate to a different community, or conform to the norm and suppress her natural feelings. The person with fluid sexual identity senses the binary gender norms of the home culture, whereas others may not even see them; the activation of love and desire in this person begs for a new type of social order where gender binaries are seen as unrealistic oversimplifications of a complex bio-psycho-social reality.

This neurobehavioral account of the human being's biologically embodied and socially embedded experience of love and desire has important implications for other classifications of love. Our diverse experiences make it obvious that there are many kinds of love and desire, and we human beings love to categorize difference in a never-ceasing quest to understand ourselves. The biologically grounded classification I offer here is far from the only way to look at things. Although it is true that all our experiences of love and desire will connect with the bodily realities I have described, and equally true that we are better off knowing than not knowing about the various love-and-desire systems, the ways we love are socially constructed and pull these pieces together in very different ways. Love of a pet, love of a friend, love of a child, love of a spouse, love of a sports team, love of a country, love of a moral ideal: it makes sense to pursue higher-order classifications of these wildly diverse realities to reflect the complex ways we put the atomic biological elements together in socially constructed patterns of love and desire. There is no need for an invidious biological reductionism here; biology constrains but does not determine human behavior. Likewise, there is no necessity to deny or delegitimate what we have discovered from the sciences about love and desire.

Similarly, there is no reason to think that the deliverances of the process of biological evolution in the form of the three (or four, if we include maternal love) love-and-desire systems should be normative for us. Social construction of reality includes social construction of the norms we rely on to catalyze moral consensus, social order, and civilizational stability. We can adopt norms that explicitly legislate against the reflexive outworking of the three love-and-desire systems. For example, we can articulate a radical form of agape love that explicitly resists the intensification of in-group–out-group boundaries associated with the bonding love-and-desire system (some neuroscientists even argue that unconditional love has not only a distinctive neural signature but special neural circuitry; see Beauregard et al. 2009). We can create a culture that ridicules infatuation as an abandonment of rational thought and a betrayal of our higher natures, thereby checking the infatuation love-and-desire system while still enjoying the intoxicating feelings it engenders in us. Or we can embrace a strictly celibate lifestyle in which sexual arousal is transmuted into love of some endorsed religious object and into loyalty to a fellowship of like-minded companions but ideally never expressed sexually, either physically or mentally. We establish such ideals all the time, pushing back against some of the deliverances of evolution and striving to realize imagined ideals that we deem superior to nature unchecked, unregulated, and unimproved – and, of course, we use what nature produces to refine what nature gives us as cognitive-emotional defaults. We must fight hard to push against the grain in this way, but with appropriate forms of social support and sufficient inner determination, we can often do it.

Individual differences matter here, as well. Not everyone loves well, or can love at all, in one or another sense of love. Men don't experience maternal love, for starters. Biological differences and psychological formation through traumatic experiences and cultural learning can also limit an individual's ability to engage in some kinds of romantic love or to achieve what some group might deem an ideal version of love. Just as personality characteristics are distributed normally across a population, so the capacity for love of various kinds varies from individual to individual. In relation to the sexual-attraction love-and-desire system, some people are essentially asexual, and love and desire do not operate in specifically sexual ways for them. In relation to the infatuation love-and-desire system, some people are too given to self-evaluation and judgment to surrender to the haze of delusional bliss on offer in the delirium of infatuation. In relation to the bonding love-and-desire system, some people's behavior patterns are so haphazard and so lacking in self-control that they can never build the trust required for bonding to grow. Every statement about human love and desire is a generalization, abstracting from the intricate details of human biology and psychology, yet rendering a serviceable approximation to messy reality. Just as it is foolish to pretend to eschew abstractions, we forget the downside of such abstractions at our peril.

Human beings are bad, often, as well as good, often. This is a serious consideration in love and desire. We desire things outside the boundaries prescribed by the social norms of our cultural worlds, creating internal psychic tension and, when self-regulation fails, social chaos. We have it within us to steal what we desire, love selfishly, and ruthlessly exploit people's vulnerabilities around love and desire. Amazingly, emerging from the swirl of culturally varied norms on our planet are a series of deep insights into love and desire that have the standing of widespread and nearly universal moral principles of love and desire that guide people away from the bad and toward the good, as defined within the scope of these principles. These principles show up in multiple wisdom traditions, despite being generated within cultures having distinctive behavioral and moral norms, confirming the depth of the corresponding insights. For instance, we know we shouldn't exempt ourselves or some special subset of people from the moral expectations we want to articulate. We know we should treat others the way we want to be treated. We know we should learn self-regulation to control desire. We know we sustain love by behaving in trustworthy ways. Monogamy might occur in only about 3 percent of mammalian species (Fisher 1992), but we know what behaviors promote happy monogamous relationships and what behaviors don't.

I employ the phrase "we know" here deliberately: these are forms of knowledge accumulated empirically from personal experience and codified in vast and long-lived traditions of moral wisdom. Knowledge of human behavioral patterns across cultures does not establish the "ought" of morality unaided – the slippery reasoning of the naturalistic fallacy is always near. Additional assumptions lock in the normative "oughts" atop descriptive information about human moral and immoral behavior we distill from world cultures and life experience. When we notice that we sometimes make exceptions – for instance, we exempt soldiers from certain widespread moral norms – we become aware of this additional layer of norm-making assumptions, which is almost invisible in most circumstances. Thus, neither the behavioral patterns made natural for human beings within the process

of biological evolution within our planetary home, nor the moral principles we detect emerging within a host of varied human cultures, can determine moral norms by themselves. We can defer to them, but that deference
expresses normative assumptions about the moral authority of nature and
culture. We can resist them, but that resistance expresses normative assumptions about the moral authority of the human imagination as it envisions
new ways of being human.

Divine love and desire

We have begun the promised shift downwards into the well of love and
desire in the depths of nature itself. What shows up for human beings with
regard to love and desire is one kind of guide to the axiological depth structures and flows of nature, but scientific inquiry presents us with other kinds
of guides as well, as does critical theory from sociology and philosophy. Let's
begin with critical theory's formalization of long-standing human insights
into the social construction of reality.

Just as it is tempting to derive moral norms from descriptive information about nature (the naturalistic fallacy), so it is all too easy to impute to
the depths of nature what we find emerging in human moral worlds (the
projection fallacy). These two fallacies of moral reasoning are perpetually
close at hand because we hesitate to accept full responsibility for adopting our preferred moral norms – indeed, we go to great lengths to evade
awareness of this responsibility. This was one of Friedrich Nietzsche's pas-
sionate points, and the point of several moral philosophers contributing to
our world's large philosophical literatures: we feel existentially disoriented
with head-spinning nausea when we sense that the crystallizing of worldly
facts into moral norms is the quintessentially human activity – that we alone
bear responsibility for the moral norms we first create, then impose, and
ultimately embrace as if they were imposed on us by an Other, be it heaven,
God, or the spirits of the ancestors. This is the critical spine of the social
construction of reality, and it doesn't apply merely to the emergence of traf-
fic conventions; it has everything to do with the moral framing of love and
desire.

A central commitment of any naturalistic moral philosophy is to accept
this fact of human life and to embrace our responsibility for moral norms
with no convenient deflections of responsibility, no evasions of the meaning
of acts of norm creation, and no collapsing into either the naturalistic fallacy or the projection fallacy. We build our world, including the norms we
employ to orient ourselves within it. Norm building is a group activity, so
it is easy to miss the all-important element of human creation; it just feels
as though moral norms hit us from outside. And they do hit us from the
outside, of course, but only because we first externalized them and made
them objective by imposing them at the group level so that subsequently
they would be encountered as rules that we need to internalize in order to

operate successfully within our group. Critical theory taught us to see the social construction of reality and generated irrefutable evidence of its presence and functions, which both ramifies and surpasses the same insight in its previous forms across cultures.

Do we make norms for love and desire? Yes, we do. We externalize behavioral expectations surrounding love and desire; we objectivate those expectations in human groups, we internalize the now-objective externalized rules; and we narrate the appearance of those norms in our lives as gifts from heaven, commandments from God, or wisdom from ancestors. They may be those things, in the demythologized, naturalistic sense of the phrases, but they are ultimately our creations, our constructions, and signs of our creaturely craving for control over anomic chaos. The raw materials for our constructions are the three (or four) neurobehavioral love-and-desire systems, along with the manifold culturally specific explorations of the multidimensional space of possibilities opened up by our biological natures. This is the domain of the *biocultural*, where biology can't be interpreted without culture and culture can't be understood without biology.

We are extremely creative in our biocultural constructions, no question. But those constructions are never random. For a socially constructed reality to survive the scrutiny that human beings reflexively apply to every act of self-and-world narration, we are inevitably forced to acknowledge the nondeterministic constraints of biology, even if we finally decide to contest or transcend those constraints. One day we may be able to deploy biotechnology to change our very brains and bodies so as to express the moral norms we prefer; for now, biology conditions and constrains but does not dictate or determine how we love and desire. Likewise, we are smart to respect the cross-cultural consensus on wisdom in relation to love and desire, because those discoveries were hard won and are probably as close to timeless human wisdom as our species possesses, but we are also smart to be suspicious of unstable generalizations masquerading as the wisdom of averages. Our journey through the multidimensional space of biocultural possibilities related to love and desire shows us that the biocultural is incredibly fecund, spawning pathways optimized for the survival and flourishing of groups that journey along them. In the patterns of similarity and difference that emerge as we compare those pathways, we detect the areas of strongest constraint, where there is cross-cultural consensus on moral principles related to love and desire, and the areas of weakest constraint, where the cross-cultural diversity spreads in every direction like a veined network of river remnants fanning out over a plain.

This line of interpretation roots the emergence of human love and desire in the biocultural background of our species, going back millions of years. A naturalistic account of this emergence requires no postulates of purposeful teleologies or primal teleonomies or reflexive entelechies or gaiaic impulses that draw the cosmos toward the realization of desire and love, as if the process were designed or somehow guaranteed because of an ultimately purposeful power at work in the cosmic environment. On the contrary, this account of human wrangling with moral norms for love and desire makes perfect sense even if the universe is wholly accidental, fundamentally random, deterministically fated, or utterly meaningless in some global sense. We make meaning where we are, locally, and it is only our narrations of meaning that we project into the cosmos in search of plausibility. If we don't check them too carefully, they pass muster and we can carry on, sensing that our working norms for love and desire match the cosmos well enough for us to feel at home there. This is delusional thinking, however, even when it produces wonderful behavioral fruits. It can be challenged only by seeking comprehensive, unrelenting correction from what we discover about the world around us.

Nature is neutral to us, affording us possibilities to exploit and presenting dangers to navigate. Eat the wrong berry and we die, with nary a tear from Mother Nature. A large asteroid will wipe out most life on Earth, as has occurred several times before in the history of our planet, and there is no cosmic or divine memorial service – not for the religious naturalist, at least, and for the personal theist there is only a monumental, finally intractable theodicy problem, as the fantasy of a personal deity smashes to pieces on the rocks of reality. Suppose we narrate love and desire all the way into the depths of nature, making the ground of being look a lot like our morally normed human adventures in love and desire, and risking that appalling theodicy problem. In that case, for the religious naturalist, we not only fall prey to anthropomorphic wish fulfillment; we also minimize and neglect the miracle of nature in which spontaneity mates with law-like regularity to yield our planetary home and eventually human love and desire, in all its complexity, and we effectively evade responsibility for the social construction of love and desire in human life. Religious naturalism may be a false worldview, I allow – and to repeat, that's a debate for another place. But in rejecting personalist framings of love and desire in the entire cosmos, from its divine roots to its biocultural floral showings, the religious naturalist is not rejecting the importance of love and desire. On the contrary, the religious naturalist treasures love and desire all the more for rightly understanding the miracle of their emergence, the miracle of their biocultural conditions, and the miracle of our ability to create norms to conform with and to confound the default cognitive-emotional-behavioral love-and-desire impulses of our species. That kind of realism is all too rare in religion, and that kind of resistance to invidious reductionism is all too rare in religious and antireligious philosophy.

But might there be evidence beyond the questionable findings of needful human projection for something deep in nature that beckons cosmic reality to manifest love and desire? The pre-Socratic philosopher Empedocles discerned two fundamental dynamic principles in nature: love and strife. Might not he be correct, all these centuries later? Empedocles was right about the pair of dynamic principles, which we today would call attraction and repulsion, thinking especially of the electromagnetic force, but also of the other fundamental forces by analogy. But in naming the two fundamental forces love (*philotes*) and strife (*neikos*), Empedocles directly tied them to phenomena in the human sphere, which is misleading. Electromagnetic attraction and repulsion are conditions for atoms, molecules, chemistry, and biology, and thereby for love and desire–aversion, but it is an instance of the projection fallacy to impute to atomic and subatomic forces human-like feelings and motivations. We have had plenty of anthropomorphism in human efforts to ground love and desire in the wider cosmos – enough already. The micro-level forces that function as conditions for the emergence at the biocultural level of complex harmonies, and even of unruly chaos, should be appreciated without anthropomorphic distortion. What those fundamental forces are, ontologically speaking, is a first-rate mystery, but we get further by constructing empirically testable mathematical theories of them and running experiments to evaluate those theories than we do by giving free rein to our imaginative powers, piling trope upon trope in a desperate attempt to give cosmic significance to human experiences of human love and desire.

For the religious naturalist, therefore, love and desire have cosmic significance not because they were in some sense always there, within a creator God or any kind of natural entelechy, but because they emerge without collusion or design within the biocultural realm as a sign and an instance of the potent axiological possibilities in the very depths of nature. In this interpretation, there is no evading responsibility for the all-too-human construction of norms to manage love and desire. Nor is there any dimming of the luminous possibilities that lie before us. We can choose what love and desire will mean for us, constrained but never determined by biocultural givens, and inspired by pictures of an ever more just and verdant world.

References

Beauregard, Mario, Jérôme Courtemanche, Vincent Paquette, and Evelyne L. St-Pierrea. 2009. "The Neural Basis of Unconditional Love." *Psychiatry Research* 172 (2): 93–98. doi:10.1016/j.pscychresns.2008.11.003

Choi, Charles Q. 2011. "A Love-Hate Relationship?: 'Feel-Good' Oxytocin May Have a Dark Side." *Scientific American*, January 12. www.scientificamerican.com/article/a-love-hate-relationship.

De Dreu, Carsten K.W., Lindred L. Greer, Gerben A. Van Kleef, Shaul Shalvi, and Michel J.J. Handgraaf. 2011. "Oxytocin Promotes Human Ethnocentrism." *Proceedings of the National Academy of Sciences of the United States of America* 108 (4): 1262–1266. doi:10.1073/pnas.1015316108

Fisher, Helen E. 1992. *Anatomy of Love: The Natural History of Monogamy, Adultery, and Divorce*. New York: W.W. Norton and Company.

Fisher, Helen E. 2004. *Why We Love: The Nature and the Chemistry of Romantic Love*. New York: Henry Holt.

Fisher, Helen E., Arthur Aron, and Lucy L. Brown. 2006. "Romantic Love: A Mammalian Brain System for Mate Choice." *Philosophical Transactions of the Royal*

Society of London B: Biological Sciences 361 (1476): 2173–2186. doi:10.1098/
    rstb.2006.1938

Fisher, Helen E., Arthur Aron, Debra Mashek, Haifang Li, and Lucy L. Brown. 2002.
    "Defining the Brain Systems of Lust, Romantic Attraction, and Attachment."
    Archives of Sexual Behavior 31 (5): 413–419. doi:10.1023/A:1019888024255

Jankowiak, William, and Edward F. Fischer. 1992. "A Cross-Cultural Perspective on
    Romantic Love." *Ethology* 31 (2): 149–155.

Wildman, Wesley J. 2009. *Science and Religious Anthropology: A Spiritually Evoca-
    tive Naturalist Interpretation of Human Life*. London and New York: Routledge.
    doi:10.1111/j.1467-9744.2010.01171.x

Wildman, Wesley J. 2017. *In Our Own Image: Anthropomorphism, Apophati-
    cism, and Ultimacy*. Oxford: Oxford University Press. doi:10.1093/oso/97
    80198815990.003.0002

Zeki, Semir. 2007. "The Neurobiology of Love." *FEBS Letters* 581 (14): 2575–
    2579. doi:10.1016/j.febslet.2007.03.094

Part IV

Theologizing in a multireligious world

Introduction

Jerry L. Martin

We now live in a global village that puts within reach a rich array of religions and worldviews. This situation poses a number of challenges: Can we really understand people and belief systems quite different from our own? How can we manage our religious lives in such a diverse religious landscape? Can we appreciate multiple religions and theologize globally without losing our own distinctive religious identity? And what about those who have been so shaken from their religious moorings that they do not identify with any tradition at all, even when they still think of themselves as spiritual?

In addressing such questions, J. R. Hutwit draws on hermeneutics, with close attention to his own "lived experiences" that have led him to several theological hypotheses. First, "the sacred, whatever its form(s), is a natural presence, equitably available to all communities." Second, one's "linguistic-cultural background" binds one to a community and limits what one understands. Third, what a person understands can be "enlarged" through dialogue. Fourth, "the pursuit of truth is the end, not the beginning, of dialogue." These points suggest that "the only way to do theology is to do it transreligiously" and "to follow the truth, even if it takes one beyond the limits of her home tradition." To do so will require dialogue, through which we will "appropriate" (in a benign sense) novel ideas and practices. This process "smuggles content into my horizon," while "differences explode its boundaries." Dialogue "traces the boundary that joins human language and the prelingusitic sacred." It proceeds in "the eschatological hope" for "an ever more complete model of the world."

How are we to live religiously among a plentitude of traditions? In the West, which has a tradition of "strong religious borders," this is a challenging question. Not so, in the East, according to Paul Hedges. The Chinese, for example, engage in what he calls "strategic religious participation" in a "shared religious landscape." "Doing 'religion'" is not seen as adhering to a set of beliefs, but as way of making use of religious traditions, ritual experts, and practices to fit the need in a particular situation. Similar patterns may be occurring within Western contexts. Transreligious theology "no longer

DOI: 10.4324/9780429000973-18

becomes a perilous venture bordering, at best, on illicit syncretism, but rather may be seen as a perfectly legitimate employment of resources" in a multiply religious setting. Theology "may need to play catch-up with the wider world."

Can one theologize without walls and simultaneously affiliate with a particular religious tradition? Yes, answers Jeanine Diller, because "TWW affiliators are expanding their knowledge of the thing that that affiliation has put them in touch with (which I will call 'the Ultimate')." After clarifying the relation between affiliation and propositional beliefs and between affiliating with a tradition and identifying with it, she takes up three challenges. First, why seek truth outside one's affiliation in the first place? One is "logically required" to look beyond one's own experiences of the Ultimate so as not to commit the fallacy of hasty generalization. Second, what if outside beliefs contradict some of one's home beliefs? Indeed, "if we are all meeting the Ultimate," why do we have "such different things to say about it?" Drawing on an analogy with Spinoza, she takes different religionists to be "in touch with different attributes of the Ultimate." She calls this view "partialism," because no one religion grasps all attributes of the Ultimate. Third, even if the core ideas of the different religions are consistent, won't they weaken one's affiliation? When that happens, there is a genuine loss, akin to the loss of one's home or first language, but there is also "a genuine gain, a new way to see the Ultimate all over again."

What about those who have been so shaken from their religious moorings that they do not identify with any tradition at all? Do the spiritual but not religious (SBNR) even need to "theologize"? Yes, says Linda Mercadante, they, too, "need to understand what they believe, why they believe it, and how this functions in their lives." They are highly diverse, such as Mercadante found in her landmark study, Belief without Borders; they agree on what they *don't* believe: a self-determining, transcendent, personal God; the drama of human resistance to God; human-made religious institutions; and an afterlife governed by divine judgment. Nevertheless, SBNRs often see themselves "on a spiritual quest, journey, or path, seeking such things as spiritual experience, greater understanding of the self, authenticity, ancient wisdom predating religion, cosmic energetic transmissions, holism, or harmony."

Can SBNRs' faith seek understanding? Yes, concepts they use provide starting points for theologizing. For example, rejecting a transcendent deity, they see themselves in what Charles Taylor calls "the immanent frame," yet they do propose a kind of "horizontal transcendence," something larger than themselves, perhaps a universal "oneness." They have beliefs in favor of "the authentic self" but against "ego," and in favor of love and compassion. They regard terms like "good" and "bad" as judgmental and insist that "everyone is born good." SBNRs are exceedingly individualistic and yet seek community and even to be of service. These are all issues with conceptual and existential stresses that beg to be thought through.

14 Dialogue and transreligious understanding

A hermeneutical approach

J. R. Hustwit

There is no common ground from which all theology should be derived. Every theologian is thrown into the middle of things – her family, education, cultural location – and makes her way from there. Heidegger describes this universal condition as having-been-thrown-ness (*Geworfenheit*). Every person comes to consciousness shaped by a world that she did not create. The result is that each person is situated differently, with different pressures, questions, and projects. For some theologians, beginning with the Gospel makes the most sense, because God created humans and their experience.[1] For others, beginning with human experience makes more sense because human experience created our narratives about God. I confess that the latter approach makes more sense to me. The situation into which I have been thrown has led me to several theological hypotheses. First, the sacred, whatever its form(s), is a natural presence, equitably available to all human communities. Second, a person's linguistic-cultural background binds them to a community and limits the possibilities of what they understand. Third, the scope of what a person can understand may be enlarged, especially through dialogue. Fourth, the pursuit of truth is the end, not the beginning, of dialogue. When these four hypotheses are considered together, they suggest that the only way to do theology is to do it transreligiously – to draw on the experiences of more than one religion and to follow the truth, even if it takes one beyond the limits of her home tradition.

Hermeneutics is the study of how humans interpret various objects in the world: texts, persons, actions, events, nature. Though originally applied only to legal or sacred texts, hermeneutics has been promoted to a universal scheme of human understanding. Everything is always interpreted. There is no such thing as an unambiguous and objective meaning. Theology, from my situation, appears to be a species of interpretation. At the same time, theology is a public and constructive task that aims at the production of metaphysical truth claims, salvific practices, and proper virtues. There is considerable tension between these two descriptions. As interpretative, theology is prone to disagreement. Radically particular backgrounds will lead to divergent perceptions of God, nature, and humanity. But as public and constructive, theology aims at universality. A person's theological

DOI: 10.4324/9780429000973-19

conclusions are not true only in a personal sense, or for her community, but true for all persons – true full stop. In order to reconcile these divergent aspects, a theology must acknowledge its private origins and public aspirations. That journey from private to public is accomplished by a never-ending process of comparative dialogue with difference. Individuals are only able to offer a narrow selection of possible experiences. The way to avoid falling into a debilitating relativism is to compare finite human perspectives to see if they converge on any commonalities. Through collaboration, theologians may strive to combine religious interpretations into an ever more refined model of human existence, the ultimate(s), and the world.

An available God

In the spirit of the private striving for public legitimacy, I offer a few biographical anecdotes to illustrate how my own private experience has served as evidence supporting theological conclusions. At seven years old, I was living in Texas. I spent a lot of time in my head, because I was not athletically talented. Two influences competed for my attention: first, the fairly bland nondenominational Christianity taught at my new private school and second, my love for superheroes. I was not alone. Most of my classmates – it was an all-boys school – were interested in comic books, aliens, or anything that was strange. I remember there were lots of discussions involving slime, blood, claws, and laser swords.

Say what you will about parochial schools, this one was pretty tolerant of diversity. There were Jewish students who sat next to me during the mandatory chapel services. However, I ended up crossing a line that startled the normally tolerant administration. I was given an assignment. The assignment was to draw what I thought God looked like. I am pretty sure that even at seven, I had been asked to do this before. I knew that drawing an old man with a beard would be the predictable answer. And I knew that at least four other boys would draw a glowing ball of light – almost as predictable as the old man. As I racked my brain about what to draw, I suddenly had an idea. It wasn't profound, and I did not take the assignment very seriously, but I did love to draw. I put my crayon to work.

The next day my parents sat me down and told me that Sister Rachel, headmistress of the Lower School, had asked to speak with them. She was slightly concerned about my drawing of God. The large piece of manila paper had been folded into fourths to fit into my desk. They unfolded it and asked me to explain what I had drawn. It was a male torso, unreasonably muscular, with the head of a stag. I'm not sure if Sister Rachel was more concerned with my poor grasp of how many abdominal muscles humans possess or if she worried that my family were neo-pagans who honored the King of the Hunt. Honestly, if you ask a room full of seven-year-old boys to draw something they've never seen, I think you should expect some weird stuff. But my parents had promised Sister Rachel they would talk to me about it. So they asked me why I drew God that way, like a deer-man. I was a little bit afraid of being in trouble, but I also sensed that for my parents there would be no wrong answer, and this gave me space to give an impromptu explanation for my deer god.

I said, "If God is the God of all creation, then He is just as much non-human as he is human." My parents awkwardly nodded, and the picture was never mentioned again. Upon reflection, I was surprised to discover that I meant what I said. An intuition about God's universality had crystallized into what was probably my first theological conviction. The divine produces nature, of which human beings are only a small part. Of course humans would claim that they are in the image of God. My little sister also claimed to be the center of the universe, but she, I knew, was not a credible source. At age seven, the propositions "We are made in God's image" and "We make God in our image" both made sense. Even deer, in so far as they are capable, must experience the deity in their own ungulate way. And if they can imagine God, they probably imagine a being with antlers. Except for the cheeky deer who shock their parents by describing an anthropomorphic God.

As I learned about other religions, my early intuition about God's abiding presence developed. How could it be moral for God to answer the prayers of some communities and not others? If God is just, God would be equally available to all humans, or even all creatures. All creatures are equally subject to the forces of gravity and electromagnetism. All should be equally subject to the divine as well. A loving and just God would be uniformly present to all of creation, so that all have relatively equal chance of experiencing the divine relative to their species. I would describe this intuition as something like egalitarian religious naturalism. Regardless of how or when God acts in history, the presence of God is a permanent feature of the natural world – a divine piece of metaphysical furniture. And though God cannot be reliably perceived with the five senses, God is able to be experienced with diverse mystical and contemplative practices.

Now I am not sure how firmly I would hold this hypothesis today. Of the four propositions in this chapter, I hold this one with the least confidence. If pressed, I would probably add a qualification. Despite God's equitable presence to all human communities, individual persons may have clearer or more obscured perceptions of God as the result of spiritual practices or distractions. This qualification, which rejects God being closer or further with communities but grants that God may be closer or further for individuals, is itself a very modern and liberal intuition. It allows for relationship and consequences for individuals, but not for groups. Nevertheless, it seemed the most adequate model of God's presence at age 7, and still does, despite my doubts, at age 39.

If God is natural furniture, this implies a negative corollary: God is equally mediated to human beings. That is to say, because humans are interpretation machines, God's presence is always hidden behind the perceiver's biases and expectations. And this is equally true for all humans. The Aleutian Islander is just as alienated from the true nature of God as the Ibizan. Getting God somewhat wrong is part of human nature. Theologians may be more or less optimistic about how thickly or thinly human subjectivity mediates the presence of the divine, but there are no human communities that are *a priori* excluded from or central to the task of theology.

Word is bond

If the divine is uniformly present to all humans, it should be the case that nearly all human beings have displayed some sort of religious sensibility. And this has more or less been the case historically. But what is really remarkable are the patterns of variation in how religious ultimates (e.g., Yahweh, Shiva, nirvana, or nirguna Brahman) are described. A survey of human beings would show that although there is no universal agreement about religious matters, there is a good deal of *piecemeal* consensus. Agreement concerning belief and practices clump together historically and geographically. Scholars of religion have attempted to classify these clumps into "religions," and the most common classification is that there are five large clumps: Judaism, Christianity, Islam, Hinduism, and Buddhism. There are also a number of smaller clumps: Sikhism, Jainism, Celtic Neo-Paganism, Shinto, Confucianism, etc. This convenient canon of world religions is by no means a perfect representation of human religiosity and needs to be continually interrogated and revised. Nevertheless, it does reveal an important fact about human religious experience. The way that the divine is experienced correlates to human communities. Presbyterians are not scattered across the continents in a perfectly random distribution. They emerge from a group of people who are able to share a way of life. Religious experience clumps together because communities clump together. And language is the primary clumping agent. Language emerges co-originally with a community of human beings who require a common set of signs in order to effectively communicate. But language is not just a code humans use to translate thoughts into sounds and back into thoughts again.

Every category of being that I use is language inherited from my family and community. When I entertain light, the concept is not speciated, but simple. Light is light. I can attribute adjectives to it. The light is bright. The light is pink. But I do not distinguish light into distinct kinds. However, I do make distinctions between kinds of pastry. A Chelsea roll is not just a swirly generic pastry; it is a kind of pastry with a definition that excludes kolaches and knish. Chelsea roll, kolache, and knish are completely distinct classes of objects in my mental filing system, unlike light, which does not admit any kinds. The simplicity of light and speciation of pastry is an arbitrary linguistic convention. Some may argue that sunlight is a different kind of thing than fluorescent light. A colleague once told me that my office's fluorescent lights will eventually kill me and I need incandescent bulbs. I don't think that way – light is light – but I can understand his worldview. Conceptual speciation, and language in general, precedes discursive thought, speech, and writing. Because it precedes even the will, many hermeneutic philosophers have noted that though human beings create language, the reverse is also true.

The influence of language upon religious experience becomes apparent when I reflect upon my early experiences in the church. Like many adolescent Methodists, I was sent to summer church camps, where I would cultivate a close relationship with the Almighty. In my experience, church camp was a week-long exercise in channeling hormones into a fervent piety. Everything was emotionally intense: the awkwardness of living with strangers, the ritualized behavior at mealtimes, and evening devotionals held at night on the top of a hill. One night, at the end of the week, I remember being instructed to pray to God – or Jesus. Honestly, it was never entirely clear to me to whom I should pray. But pray I did. I asked God, if He[2] existed, to show me an unmistakable sign. As I prayed, the sky lit up with flashes of lightning, right on cue. There were no storms – this would have been described as "heat lightning." But the timing was unmistakable. I prayed, and the lightning flashed. God was listening. I was certain.

Even though this event relied on acts of nature, it was human language that made this religious experience possible. What counts as a sign from God are culturally transmitted criteria. There is certainly a natural spectacle to lightning: it is vast, above, bright, intense, fleeting. But these traits are meaningless without a history of association. The shopping mall parking lot seems vast, the ceiling fan is above, the sun is bright, vinegar is intense, and birthdays are fleeting. None of these objects signify the divine in my home clumps. Conversely, it would be absurd for me, given my clumps, to find a sign from God in an unusually quiet toilet flush or a surprisingly stale donut in an unopened package. Toilets and stale food do not have a history of association with God in the texts of Christianity, nor more immediately in the popular culture of my childhood. Scripture, novels, television shows, and comic books all repeat certain linguistic signs: the lightning bolt is divine, a tool of the sky father, weapon of Zeus and Thor. But it is possible to imagine a culture that had a different tradition in which the stories surrounding the divine involved the silencing of troubled waters. For that culture, a quiet faucet, or even a flush might signify the presence of the sacred.

My intention is not to reduce all religious experience to cultural projection. But rather to point out that whatever religious experience humans can understand is always clothed in language. I do believe there is a real nonhuman component to many types of religious experience, because that is the most plausible explanation for the amount of similarity between religious experiences. But if there are any naked undigested alien epiphanies, they do not last for long. Our brains do not work that way. As experience comes to consciousness, it is interpreted into linguistic concepts and categories. Untangling the contributions of the divine from the contributions of human culture is tricky business. How much is authentic revelation and how much is contributed by my own preunderstanding? Is it 50/50? 20/80? I do not think there is an easy or certain way to determine that. Nevertheless, I continue to search for the presence of the sacred behind the cliché of the lightning.

I struggle with discerning the purity of religious experience. Our inability to step outside of our own perspective to see the matter "objectively" is precisely why interreligious dialogue is necessary. We may be too embedded in our own experience to judge the authenticity of our own experiences, but by having authentic dialogue with persons embedded in different traditions, we may detect patterns amid the interference, signal amid the noise. But authentic dialogue is not as it easy as some may assume. Communication within a clump of common meaning encounters fewer incidents of problematic meaning, but understanding between clumps is problematic. Because I was raised to look for lightning, I will not notice when the toilet is quiet.

In defense of appropriation

So far, I have given a few experiences that support my own hypotheses for the basic theological situation of human beings. First, the sacred is, on the whole, equally available to all humans. Second, all persons experience the sacred in terms of a finite linguistic community, and this finitude routinely causes conflicts of interpretation both in and among communities. These first two hypotheses have several implications. If the sacred is equally present and equally mediated to all cultures, more than one religious tradition may disclose truth (propositional or salvific) despite incompatibilities of doctrine and practice among them. This is not to say that all religious traditions are equally good, or even partially good. It is perfectly possible that an entirely bogus religion may arise and perpetuate into an enduring tradition. Bogus religions aside, some theological claims are truer than others. Some are more fruitful or coherent. Interreligious dialogue is that process that allows theologians to make comparative judgments about religions. But in order for this to happen, for transreligious theology to get its legs, humans must be able to expand the horizons that constrain possible meaning. Every person only sees the divine through the lens of her cultural categories, but that lens can be polished, enlarged, and bent by talking with others. A third hypothesis is necessary: one's worldview is not set at birth or at some later point in childhood. The lens changing occurs through an ongoing process called appropriation. This is not a controversial hypothesis. People learn new things every day. But some learning simply combines elements of a worldview in a new way, and some learning introduces genuine novelty into the worldview. Theologians are able to understand new and other religions because they are able to appropriate novel ideas and practices and make them relevant to their own situations.

School, ideally, should provide many easy examples of appropriation. Having left the private boys' school for a public high school, I was fortunate to participate in a humanities curriculum, which combined history, art, literature, and philosophy into a single course that lasted two years and covered Europe from the sixth century BCE to the present. During the ancient Greek unit, the class was divided into five or six *polises*, and we were encouraged to adopt the culture of the polis and stay in character. Our research was fairly shallow, so for us, this meant that the Spartans knocked down everyone else's temples and the Corinthians pretended to drink a lot. Because the role playing was immersive, we were not learning history at one time, then doing art at a later time. The subjects were all mixed together – because life in ancient Greece was all mixed together. It slowly dawned on me that the practice of learning subjects in isolation from each other was at odds with the natural state of things. Art does not exist in isolation from science, and neither is immune to politics. This caused a relatively drastic transformations in my conceptual categories. My worldview had been one that had received the school disciplines uncritically (i.e., as unrelated skills to facilitate a future career). Suddenly, there was a problem reconciling those distinct disciplines with the newly perceived messiness of the world. From then on, every course seemed to me like a compromised endeavor – a failure to mirror the real world.

Though this class was not what anyone would typically think of as interreligious dialogue, it was structurally the same. I experienced a new way of dividing the world of experiences, which was gradually adopted. This was not a revelatory bolt, but a process of comparing my new insight, "world resists disciplinarity," with a previous assumption, "world facilitated by disciplinarity." I had appropriated something from my teachers, and it had caused discomfort, followed by an appropriation of a new idea. Phenomenologically, appropriation is an oscillation between my own horizon and the alterity of the object of interpretation. Philosopher Paul Ricoeur describes it as a three-part cycle of guessing, validation, and then comprehension (Ricoeur 1976, 75–88). And the process of guess–validation–comprehension repeats. Endlessly. A new meaning of the world – "world resists disciplinarity" – was guessed, then tested for coherence with the text (i.e., the structure of the course I was taking). Once the differences between my own worldview and the alterity of the text had been negotiated, I understood the text as applicable to my world. I did not assent to "world resists disciplinarity" as a sterile fact, but as a quality of the world in which I make plans and love things. In order for something to be understood, it must *matter* to the person. For this reason, Heidegger describes the world of our experience as characterized by my-own-most-ness (*Jemeinigkeit*). We are only aware of a thing when it serves a purpose for us.

And because hermeneutics is cyclical, I was not done with the notion of disciplinarity resistance. Later experiences would cause me to re-examine it and adjust its application to my own-most world. As a university student,

I had been assigned the *Dao De Jing*. I confess to not reading much of it, but I did notice its argument against formal education. Take, for example, Chapter 32:

> The Way is forever nameless.
> Unhewn wood is insignificant, yet no one in the world can master it . . .
> When unhewn wood is carved up, then there are names.
> Now that there are names, know enough to stop!
> To know when to stop is how to stay out of danger.
>
> (Ivanhoe and Van Norden 2011,
> 32, 178–179)

Unhewn wood, representing the cosmos as it truly is (i.e., uncomplicated by distinctions), is here contrasted with human conceptualizations. Such concepts, which formal education reinforces, inevitably chop up the wholeness of the Dao. The result is distorted thinking and, the *Dao De Jing* argues, human misery. My own appropriation of this text was based on the previous understanding of disciplinarity resistance from my earlier humanities course. Ah-ha! The *Dao De Jing* is saying something similar to what I had already understood. "Names" are like "disciplines." "Unhewn wood" is like "life outside of the classroom." There is a similarity-in-difference. In that respect, appropriation is thoroughly metaphorical. When we appropriate a term, we use similarities to analogize the foreign to our own experience, while maintaining a tension with the differences. The goal is to suss out the interaction between resemblance and difference. The similarities are the vehicle that smuggles content into my horizon, and the differences explode its boundaries, enlarging the possibilities I may imagine.

The word "appropriation" is frequently criticized in discussion of cultural appropriation. When a person adopts the fashion or customs of another culture without sufficient understanding of the meaning, we argue that they do violence to the culture by appropriating it. But in these cases, we should say that the insensitive person has *malappropriated* the custom. For all understanding is appropriation, and it can be done skillfully or clumsily. The term "appropriation" ought to be rehabilitated, much as Gadamer sought to rehabilitate the term "prejudice" (*Vorurteil*; Gadamer 2000, 277–306). Appropriation itself is inescapable and only a vice if we fail to validate the meaning we have guessed against the structure of the text. We cannot complacently assume that we have correctly guessed the meaning of another religion when we see the first resemblance.

It is crucial for me, as a Christian, to note that the *Dao De Jing*'s idea of nature is quite different from what I may imagine. Likewise, the *Dao De Jing*'s claims about human nature and the ability of the mind to perceive the world probably differ from mine. All of these points of difference must be maintained along with the similarities. If I neglect the differences between religions, I assimilate the other religion into my own. If I neglect the similarities between religions, I am unable to comprehend anything unfamiliar. But if we grant that our worldview is changeable, then we have the ability to expand it to appropriate other religions. Healthy appropriation is always in danger of collapsing into assimilation or exoticization, but if the sacred is disclosed in other religions, it is worth our while. Understanding other religions is required to live together in peace, but also required to judge truth claims as "better" and "worse" hypotheses.

Truth deferred

Not everybody loves to argue. I have been slow to come to this realization. I love to argue. I love to be right. I sometimes spend too much time trying to poke holes in the arguments of others. There are a couple of cultural-linguistic facts that could explain why I tend to behave this way. The most immediate cause is probably the years studying for a philosophy degree, which enculturated me to focus on argumentation and logic. I was taught that philosophy is mostly a critical task and rarely constructive. Philosophy courses, until the advanced stages of the degree, present a text to the student, ask the student to distill an argument from the prose, and then require the student to criticize the argument. After so many years, this training leads to a particularly critical temperament – a tendency to look for the weaknesses of things first. My classmates and I were great at tearing things down, but not very good at building things on our own. Although critical analysis is an essential skill, it is not the only skill worth developing.

But why is philosophy taught this way? Without going into an elaborate intellectual history, I think Christian theology deserves much of the blame for why I am no fun at parties. Christianity has always placed an emphasis on orthodoxy, or correct belief. Believing certain propositions to be true and others false has the chief criterion for determining Christian identity and value. The first seven ecumenical councils of the Christian church are striking examples. A tremendous amount of time and mental energy went into deciding exactly which propositional truth claims should be endorsed and which should be condemned as heresy. It is no coincidence that Christian theology has historically focused on doctrine much more than practice, dialogue, or affect. So, the Christian theology that dominated the medieval university as "queen of the sciences"[3] passed on its preoccupation with propositional truth claims to the teaching of philosophy, first in Europe and then its colonies. So even for those philosophers today who consider themselves to be completely divorced from Christian belief and practice, Christianity has shaped their academic discipline, their cognitive training, and thus their temperament. And that is one reason why they – and I – argue too much.

With this temperament as a liability, I took a job teaching religion at a small university in the American South, and with encouragement from the administration, began an interreligious club for students. This was challenging. Though our student population contains a relatively high proportion of international students, our domestic students tend to be fairly sheltered and uncurious. The result was a lot of potential for expanded horizons for those who participated and a lot of resistance to those programs from those who would not participate.

My first attempts at getting college students to sit together and talk were based on my idealized vision of what interreligious dialogue should be: a round table of persons steeped in their own traditions, arguing over metaphysical claims in good cheer until everyone agreed about the nature of reality. I invited a number of students to gather over some pizza and threw down some of my most combustible debate kindling: "Is the sacred personal or nonpersonal?" "Is the universe infinite or discretely bounded?" Nothing. Awkward silence. Polite thanks for the pizza and excuses to be somewhere else.

My vision of interreligious dialogue could not have been further from how dialogue – on any topic – actually begins. My students are not steeped in their own traditions, much less anyone else's. They frequently come from secular families, and when they do have a background in religious participation, they are hesitant to speak for their tradition. Even if they were informed and willing, they would not be interested in doing so. My own project of transreligious theology does not matter to my students. What they do value highly (besides food) is relationships. Ultimately, I found that if I organized a social event, like a halal potluck during Eid al Adha, attendance was much higher. By the end of the school year, after a series of well-attended social events, the students had organized their own small interreligious discussion group in the evenings.

I think that in the situation of interreligious dialogue, whether one's dialogue partner is a human, a written text, or some other symbol, care precedes knowledge.[4] That is to say, human beings cannot understand a thing unless it first has a place in their own-most concerns. This is why it is a mistake to begin interreligious dialogue with a contest of truth claims. Truth-directed inquiry requires concern, which manifests as goodwill, open-mindedness, and curiosity about other religions. Dialogue does not require its participants to agree beforehand, share a worldview, or even like each other. But it does require an openness to the legitimacy of the other and an interest in the message of the other. Dialogue begins with a mutual recognition of humanity and only later takes up competing truth claims.

Of course, we may find ourselves in a contest of truth claims with someone we have just met, with no established relationship. But even when we argue with strangers about religion, this is not a case of truth questions preceding relationship. Rather, the stranger is assigned a relationship status as the argument commences. This status may have been assigned even before the stranger appeared. We may have an imaginary adversary in some matter, and we project it on to the person before us. It is precisely because there has been so little time for the relationship with the stranger to develop that these encounters usually end unhappily.

My experience with students and student organizations has moderated my hard-nosed philosophical instincts and taught me that relationships of some kind are necessary before arguments can be entertained. Practically speaking, the truth is a concern for advanced stages of dialogue. Philosophically speaking, the truth should be a heuristic device. It guides and regulates the process of dialogue even if it is never permanently achieved. For no matter how firm my conviction, there is always another dialogue partner around the corner.

Conclusion

So, I am left with four theological hypotheses: 1) The Ultimate is equally available and equally mediated to all humans. 2) This mediation is largely due to the conceptual schemes that emerge from communities of humans. 3) Human conceptual schemes are routinely enlarged or transformed through the act of appropriation, which is a species of interpretation. Finally, 4) the adjudication of truth claims submits to the demands of an existential relationship and not vice versa. Taken together, the claims suggest to me an infinitely long process for theology. It is almost Hegelian. We *should* engage the other – person or text – in interreligious dialogue. The dialogue is usually productive. It produces an enlarged horizon, a new synthesis, which then is brought into the next dialogue. But unlike Hegel, this process does not unfold according to the logic of Absolute Spirit. Instead, it traces the boundary that joins human language and the prelinguistic sacred. There is a pessimistic interpretation of transreligious dialogue, that while it may foster goodwill among religious communities, it is a metaphysical goose chase. However, there is an eschatological hope that it is more than that. As we perpetually dialogue with otherness, we trace an ever more complete model of the world.

Notes

1 Experience should be understood widely, not as just experience gained through the five sense organs. Theology employs a wider range of experience than just the five senses. Ethical intuitions, aesthetic sensibilities, emotive states, and recognition of authority are also modes of perception, though more susceptible to idiosyncratic interpretation than the five senses.

2 In the language of my church community, the masculine pronoun was always used to refer to the divine. This set up my own uncritical expectation of God's masculinity. In fact, I remember imagining that God probably looked a lot like my grandfather: dark oily hair, olive skin, a large nose, and pale yellow golf shirt with a chest pocket. The shirt was by far the most vivid part of the image.

3 Here, *science* is defined broadly. It is derived from the German *Wissenschaft*, which is perhaps better translated as a *method of production of knowledge*.

4 This insight is present throughout the hermeneutic tradition, but is most clearly articulated by Heidgger. *Care (Sorge)* is the fundamental mode of being in the world. Metaphysical truth claims are but one species of existential concern.

References

Gadamer, Hans-Georg. 2000. *Truth and Method.* trans and edited by Joel Weinsheimer. 2nd rev. ed. New York: Continuum.

Ivanhoe, Philip J., and Bryan W. Van Norden, eds. 2011. *Readings in Classical Chinese Philosophy.* 2nd ed. Indianapolis: Hackett Publishing.

Ricoeur, Paul. 1976. *Interpretation Theory: Discourse and the Surplus of Meaning.* Fort Worth, TX: Texas Christian University Press.

15 Strategic religious participation in a shared religious landscape

A model for Westerners?

Paul Hedges

Introduction

Can one person participate in the rituals and beliefs of more than a single religion? For most modern Westerners, this seems almost like a non-question. Of course not! You are either Buddhist, Christian, Sikh, or Muslim. You cannot, in any coherent sense, do the rituals of a certain tradition one day and then engage in the rites of another the next day. However, this common-sense Western norm has not been the standard global pattern through most of history. People have, and still do, participate in, belong to, and identify beyond the boundaries of a single religious tradition – and in many places this is perfectly normal and acceptable.

Moreover, in the West today, many people are engaging in what is often termed multiple (or dual) religious belonging (or identity). However, this is generally seen – by scholars, religious professionals, and many of the public – as some form of spiritual dilettantism or illegitimate syncretism. It is frequently frowned on or dismissed as lacking seriousness or credibility. The argument of this chapter is that we should not so readily dismiss these practices and that we may simply be looking at a different way of doing religion. To this end, we will explore the traditional way in which such boundary crossing between religions has occurred in the Chinese context (and beyond), which I have elsewhere described as strategic religious participation (SRP) in a shared religious landscape (SRL). My argument is not to suggest that Westerners should start copying East Asian patterns of religiosity. Rather, it is to suggest that patterns of religiosity may now be occurring within Western contexts. We are simply doing religion differently. As such, rather than dismissing this as illegitimate, some form of spiritual pick'n'mix, or superficial dabbling it is actually a way of doing religion that is credible, serious, and profound. If an individual, family, or community can use one tradition for marriage, another for death, a third for meditation, and so on, why should we not see this as normal?[1] It is certainly increasingly common and arguably has implications not just for the people doing it but also for scholars of religion studying the phenomenon and for Christian (and other) theologians and religious professionals who are thinking about what

DOI: 10.4324/9780429000973-20

religious identity, belonging, and participation mean. Does it even have implications for thinking about a transreligious, or interreligious, theology?

In this chapter, I will briefly address the way that Western scholars have typically thought about multiple religious belonging and the paradigm for thinking religion that informs this. I will then describe in general terms the East Asian context of SRP in an SRL.[2] I will then briefly address some ways in which this phenomenon could describe some contemporary Western trends found in America, Europe, and elsewhere concerning the way that people are engaging with multiple religious traditions. Finally, I will address at more length some potential consequences from this about how we may come to think about theological issues in light of this.

The West: the world religions paradigm and strong religious borders

Why do we assume that people cannot belong to more than one religion at any one time? Nor participate in the rites and rituals of different traditions? Such activity is often spoken of as a transgression of "natural" boundaries, or even compared to some form of spiritual adultery.[3] It is seen as something that goes against what religion is or truly should be. All these attitudes come from a context in which what are often termed the Abrahamic monotheisms (Judaism, Christianity, and Islam) have been predominant. Especially in certain forms, including the Protestant strands that have dominated North Western Europe and North America for the last couple of centuries, singular and exclusive identity and belonging are affirmed. Strict creedal confessions of belief demarcate each religion, even each denomination or sect within each religion, such that seeking to belong to more than one seems intellectually incoherent. It also violates the strict teachings and representations of these religions. Given several centuries of Western colonialism, and over the last couple of centuries a military and economic dominance that has ensured cultural and intellectual global hegemony, this has become the predominant model. Without entering into the intricacies, the models of what religion is within Western Protestant religious imaginaries have been taken by scholars and others as defining and definitive of the very essence of religion. It has shaped what has come to be called the world religions paradigm (WRP).

Within the WRP, each religion is imagined to exist as a clearly demarcated monolith. It has distinctive and unique beliefs, as well as its own defining rituals and practices. It claims sole allegiance of its members, who must adhere strictly to the confessions set out in the foundational books, which state what it says. If you have done any courses in religion, you may well have been taught according to this kind of "world religions" model, which presents each religion in turn by a set of common criteria: beliefs, scriptures, priests, history, rituals, etc. Each religion becomes a distinct and bounded entity of belonging and belief. However, although this – to some extent – maps out some dominant trends within the Abrahamic traditions, it is far from normative or representative of the world's wider religious landscape.

In short, the way in which one part of the world does religion has become a pattern and map to presume to say how all religion works, or should work. It is a deeply colonial, or orientalist, set of presuppositions, which has taken a Western model and applied it globally. We shall see, though, that this model is far from normative in the East Asian context, where we will focus on China but also look broadly.

The East: strategic religious participation in a shared religious landscape

If you wandered into a traditional Chinese temple across much of Asia, you may be surprised that inside you would find statues of such figures as the Buddha, the bodhisattva Guanyin, Confucius, figures from Chinese folk tradition such as Sun Wu Kong (the Monkey King), and Daoist deities, including perhaps the popular Eight Immortals, or maybe the Jade Emperor. How to reconcile that one temple (even if nominally Buddhist or Daoist) may contain figures from seemingly four different "religions" (Buddhism, Daoism, Confucianism, and Chinese folk religion)?

Our question perhaps only seems strange because of where we are viewing it from. In the East Asian Sinitic world (i.e., primarily China but also those territories affected by Chinese cultural mores), what we may term SRP in a SRL has been the norm. Let us break this down into its two component parts to discuss it. First, SRP. This denotes that doing "religion" in East Asia has not primarily been about belonging to a particular tradition, nor adherence to a set of doctrines and beliefs (creedal statements) that define what it means to be a member of one religion as opposed to any others. Rather, one will make use of religious traditions, ritual experts, and ways of doing religion as are useful and appropriate. For instance, Buddhists are known for doing funerals and so may be called upon for such services, Tianshi Dao (Heavenly Master Daoist tradition) Masters were often considered the best exorcists and so may be sought out for this, and any passing itinerant monk may be asked to do services at the local village temple as and when the need arises. Meanwhile, in some rituals, Daoists, Buddhists, and local ritual (folk religion) priests may all have a role in some contexts. Religion is therefore not about believing and belonging to a single tradition. Rather, one will strategically employ the services of whichever tradition(s) and its (their) ritual experts that are available, suitable, or customarily required for certain acts. This is what is meant by SRP. We should also note that in imperial China, the three dominant traditions (Buddhism, Confucianism, and Daoism) were often seen as complementary, in what was termed the *sanjiao* (three traditions) teaching. This was variously understood by different figures at different times, but as one way of conceiving it: Buddhism dealt with our eternal concerns and certain rituals; Confucianism deals with our outer relationship with family and society; and Daoism concerns our personal bodily/spiritual cultivation.

SRL meanwhile signifies that despite considering several different traditions, a fairly common cosmological system underlies it all. This, in the Chinese context, may be concerned with the fact that everything is composed of *qi* (often translated as breath, but signifying also psycho-spiritual matter: it is the stuff that everything is made of), a belief in the interaction of yin and yang and the so-called five agents (or sometimes five elements), and often reincarnation. These were taken, to a large degree (even if sometimes contested), as a common ground, such that the different doctrinal teachings of the varying traditions could be seen as not significant differences compared to what was held in common. As such, mixing traditions or taking bits from each was not typically seen as violating core doctrinal systems or some illicit form of mixing.

It may be objected, as has been argued by some, that this context of SRP in a SRL may have been a common grassroots viewpoint but was rejected by elites, who demanded strict allegiance to only one tradition and fiercely rejected the others. However, this does not do justice to the context. First, at the most elite level – in some senses – of imperial decrees, the *sanjiao* teaching was often pronounced and officially taught. Second, although strong disputes and even vehement rejection of the other traditions was heard at times, it is not the whole story. Confucianism, when it adopted meditational teachings (in the Neo-Confucian tradition) borrowed directly from Daoism and Buddhism, even while often derogatorily condemning those traditions (as it, in some ways, became more like them). Confucian scholars would be known in retirement to go live in Buddhist or Daoist temples, without any sense that they stopped being a Confucian. Third, in training, Daoist masters would often send their disciples to Buddhist monks (and vice versa), believing they had particular skills they could learn. All of this is only possible because of a sense that all lived within a SRL. It even shows elite practice and acceptance of SRP. Notably, we could expand examples, and these are only mentioned here as indicative.

Eastern ways in Western landscapes: crossing boundaries and multiple belonging

Arguably, in the contemporary Western context, we are seeing people engaging in what looks like SRP in a SRL. In the West, because of the WRP, such crossing between traditions has traditionally been viewed as at least difficult, if not deeply problematic, and even illegitimate. Certainly, much of the literature suggests this. Nevertheless, particularly among millennials the sense that what is often termed multiple religious belonging (MRB) is neither problematic nor some form of dangerous syncretism. It is considered perfectly fine to learn or borrow, rituals/techniques from such places as Hindu yoga, Buddhist meditation, Christian and Jewish rituals, Native

American traditions, etc. Scholarship in the study of religion, not to mention Christian theologians, have often condemned this. However, the Chinese and East Asian context suggests that we should not be so troubled. Although some ways of doing or thinking about religion make this seem illegitimate, other ways of doing or thinking about religion make it seem natural and expected. The issue is that engaging in MRB is often misunderstood, so the question becomes: How this can be changed in our ways of conceiving the religious field?

Interreligious streams: transgressions and interventions in the religious fields

What implications does this have for the way that we do theology today and think about spirituality and religious performance? I would argue that for those exploring what we may term transreligious or interreligious theologies, the implications are immense. First, as should be clear, it to some extent tears up the rule book. Scholars have argued, for many years, that doing MRB or engaging in rituals across traditions is not simply theologically illegitimate (which, arguably, in some traditions it may be) but that it is also doing "religion" wrong. These, we should realize, are two entirely separate issues. What regulations cover what religious leaders say is legitimate within their tradition is not coterminous with what religion is or what it should look like. Indeed, here we should note that the very term and concept of "religion" itself is one that has a particular Western and colonial backdrop that has shaped how we envisage it (and, for some, is even why we envisage such a thing exists);[4] as such, we speak of "religion" here not as a "thing" but as a social reality.[5] This is an important caveat, because it means that we cannot even speak of there being a right or wrong way of understanding "religion" or regulating the way we see it. Those parts of society that we see as religious vary due to various social and cultural factors that have shaped them.

Second, and following from our first point, we can see the regulation of whether religious worldviews permit some form of MRB or SRP in a SRL as socially and culturally determined. They are not set in stone. As such, the parameters that have made the Abrahamic traditions seem less liable to MRB or SRP in a SRL are not prescriptive. Indeed, knowing that worlds of religious understanding give different perspectives on this also suggests that these different ways are not getting it wrong, but have equal validity. It can thus lead to a rethinking of how we think about the "natural" barriers between religions, and even whether we should see them as such. Further, the notion of the complementary nature of traditions or what disagreements may mean can also be seen through different lenses.

Third, doing what we may term a transreligious or an interreligious theological task no longer becomes a perilous venture bordering, at best, on illicit syncretism. Rather, such ventures may be seen as a perfectly legitimate employment of resources in a SRL. Much of the literature not just on MRB,[6] but also on inter-riting (the sharing of rituals across religious boundaries; Moyaert and Geldhof (2015)), and on interreligious encounters and theologies in general,[7] has tended to come from Western contexts and is reflective of the WRP as normative. However, for those who come from a context where SRP in a SRL is normative, this may seem irrelevant. Whether in the East Asian context[8] or in today's Western context, doing transreligious or interreligious theology is not a marginal or dangerous pursuit, but rather arguably the new norm. We are still certainly a long way from this, certainly in ecclesial contexts or academic theology and understanding; nevertheless, the situation on the ground may be more fluid and changing faster. As is often the case, theology may need to play catch-up with the wider world.

Notes

1 A recent exploration of such patterns in the US context is found in Bidwell (2018).
2 The first two parts of this chapter will draw heavily from my paper, Hedges (2017). Readers are encouraged to go there for references and further resources on the issues discussed.
3 See Knitter (2009).
4 On such debates see King and Hedges (2014, 1–30).
5 See Schilbrack (2017, 161–178). This is explored further in Hedges (Forthcoming, chapter 1).
6 See e.g. Cornille (2002, 1–6) and Berthrong (2000).
7 See Hedges and Race (2008) and Harris, Hedges, and Hettiararchi (2016) as two overviews on the typical theology of religions literature,
8 However, it has been noted that although this has reflected historical practices and understandings influenced by Western norms and the hegemonic imposition of the WRP standard, we are seeing a change in understanding in East Asia and elsewhere to a context where singular belonging and identity in religion is being enforced.

References

Berthrong, John. 2000. *The Divine Deli: Religious Identity in the North American Cultural Mosaic*. Maryknoll, NY: Orbis.
Bidwell, Duane. 2018. *When One Religion Isn't Enough: The Lives of Spiritually Fluid People*. Boston, MA: Beacon Press. doi:10.1353/scs.2019.0018
Cornille, Catherine. 2002. "Introduction: The Dynamics of Multiple Belonging." In *Many Mansions? Multiple Belonging and Christian Identity*, edited by Catherine Cornille, 1–6. Maryknoll, NY: Orbis.
Harris, Elizabeth, Paul Hedges, and Shantikumar Hettiararchi, eds. 2016. *Twenty-First Century Theologies of Religions: Retrospective and Future Prospects*. Leiden: Brill.
Hedges, Paul, and Allan Race, eds. 2008. *Christian Approaches to Other Faiths*. London: SCM Press.
Hedges, Paul. 2017. "Multiple Religious Belonging After Religion: Theorising Strategic Religious Participation in a Shared Religious Landscape as a Chinese Model." *Open Theology* 3 (1), 48–72. doi:10.1515/opth-2017–0005

Hedges, Paul. Forthcoming. *Understanding Religion: Method and Theory for Studying Religiously Diverse Societies*, Chapter 1. Berkeley, CA: University of California Press.

King, Anna, and Paul Hedges. 2014. "What Is Religion? Or What Is It We're Talking About?." In *Controversies in Contemporary Religion*, edited by Paul Hedges. Vol. I, 1–30. Santa Barbara, CA: Praeger.

Knitter, Paul. 2009. *Without the Buddha I Could Not Be a Christian*. Oxford: Oneworld.

Moyaert, Marianne, and Joris Geldhof, eds. 2015. *Ritual Participation and Interreligious Dialogue: Boundaries, Transgressions and Innovations*. London: Bloomsbury Academic. doi:10.1558/firn.32269

Schilbrack, Kevin. 2017. "A Realist Social Ontology of Religion." *Religion* 47 (2): 161–178. doi:10.1080/0048721x.2016.1203834

16 How to think globally and affiliate locally

Jeanine Diller

Can one theologize without walls and simultaneously affiliate with a particular religious tradition? Or, as Jerry L. Martin phrased the question in conversation: Can a transreligious theologian take account of spiritual truths outside their confession, or would they have to give up or loosen their affiliation to do this?

I will argue that it is *not* a contradiction in terms to affiliate and do Theology Without Walls (TWW), both in a serious way. It is possible to do both. Why? In short, it makes sense to affiliate and do TWW because through TWW, affiliators are expanding their knowledge of the thing that their affiliation has put them in touch with (which I will call "the Ultimate"). That is, despite appearances, they are not *undoing* what they have found from affiliation by thinking outside it; they are rather *adding* knowledge to it.

This "expanding knowledge" sentiment is all well and good, you might be thinking, until an affiliator tries it and finds their search for more exploding into confusing and contradictory news about the Ultimate that challenges their affiliation's view of It. True. The burden of this chapter will be to state more carefully this and two other specific challenges that TWW seems to present for affiliation and then to identify views on religious diversity that address them.

Preliminaries: TWW, affiliation, and belief

TWW seeks the truth of ultimate matters by drawing on the resources of multiple traditions. Because it is about seeking truth, TWW focuses on the propositions associated with religions. To think there is a tension between TWW and affiliation thus seems to assume that affiliation is also, at least in part, about propositions (i.e., that affiliation entails belief). Though I will be assuming for the bulk of the chapter that affiliation does entail belief, I want to explain why this is not obvious as we begin.

By "affiliating with" a religion, I will mean here either belonging to it or identifying with it. *Belonging* to a religion is generally a joint act of the person who is presented to belong and leaders within the religion granting belonging to them under certain conditions. For example, an individual goes

DOI: 10.4324/9780429000973-21

through jukai to enter a Buddhist community, baptism to enter a Christian one, etc. These processes may be more or less elaborate, depending on the religion or community, but for most religions[1] they require a leader. This fact makes belonging to most religions an invite-only affair, though most religions are very free with the invitations. In contrast, *identifying* with a religion is decided by the individual himself or herself. All identity entails is that one considers oneself involved with the tradition enough to call oneself a "Daoist," a "Muslim," etc. Though this analogy borders on the sacrilegious, identifying oneself with a religion is as easy as becoming a fan of a sports team. Nobody except me decides that I am a University of Michigan football fan, and I can choose to live out my fanhood with as much or as little devotion as I please.

The wide welcome for belonging and even wider welcome for identifying makes affiliation relatively easy. The complex nature of religion makes it even easier because one can affiliate by participating in only some of a religion's many dimensions, e.g., creed, code, community, and cult, to use Scott Appleby's gloss. The relevant question here is: Can one affiliate while dropping creed in particular? Sometimes no; sometimes yes. I know firsthand of several Christian communities where a fair number of beliefs are required for belonging, and of a Jewish community whose rabbi stated was about "deed, not creed." Still, to guard against setting up a straw man here, I will follow Samuel Ruhmkorff in taking religions "to involve a core area of doctrine even cluster concepts cannot bypass"[2] and focus on communities that take belief to be necessary for affiliation. Even there, I will argue, one can *still* affiliate and do TWW.

Three challenges to affiliating and doing TWW

But how exactly can one affiliate and do TWW? Doesn't seeking truth outside one's tradition *challenge* the beliefs one affirms inside it?

It does, in at least three ways:

Challenge 1: Why seek truth outside one's affiliation in the first place?
Challenge 2: If I do seek truth outside my affiliation, some outside beliefs seem to contradict some of my home beliefs. That risks a denial of the home beliefs, thereby wearing away at affiliation.
Challenge 3: Even for new beliefs that are consistent with home beliefs, adding new beliefs shifts one's focus away from home beliefs. That shift weakens one's affiliation.

Both Challenges 2 and 3 arise from how beliefs within and outside one's tradition might relate to each other. There are three possible relations, pictured in Figure 16.1:

1   The outside beliefs might *confirm* a home belief: for home beliefs *a* and *b*, one can rediscover *b* outside.

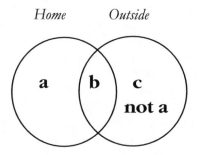

Figure 16.1 Home and outside beliefs

2   The outside beliefs might *contradict* a home belief: for home beliefs *a* and *b*, one finds *not a* outside.
3   The outside beliefs might *add* to the home beliefs: for home beliefs *a* and *b*, one finds *c* outside.

Confirmation of a home belief from the outside as in 1) is all good: it suggests anew that what one thought *was* true *is* true, at least according to the outside tradition too. If anything, such confirmation deepens one's affiliation. For example, imagine I had always believed that the Ultimate was good and then found that same belief in another religion. That makes me even more sure that I was right about the Ultimate's goodness all along.

However, if an outside belief contradicts a home belief as in 2), which belief should one take to be true? If one chooses the outside belief and loses the home belief, this is a hit to one's affiliation – a "loosening" of it, as Martin says. Say I am a Christian who believes in the Trinity and become concerned by a Muslim view that it constitutes polytheism and should be dropped. I become less Christian, it seems, if I drop it. Contradiction and its attendant risk of possible loss of belief is Challenge 2.

Finally, even an outside belief that does not require subtracting but merely adds to the home beliefs as in 3) still distracts from the home beliefs. This loss of focus on, perhaps even loss of love for, the beliefs of one's affiliation is Challenge 3. I had thought for some time that contradiction was the hardest challenge TWW presented for affiliation but, oddly, dwelling on outside beliefs turns out to be an even deeper threat in the end, as we shall see.

Challenge 1 and some preliminary reasons to step outside one's affiliation

One affiliates presumably because, among other things, one is convinced of the truth of the core doctrines of one's religion. So why go elsewhere looking for truth? This is a very fundamental question, and I think many affiliators never get past it. I think of one colleague who said: Why not look to another religion for truth? Because I might go to hell, that's why!

My main reply to this challenge, and my main point of this whole piece as intimated at the start, can be summed up with what Bilbo writes to Frodo at the start of the movie version of *The Hobbit*: "You asked me once if I had told you everything there was to know about my adventures. And while I can honestly say I have told you the truth, I may not have told you all of it."

Long-standing affiliators with a religion are like Frodo and the Ultimate is like Bilbo in this quote. Their affiliation has brought them in touch with something they perceive as Ultimate. Due to the renowned magnetic attraction of the Ultimate – a "to-be-pursuedness" about it, as J. L. Mackie has said about the good – affiliators may have a keen desire to know everything there is to know about the Ultimate. As they live out their affiliation, they come to know truths about the Ultimate. But in this very process, they also may glimpse how vast the Ultimate is, how it transcends human thought. So they may come to think that, though they have heard the truth from their religion, they may not have heard all of it. So, ironically, it is touching the Ultimate through affiliation that can ready someone to go outside it.

In fact, it is not only natural but also logically required to look beyond one's own experiences of the Ultimate in order to generalize about It, on pain of committing the fallacy of hasty generalization. As Toulmin, Rieke, and Janik (1984) say well:

> We commit fallacies of hasty generalization when we (1) *Draw a conclusion from* too few *specific instances*, for example, basing the general statement "All Audis are lemons" on a few individual reports from friends who have happened to have trouble with their own Audis, or alternatively when we: (2) *Draw a conclusion from* untypical *examples*, for example, concluding that we do not care for Woody Allen movies (which are normally comedies) on the basis of our reaction to *The Front* (one of [his] rare serious films). . . . Though the relevance of the data to the claim being made is beyond question, there simply isn't enough data available for making the sweeping claim that is alleged to follow from it.
>
> (151–153, emphases theirs)

It is fallacious to generalize from one's own experience to the way the whole world is. So also it is fallacious to generalize from our own personal experience of the Ultimate to claims about the way It actually is. The move from, for example, "I experience the Ultimate as kind" to "the Ultimate is kind" commits the fallacy. To avoid the fallacy, we need to look further for 1) more examples that will help us 2) determine whether our experiences are atypical, as Toulmin says. The more examples we find, the surer we can be about the Ultimate in general.

Challenge 2: meeting contradiction

Still, it is genuinely puzzling why, if we are all meeting the Ultimate, we have such different things to say about it. It is easy to understand how I might hear from another religion about a belief that is *different but adds*, as belief *c* in Figure 16.1 illustrates. If I know someone and you do too, it is not unusual that you know things about them that I don't, so I can learn new things about them from you. But the beliefs that are *different and contradict* as belief *a* and *not a* are in Figure 16.1 – especially numerous such beliefs that contradict – are confusing. If I hear from you that this person is not like I thought and then from several others as well, I start to wonder: Am I wrong? Are you wrong? Are we all wrong? Should we just call the whole thing off?

These questions are the stuff of Challenge 2, and I have asked them over and over again as I, affiliated with one religion, listen to people from other religions talk about the Ultimate. Interestingly, it turns out, there are many ways theorists are meeting Challenge 2.

The landscape of views of religious diversity

The many ways to understand contradictions between the world's religions are "theologies of religious pluralism" – or what I call "views of religious diversity."[3] It will help to talk about these views in the more subtle ways that Perry Schmidt Leukel's view of them allows. He reads views of religious diversity as answers to the question: How many religions "[mediate] salvific knowledge of ultimate/transcendent reality?"[4] Because this is a "how-many" question, the answers define the usual range with numbers: exclusivists answer "1"; inclusivists answer "1 but others work or help in some way"; pluralists answer "more than 1" (*n.b.* pluralists need not say "all"; as Ruhmkorff (2013) says wonderfully, they are allowed to think "there are some sketchy religions out there"). To complete the logical range, let's add the answer "0" for those who think that no religions mediate salvific knowledge of the Ultimate – either because no religion is good at that yet or because no religion ever can be, say if such knowledge is beyond us or if there is no Ultimate to know in the first place.

The range of views on religious diversity is often displayed with mountains. In Schmidt-Leukel's phrasing, the top of the mountain is "mediating salvific knowledge of the Ultimate" and the arrows represent various religions' ability to do that (see Figure 16.2). On the exclusivist mountain, only one religion makes it to the top while all the others have false starts. On the inclusivist mountain, though only one religion makes it all the way to the top, others might help in the foothills, for example, the Dalai Lama's view that even if it turns out that only Buddhism has saving truths, other religions have partial truths useful for working toward salvation. On the pluralist's mountain, multiple religions make it to the top, and on the error theorist's, none of them do.

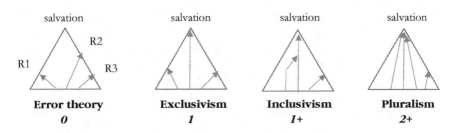

Figure 16.2 Soteriological diversity in Schmidt-Leukel

Ruhmkorff noticed that we can convert Schmidt-Leukel's question into a *form* of a "how-many religions x" question and thereby produce different diversity questions with different fillings for x. So one can ask Schmidt-Leukel's instance of the form (put more simply): "how many religions *lead to salvation?*" (a soteriological question); or other instances, such as "how many religions *have true claims about the Ultimate?*" (an alethic question); "how many religions *provide experience of the Ultimate?*" (an experiential question); etc.[5]

The key point is that someone might not answer each of these questions with the same number. For example, think of Kierkegaard's lovely saying that it is better to pray to a false God truly than a true God falsely. Kierkegaard might hold an *alethic* exclusivism, that the fundamental claims of only *one* religion can be true (there is a true God and there are false Gods) mixed with an *experiential* pluralism, that nevertheless faithful adherents of *many* religions actually experience the divine (God honors their true spirit of prayer). If so, it would be misleading to call Kierkegaard "an exclusivist" or "a pluralist," full stop, because which word applies depends on the diversity question at issue. So people do not hold a single, all-purpose view of religious diversity. They hold views on religious diversity. To picture someone's view, you would be obliged to draw the whole range multiple times, once for each question with the *telos* it discusses at the summit.

As if Ruhmkorff's insight doesn't complicate our lives enough, S. Mark Heim and John Cobb have expanded the range of options even further by noticing that each of the views discussed so far assumes there is just *one* mountain with *one* top – one salvation, one Ultimate, etc. – which none, one, or more religions might reach. To lay bare this assumption, Heim and Cobb each decided to ask not only the questions of the form "How many religions x" but also questions of the form "How many x's are there in the first place?" In particular, to "How many religions lead to salvation?" Heim has added "How many salvations are there?" And to "how many religions involve veridical experience the Ultimate?" Cobb has added: "how many kinds of religious experience are there? And how many Ultimates are there to experience?"[6]

As Griffin noted, Heim's and Cobb's new questions have the effect of distinguishing the original views earlier as all "identist" because they assume there's just one mountain top (e.g., one salvation or one kind of religious experience or one Ultimate). In contrast, the "differentialist" views assume there are irreducibly multiple salvations, religious experiences, Ultimates, etc., thus multiple mountain tops. Though Heim and Cobb both seem to be differentialist pluralists, it is in principle possible for someone to be an error theorist, exclusivist, inclusivist, or pluralist about differentialism just as people are about identism. Such views, though possible, might sound odd, for example, a differentialist exclusivist would believe there is one very handy religion that helps you reach theistic salvation *and* nirvana *and* moksha simultaneously!

Putting the old and new questions together makes the landscape of views of religious diversity contain two kinds of mountain ranges, that is, the identist range that answers "1" to the question "how many x" (where x is salvation, the Ultimate, etc.) and the differentialist range that answers "more than 1." Both ranges display various answers to the "how many religions do x" in the usual exclusivist, inclusivist, etc., terms. And both ranges need to be redrawn for each diversity question that gets asked. To illustrate the new shape of the resulting landscape, I have drawn it in Figure 16.3, just for the question Heim asks about salvations.

Now we can talk more exactly about these theorists' varying views of religious diversity. Take Hick (2004). He's an identist pluralist about *salvation*: he thinks there is one salvation he calls "Reality-centeredness" (identist) and

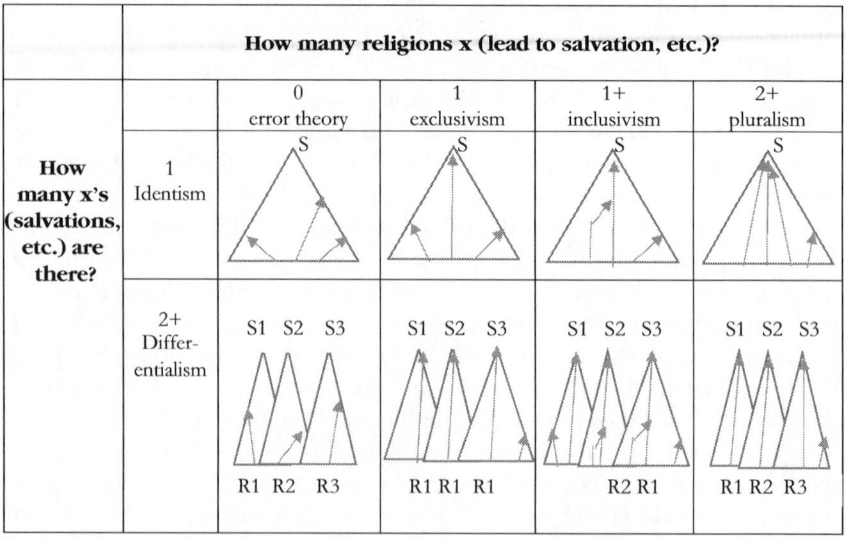

		How many religions x (lead to salvation, etc.)?			
		0 error theory	1 exclusivism	1+ inclusivism	2+ pluralism
How many x's (salvations, etc.) are there?	1 Identism				
	2+ Differentialism	S1 S2 S3 R1 R2 R3	S1 S2 S3 R1 R1 R1	S1 S2 S3 R2 R1	S1 S2 S3 R1 R2 R3

Figure 16.3 Example of soteriological diversity after Heim and Cobb

that every major religion can help you get from self-centeredness to Reality-centeredness (pluralist, so first row, last box). But Hick is *not* an identist pluralist about *truth*. As Ruhmkorff says well, for Hick "claims made by different religions about the Real are noumenally false (because they do not describe the Real as it is in itself) but phenomenally true" because they describe "the Real as mediated by their religious and cultural understandings." So Hick is an identist error theorist about *noumenal* truth: no religion has true claims about the one Ultimate as it is in itself. He is simultaneously an identist pluralist about *phenomenal* truth: each religion succeeds in knowing the one Ultimate (identist) phenomenally, because there is nobody better than the perceiver to report their perceptions of It (pluralist).

Or consider Heim. He is a differentialist pluralist about *salvation*: he thinks there are many salvations, for example, nirvana, moksha, and theistic salvation are each different spiritual summits (differentialist), and the many religions train you to reach those salvations, for example, vipassana helps you reach nirvana; the yogas, moksha; prayer, salvation (pluralist, so second row, last box). At the same time, if I read him right, Heim is a Christian identist inclusivist about *truth*: he is a realist who thinks there is only one Ultimate to be known (identist) and that only Christianity's fundamental claims are true about It, though other religions know it in part, too (inclusivist).

Finally, consider Cobb and Griffin's complementary pluralism, which focuses on at least two different topics in religious diversity. First, they are impressed by how deeply different *religious experiences* are, expressed well by a quote they offer from Steven Katz: "There is no intelligible way that anyone can argue that a 'no-self' experience of 'empty' calm is the same experience as the experience of intense, loving, intimate relationship between two substantial selves" (Griffin 2005, 46), or the same experience as a sacred experience of the cosmos (49). Inspired by Katz, Cobb is a differentialist pluralist about religious experience. He looks at the wide sweep of human religious experience and sees three durable, radically different, irreducible kinds of religious experience that he calls "theistic, acosmic, and cosmic" (49, differentialist), and he thinks multiple religions help you reach these experiences (pluralist). Specifically, he thinks the theistic religions such as the major monotheisms and some forms of Hinduism involve theistic experiences; the acosmic ones such as Buddhism and other forms of Hinduism involve acosmic experiences; and the cosmic traditions such as Daoism and Native American spiritualities – and the sciences, I would add – involve cosmic experiences.[7]

Cobb's second move is even more radical. As Griffin says, Cobb "finds it unilluminating to claim . . . that . . . radically different kinds of experience are experiences of the same ultimate reality. '[The] evidence,' suggests Cobb, 'points to a different hypothesis'" (2005, 47). He believes there are three different kinds of religious experience because there are three different Ultimates getting experienced. Theistic experiences are experiences of the

Supreme Being, "in-formed and the source of forms (such as truth, beauty and justice)," variously named and understood as God (the monotheistic traditions), as Amida Buddha (Buddhism), as Saguna Brahman (Advaita Vedanta in Hinduism), etc. (47). Acosmic experiences are of *Being Itself*, a formless ultimate reality, again variously understood as Emptiness (Buddhism), as Nirguna Brahman (Advaita Vedanta) and as the Godhead (Eckhart in Christianity) (47). Cosmic experiences are of the *Cosmos*, variously understood as the Dao (Daoism) and other cosmic sacreds in Native American spiritualities and more (49). So in addition to being a differentialist pluralist about veridical religious experience, Cobb is a differentialist pluralist about the Ultimate: he thinks there are multiple Ultimates to reach (differentialist), and that multiple religions and spiritualities are doing the reaching (pluralist). So I read him as a differentialist pluralist about knowledge of Ultimacy: the contact with the three Ultimates in the three kinds of religious experiences provides at least some true beliefs about them, though it is an open question whether he would take these beliefs to be merely phenomenally true ("I know that the acosmic ultimate felt thus to me") or noumenally so ("I know that the acosmic ultimate is thus"). Table 16.1 summarizes the views relayed in this section.

How views on religious diversity help meet Challenges 1 and 2

Here I want to show how holding certain combinations of views on religious diversity can make doing TWW and affiliation natural. I will be using my own current combination of views as a case in point.

About *religious experiences*: Like Cobb and Katz, I suspect that there are truly distinct experiences of the Ultimate by people from various religions (differential pluralism). My own forays into Christianity and Buddhism and what I know of reports of religious experiences confirm their view that there are at least two different kinds of experiences of Ultimacy that are distinct and possibly irreducibly so, viz., the theistic and "empty calm" kinds. It may be that experiences of the cosmos are a distinct third kind. That would explain, for instance, why my long-distance experiences of the silent expanse of outer space and my actual experiences of the spiritually moving places on earth feel so very holy.

I also gravitate toward Heim's differentialist pluralism about *salvations*. Heim makes sense of the undeniably advanced spiritual states, which adepts in the many religions reach, and does justice to their substantial differences in a way that Hick's identist pluralism famously does not.[8]

So let's assume there are radically different religious experiences and irreducibly multiple salvations. *Why* do we have this deep diversity of experiences and salvations? My guess is that they are genuine responses to one Ultimate as Hick and Heim say, not to multiple Ultimates as Cobb says. The empirical facts alone actually underdetermine this choice: in philosophical

Table 16.1 Summary of views on religious diversities in Hick, Heim, and Cobb

Soteriology — How many religions lead to salvation?

	0 error theory	1 exclusivism	1+ inclusivism	2+ pluralism
1 Identism				Hick
2+ Differentialism				Heim

Knowledge — How many religions have true claims about Ultimacy?

	0 error theory	1 exclusivism	1+ inclusivism	2+ pluralism
1 Identism	Hick for noumenal truth		Heim	Hick for phenomenal truth
2+ Differentialism				Cobb

Religious experience — How many religions involve veridical religious experience?

	0 error theory	1 exclusivism	1+ inclusivism	2+ pluralism
1 Identism				
2+ Differentialism				Cobb

terms, either one or multiple Ultimates could be the "truthmaker" of these deeply diverse experiences; both theories explain the data. Still, I gravitate toward the one-Ultimate hypothesis for a few reasons. First is an empirical reason complicated enough that I am relegating it to a footnote.[9] Second is Ockham's razor, an old workhorse in theory choice: all else being equal, "entities should not be multiplied beyond necessity." The third reason comes from thinking of multiple ultimacy itself. Imagine for a moment that the Cosmos, the Supreme Being and Being Itself are distinct Ultimates. They might, or perhaps must, bear some relation to each other. If so, whatever that totality of Ultimates relating to each other is, why that would be the whole truth, and thus the most total Ultimate (singular), perhaps.[10]

Though the one-Ultimate view seems right, it actually heightens the problem of contradiction mentioned in Challenge 2. That is, I cannot say, like Cobb, that it is no wonder we make different claims about Ultimacy: we are talking about different Ultimates! On the one-Ultimate view, we are all talking about the same thing, so why do we contradict each other? To make matters worse, Hick managed to find a way to resolve the contradictions even with just one Ultimate, but I can't use his way either, because it trades on his idea that no religion involves genuine knowledge of the Ultimate and I think multiple religions do (he is an identist error theorist about knowledge and I am an identist pluralist). I agree with how Hick begins: we each experience the Ultimate through our religious and cultural traditions. But I disagree with how he ends: so none of us are describing the Ultimate as it is in Itself. His ending avoids contradiction because all claims including contradictory ones are relativized to a religion: "Jesus is God" is true about God *as Christians experience God*, "Jesus is not God" is true of God *as Jews experience God*. I, on the other hand, suspect that, if there is an Ultimate and if we are having experiences of It, we sometimes are describing the Ultimate. We almost always fail, because the Ultimate is beyond us in kind and in scope, for example, as Leibniz's cosmological argument shows deeply. Still, as Maimonides has helped me see, I think we can know some very limited truths about It (e.g., about its actions and some disjunctive claims about Its nature that those actions entail).[11] If so, we are in these limited ways (big breath!) really accessing the Ultimate.

These commitments leave me still saddled with the contradictions that Cobb and Hick avoided: How can it be that different religionists say contradictory things about the Ultimate if they are each really accessing It at least sometimes? I can think of at least three ways to read such contradictions given all my commitments earlier. First, because it is so hard to say true things about the Ultimate, sometimes I may be wrong, or you may be wrong, or we may both be wrong, and it may be decades or another lifetime until we know which. If at least one of us is wrong, the contradiction is defused.

Second, sometimes our claims about ultimate things may not be literally true, but rather, for example, a metaphor for, an allegory for, or an instance of some universal truth. This is the stuff of myth that Mircea Eliade and Joseph Campbell and others have spoken of so eloquently. For example, the Christian belief that Jesus rose again from the dead to save us from sin may be an instance of a universal truth that, for example, the forces of good are stronger than the forces of death. Perhaps a Hindu might deny that story about Jesus but affirm the story that Prahlad survived Holika's fire, and perhaps the Prahlad story is also an instance of that very same universal truth. If so, what is contradiction at the particular level is actually agreement at the universal level, so the apparent contradiction is defused in an important sense.[12]

The third way to defuse contradiction is inspired by Baruch Spinoza's thought about what he calls "God" – an Ultimate that is read sometimes monistically, sometimes panentheistically. Though I will not aim to stay true to Spinoza here, he has a wonderful idea of the infinite *attributes* of God. He reads each attribute as a different way we can *perceive* God's essence,[13] each of which is "*complete*" in itself and "*incommensurate*" with the other attributes. Roger Scruton explains Spinoza's attributes with a really helpful analogy:

> Imagine two people looking at a picture painted on a board, one an optician, the other a critic. And suppose you ask them to describe what they see. The optician arranges the picture on two axes, and describes it thus: "At x = 4, y = 5.2, there is a patch of chrome yellow; this continues along the horizontal axis until x = 5.1, when it changes to Prussian blue." The critic says: "It is a man in a yellow coat, with a lowering expression, and steely blue eyes." You could imagine these descriptions being *complete* – so complete that they would enable a third party to reconstruct the picture by using them as a set of instructions. But they would have nothing whatever in common [*incommensurate*]. One is about colors arranged on a matrix, the other about the scene that we see in them. You cannot switch from one narrative to the other and still make sense: the man is not standing next to a patch of Prussian blue, but next to the shadow of an oak tree. The Prussian blue is not situated next to a coat sleeve, but next to a patch of chrome yellow.
>
> (9–10, emphases mine)

Though Spinoza most definitely did not put his attributes to work in this way, I take different religionists to be in touch with different attributes of the Ultimate, just as the optician and critic are in touch with different attributes of the painting. This view captures at once both my differentialist pluralism about religious experiences (like Cobb's) and my identism about ultimacy (like Hick's): some religionists experience the acosmic attribute of the Ultimate; others, the cosmic, and still others, the theistic, but these are all experiences of the same Ultimate, just different attributes of It. Unlike Hick,

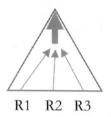

R1   R2   R3

Figure 16.4 Partialism about knowledge of the Ultimate

these experiences of the attributes can produce knowledge of the Ultimate itself. In the same way that both the optician's and critic's accounts of the painting are actually *true* of the painting – it really does have those colors in that order and it really does contain that scene – so also each religionist's account of the Ultimate can be actually true of it. Call this Scruton-Spinozistic inspired view "partialism," and give it a place between inclusivism and pluralism on the identist mountains in the question about *knowledge* of the Ultimate (the second question in Table 16.1).

Partialism addresses Challenge 1. Because the Ultimate has multiple (maybe infinite) attributes and each religion grasps just one of these, no religion has full knowledge of the Ultimate solo. Affiliators must go outside their affiliation and pool their knowledge with other affiliators to know the Ultimate more fully (see Figure 16.4).[14]

Partialism also addresses Challenge 2. Different religionists can seem to contradict each other, but that is because they are describing different attributes of the Ultimate. We can see that the contradiction is merely apparent when we relativize the religionists' claims to their respective attributes, just as Hick did when he relativized claims to their respective phenomena.

Challenge 3: a change of heart

There remains Challenge 3, the risk of adding new beliefs that, though consistent with the home beliefs, distract a person from the home beliefs and thereby weaken affiliation.

Challenge 3 is embodied in the story of the one-time Henri Le Saux turned Swami Abishiktananda. Born in France in 1910, he began his formal spiritual journey as a Christian Benedictine monk who eventually felt called to India to seek an even deeper contemplative life. Over decades of life in India, his attraction to Hindu over Christian forms grew so much that by the last year of his life in 1973, he wrote: "The discovery of Christ's 'I AM' is the ruin of any Christic 'theology,' for all notions are burnt within the fire of experience" (said in 1973, see 2019). Swami Abishiktananda seems to have failed Challenge 3, for worse or for better. His focus on Hindu truths outside his Christianity, though not formally inconsistent with it, eventually transformed his focus and spirit enough that he lost his Christian affiliation altogether.

Even though such loss of affiliation can happen in the face of new truths from an outside tradition, it also can *not* happen. In fact, in many of the other cases I have read of people who have gone out seriously enough to other affiliations that they identify with a hybrid or double belong, the person has kept their home affiliation.[15] They are living proof that it is possible to affiliate seriously and do TWW seriously.

Conclusion

To return to our initial question: "Can a transreligious theologian take account of spiritual truths outside their confession, or would they have to give up or loosen their affiliation to do this?" There are three good reasons to think that one cannot retain affiliation while doing TWW: one's affiliation should be truth enough; going beyond affiliation risks being persuaded by outside beliefs that contradict one's affiliation; and being distracted by them, too. Though the story of Swami Abishiktananda shows us that these three challenges are real, we also confirmed that they all can be and sometimes are met. In particular, if one adopts partialism and thinks that one's own religion is a way of coming to know just one of the possibly infinite attributes of the Ultimate, and that other religions are too, then an Ultimate-besotted affiliator may well venture out to other religions to get a fuller picture of the Ultimate she loves. With partialism, she also expects contradiction on the way: perhaps one of us is wrong, or perhaps there is some more universal truth we both believe here, or perhaps we are talking in incommensurate ways, you tracing one of the attributes, I another. Finally, if in this process of learning she should fall for another religion's path, and though this disaffiliation is a genuine loss – akin to loss of one's home or first language – provided there really is an Ultimate, and provided both religions are dwelling in Its attributes, then the genuine loss gives way to a genuine gain, a new way to see the Ultimate all over again.[16]

Notes

1 Islam may be an exception, because it requires only saying the *Shahadah* three times earnestly, not necessarily even in the presence of another Muslim, let alone an imam or other leader.

2 I also follow Ruhmkorff in thinking this applies just to "core" propositions, however these may get identified, because "it would be absurdly stringent to insist that all propositions associated with a religion be true." That would, for example, rule out denominational differences and more.

3 "Views of religious diversity" drops the etymological reference to God in "theology" and drops the word "pluralism" to make it clear that the views under consideration do not all talk about God and are not all species of pluralism – whatever exactly that might be (see Griffin (2005, chapter 1) for the ambiguity of "pluralism".

4 My exposition here is taken from Ruhmkorff (2013).

5 In the first section, he writes: "We can think of the debate between pluralism, exclusivism, and inclusivism at the level of salvation (are only faithful adherents to one tradition saved?), rationality (are only faithful adherents to one religious tradition rational?), doctrine (are the fundamental claims of only one religion true?), religious experience (do members of only one tradition experience the divine?), and so on."

6 These questions are my paraphrases. Heim's question is a major point in *Salvations*. Apparently Cobb had this same idea before Heim, see Griffin (2005, chapter 2). Both have good company in the other. See Cobb's additional questions laid out in Griffin (2005, chapters 1 and 2).

7 Note that an identist about religious experiences would think that human religious experience across time and place is really all the same. Such a view may sound like a nonstarter, given the differences between individuals, but think of it as close to the way many people read the experience of seeing green (to couch one vexed topic in the terms of another!). An identist view of seeing green would say that the experience of seeing green is the same among humans, given our similar biologies and the fact that green things emit light at the same wavelength worldwide. That sameness is there, someone might say, even if it expressed in different words and reactions across cultures. So also, perhaps, with religious experiences, given our similar needs for the Ultimate and the Ultimate's constancy across space-time.

8 I wonder if the fact that I am a differentialist pluralist on both counts follows from a genus–species relationship between religious experiences and salvations respectively, e.g., if salvation necessarily involves a religious experience that ushers in a new spiritual way of being, then the salvations would be multiple *because* they involve religious experiences that are.

9 Cobb's own description of the experiences indicates that it is not unusual for a single person to have multiple kinds of religious experience at one go: "The religious experience of Western mystics seems to be at once of theistic and acosmic reality – one might say that it is of the theistic as embodying the acosmic reality or of the acosmic as qualified by the theistic reality" (Griffin 2005, 50). Although these double experiences could be genuine responses to two Ultimates that are really there to be experienced (I see the painting while hearing the clock tick), it seems more likely that they come from a single Ultimate complex enough to produce both at once (I see the hands on the clock and hear *it* tick). Otherwise, we need the two Ultimates to coordinate in a way that permits multiple mystics over centuries and across the globe to keep being able to access them both simultaneously. That sort of relation between the Ultimates and constant co-access by the mystics is guaranteed if the two Ultimates are one thing.

10 There is a deep metaphysical question here: What is the difference really between three separate Ultimates and a single Ultimate that has three parts? Perhaps the difference is the kind of unity in the single Ultimate. If it is merely formal – that all we are doing is drawing a circle around the three Ultimates and saying their unity consists in being able to be "setted," as it were – why then the difference between the One and the Many is not real, at least not concrete. But if the unity consists in something substantial, e.g. if they bear a relationship of love to each other as in social Trinitarian views, and if this love is itself a "thing" they bring forth in the universe, above and beyond the Ultimates themselves, why then there *is* a real difference between a single Ultimate and the three distinct Ultimates, and in this example you can even name it. It is love.

11 See Leibniz (2017) in Clark and Maimonides's *The Guide of the Perplexed*, as well as Diller (2019) for more.
12 I used to think the move to the abstract level was a last gasp – that if a claim was not literally true, it was false in the most important sense. But lately I have been thinking that a claim that is universally true is true in the most important sense because such claims hold everywhere and everywhen, not just at one point in space-time.
13 Spinoza wrote: "By attribute I understand what the intellect perceives of a substance, as constituting its essence." (D4 in his *Ethics*)
14 All three of these views are echoed in Martin's (2016) *God: An Autobiography*: "'One of the things I put into the universe, one of the things I am, is the natural order . . . There is a frequency . . . and I am it. This is one way I make myself available to men and animals.' . . . 'And the Chinese were adept at picking up the signal?' 'Of course. . . . People cannot take everything in at once. They have to specialize and the Chinese have specialized in this.' [Cobb's cosmic experience]. 'With little or no sense of a personal God [Cobb's theistic experience], didn't they lose a lot?' 'Everybody loses a lot. No one gets it all [partialism about knowledge]. That is fine. They all help me realize, express Myself. They are all part of the big story'" (chapter 29, 196–197, unpublished manuscript).
15 Francis Clooney is a good example of someone who maintains his Christian affiliation in Hindu-Christian hybridity. Robert Kennedy, SJ, and Paul Knitter are both good examples of double-belongers who maintain their Christian affiliation while adding a second Buddhist affiliation to it. For explanations of hybridity and double belonging, see Diller (2016), especially the section on Religious Orientations.
16 My sincere thanks to Jerry Martin and Linda Mercadante for their helpful comments as this chapter took shape.

References

Diller, Jeanine, 2016. "Multiple Religious Orientation." *Open Theology* 2: 338–353.

Diller, Jeanine. 2019. "Being Perfect is Not Necessary for Being God." *European Journal for Philosophy of Religion*. 11 (2): 43–64.

Griffin, David Ray, ed. 2005. *Deep Religious Pluralism*. Louisville, KY: Westminster John Knox Press.

Heim, Mark S. 2006. *Salvations: Truth and Difference in Religion*. Maryknoll, NY: Orbis Books. doi:10.1163/157254397x00313

Hick, John. 2004. *An Interpretation of Religion: Human Responses to the Transcendent*. 2nd ed. New Haven, CT: Yale Press.

Knitter, Paul F. 2013. *Without Buddha I Could Not Be a Christian*. Croydon, UK: Oneworld.

Leibniz, Gottfried W. 2017. "On the Ultimate Origination of Things." In *Readings in the Philosophy of Religion*, edited by Kelly James Clark. Peterborough, Ontario, Canada: Broadview Press.

Martin, Jerry L. 2016. *God: An Autobiography*. Doylestown, PA: Calladium Publishing Company.

McEntee, Rory, and Adam Bucko. 2016. *The New Monasticism: An Interspiritual Manifesto for Contemplative Living*. Maryknoll, NY: Orbis Books. doi:10.1017/hor.2016.103

Ruhmkorff, Samuel. 2013. "The Incompatibility Problem and Religious Pluralism Beyond Hick." *Philosophy Compass* 8 (5): 510–522. doi:10.1111/phc3.12032

Scruton, Roger. 1999. *Spinoza*. New York, NY: Routledge.

Swami Abishiktananda. 2019. "The Call of the Self." www.abhishiktananda.org.in/html/life-of-swami-abhishiktananda.php (accessed February 9, 2019).

Toulmin, Stephen, Richard Rieke, and Allan Janik. 1984. *An Introduction to Reasoning*. 2nd ed. New York: Macmillan Publishing Company.

17 Theology Without Walls

Is a theology for SBNRs possible?

Linda Mercadante

Sheer numbers are enough of a reason to suggest a theology for the "spiritual but not religious" (SBNR). The SBNR population now comprises more than a quarter of Americans and is slated to keep growing. Already their numbers are greater than the total of all types of Protestants in the United States.[1] There is also a more critical reason. In a globally challenged, polarized, violence-ridden, climate-endangered world, the tasks we face are so critical, so massive, and so vital to world survival that some common spiritual and social principles are needed to foster cooperation. Yet the common principles and networks of relationships that have long helped society function are dwindling.

In other words, America is losing much of its social and spiritual "capital." Social capital is the fruit of community. It is the links that join us together as a society, fostering trust, cooperation, and mutual productivity. Traditionally, social capital has been greatly fostered by religion. In fact, it is estimated that half of America's social capital comes from religion (Putnam 2001, 66). Spiritual capital are those nonmaterial factors that arise from religious practices, beliefs, institutions, and relationships. These provide behavioral norms; a sense of meaning for life; and even economic, social and political effects.[2]

This means that the loss of religious attendance, belief, and practices is not just a loss for actual religion. This also does not bode well for American society in general. It follows that even SBNRs and secularists should understand they benefit from religion. But they also can benefit from practicing a form of "theology." Why is this so, when "theology" seems so deeply linked with organized religion? For even the nonreligious need to understand what they believe, why they believe it, and how this functions in their lives. This could make this rapidly expanding population a force for good in society, rather than simply a disjointed societal sea-change with unclear effects.

The difficulties are real

The difficulties of suggesting a theology for SBNRs must be acknowledged up front. First, SBNRs are hard to characterize and are often maligned,

DOI: 10.4324/9780429000973-22

especially by religious people. They are sometimes stereotyped as "salad bar spiritualists"; proudly eclectic; "poachers" of other cultures' spiritual practices; New Agers; and shallow, self-serving individuals. Although these are often exaggerations, this does not sound like a population that would attract the efforts of theologians.

Second, SBNRs are not really an integrated identifiable group. Instead, they are more of a "demographic" or "gerrymandered set." As philosopher Jeanine Diller explains, this means: "It's not clear that there is anything every member of the set has in common; there is no governing principle for why they are all in the set."[3] What they have most in common, I would add, is what they are "not," that is, religious. Even many of those who still actively participate in organized religion now identify as SBNR.[4]

In addition, SBNRs are a self-selected set with a somewhat exclusivist quality. Its activities require both time and resources, which many people don't have. Thus, there is an aspect of "spiritual privilege" to the SBNR designation. As Stephen T. Asma says: "The dismissal of religion . . . is often a luxury position of prosperous and comfortable groups. . . . Perhaps they have not suffered much. . . . For the rest of us, religion is vital to our well-being."[5]

Third, the definition of the phrase "spiritual but not religious" is far from precise. The nutshell description implies that spirituality is personal and heart-felt, whereas religion consists of human-created doctrines, institutions, and outward rituals. But in the diverse SBNR population, this sharp divide does not always hold. The SBNR set can include secular humanists, atheists, and those who simply do not identify with any religion: the "nones." It encompasses people who draw on aspects of "metaphysical religion," read popular works on the topic, create rituals, and revive others. Alternatively, it includes those who focus primarily on alternative health practices, energy work, and self-authenticity, often with a basis in what is "natural" or of the earth. Thus, what it means to be SBNR often includes a hybrid or syncretic assembly of spiritual practices and beliefs.[6] Increasingly, it also includes growing numbers who retain some practices, beliefs, and even regular participation in organized religion.

Fourth, as I demonstrated in my book, *Belief without Borders: Inside the Minds of the Spiritual but not Religious*, the most common denominator for a majority of SBNRs is not simply that they are not religious. It goes further than that. For I found SBNRs, as diverse as they are, to have an impressive agreement on the specific concepts in which they *don't* believe.[7] The rejected beliefs include such things as a self-determining, transcendent, personal God; humans created in God's image but with a propensity to turn their backs on this God; spirit-infused, yet human-created, institutions; and some kind of afterlife dependent upon God's judgment. Not surprisingly, because SBNR is more a boundary-setting rhetoric than a clear-cut set of positions, many of these beliefs are the hallmarks of religion, in particular, Christianity.

Fifth, although the SBNRs are not without an array of guides, at present they are without any agreed-upon texts, leaders, or groups. There are no widely recognized programs to promote intellectual and ethical harmony or solidarity outside the revolving door of trends and teachers. Although there are some widely respected teachers – such as Thich Nhat Hanh, the Dalai Lama, and Pema Chodron (who actually represent traditional religions) – and a few common principles, such as compassion, tolerance, or goodwill to all, these have not yet led to organization. Instead, they have bred a culture in which this growing population learns its catechism in yoga studios, fitness programs, self-help books, television shows, and internet sites.

Sixth, the vested interests of theologians and religious leaders would likely not be served by this task. As counterintuitive as this may sound to clergy, it is probably unrealistic for religions to consider the SBNR population a new "mission field." Perhaps religious leaders would do better to promote the positive teachings and values of their respective faiths and correct what has led to misinterpretations.[8]

Is creating an SBNR theology useful when it might be more effective to focus on the fact that "real religion is about human flourishing" (Asma 2018, 1)? After all, sociologists project that certain characteristics of this group – especially their anti-institutional bent – make it unlikely that they will lead to a reformation for organized religion or the creation of a new religion.

As Mark Chaves concludes in *American Religion:*

> This growing segment of the population is unlikely to reenergize existing religious institutions. Nor will it provide a solid foundation for new kinds of religious institutions or new religious movements. The spiritual but not religious should not be seen as yearning people ready to be won over by a new type of religion specifically targeted to them. They may provide a market for certain kinds of religious products, such as self-help books with spiritual themes, but they probably will not create a stable, socially and politically significant organizational expression. The spiritual-but-not-religious phenomenon is too vague, unfocused, and anti-institutional for that.
>
> (Chaves 2017, 40)

Can we use the word "theology?"

As hinted earlier, the word "theology" can present another problem if by that we mean *theos logos*, words about God. Most of the hundreds of SBNRs I interviewed for my book *Belief without Borders* scrupulously avoid using the word "God." Although this appears to be happening culture-wide and even in some religious settings, it is more explicit and intentional among SBNRs.[9] Even if they believe there is some primal source, ultimate reality, or universal energy, they largely reject the idea that it is a divine personal being and transcendent/immanent spirit. Although they may search for some type of "bottom line" or ultimacy, they generally do not believe in a God who is personally involved with humans, one who creates, acts, relates, controls, persuades, sets goals, makes promises, judges, communicates, or works for individual growth and continuity.

The theological focus on normativity, truth, and questions of good and evil also becomes problematic, because SBNRs protest religious norms, hold back from declaring things good or evil, and find truth to be relative.[10] In addition to resisting the authority of any religious doctrine, tradition, leadership, sacred text, or organization, they increasingly identify religion with right-wing politics and harmful conservative agendas. Religious morality, standards of behavior, communal mission, and other practical facets of organized religions hold little import. These many factors are what SBNRs consider retrograde, backward looking, repressive, and lacking in creativity about organized religions, even if they grant that religions do some good things now and then.

Some traction is gained if we define theology more generally as "faith seeking understanding." Oftentimes SBNRs see themselves on a spiritual quest, journey, or path, seeking such things as spiritual experience, greater understanding of the self, authenticity, ancient wisdom predating religion, cosmic energetic transmissions, holism, or harmony. Although this may be a place to start, it does not yet provide a sufficient theological basis. It is not clear what or whom this faith is in, how to reach understanding, and what that would mean.

But cynicism is not wisdom, and hope takes courage. Lending a hand is a hopeful move that people who think for a living can do. Religious intellectuals, in particular theologians, are equipped to suggest cognitive tools, historical and philosophical principles, and the wisdom of great mystics and theologians. They can promote common ethical standards, organize socially helpful projects, and propose missions that take all humanity under those umbrellas. They stand on faith traditions that live in hope for the human race, the Earth, and the entire universe. Even if the ground of their hope is questioned by SBNRs, they bring that hope to the task anyway.

In fact, the designation "spiritual but not religious" suggests a false dichotomy. SBNRs are not without ties to traditions, religious thought, and other influences. Although they borrow and adapt at will, this population is not totally eclectic and negative. SBNRs do not just disbelieve, disaffiliate, and distrust. There are some common affirmative factors in the SBNR movement that can give theologians starting places. In my interviews with SBNRs, I discovered that there are clusters of beliefs that they hold in common, especially around the four major concepts I examined: transcendence/immanence, human nature, community, and afterlife.

Common concepts

The hundreds of SBNRs I interviewed were not trained in theological inquiry. In fact, many had scant exposure to basic religious education. Even so, they routinely raised issues ripe for theological engagement. I found that an array of common concepts emerges as one talks with SBNRs.

Transcendence/immanence

Their near-unanimity on transcendence and immanence was striking. Although they rejected a fully transcendent deity who personally interacts – thus seeing themselves entirely in what Charles Taylor calls "the immanent frame" (Taylor 2007) – they did propose a kind of horizontal transcendence. That is, they felt connected to something larger than themselves, be it the human race, the Earth, or an ultimate universal "oneness."

They leaned toward "monism" and professed "all is one." Thus, when proposing a connecting principle, many suggested that some kind of "universal energy source" permeates everything. Sometimes the SBNR interviewees spoke of "the Universe" in a way similar to how others speak of God, but more often they saw this as an impersonal, benign, constantly flowing source of guidance, help, and empowerment. They leaned toward a "re-enchantment" of the world such that more goes on under the surface than mere scientific materialism can reveal.

Human nature

Most felt confident when I asked them about human nature. In spite of their implicit monism, most did not see individuality as an illusion. Although a few echoed their attraction to Eastern religions by insisting the ultimate problem was "the ego," most felt individuality was important and lasting. Freedom of choice and authority lodged in the self were sacrosanct principles, as was a belief in unlimited human potential. Some claimed immanent divinity resided in the depths of the self, with a few saying, "I am God."

Common goals included finding one's "authentic self" and clearing the energy blocks that make self-fulfillment difficult. Many agree that individual spiritual experience, unmediated by religious tradition – and especially as felt in natural settings – is the key to these things. Yet SBNRs often hope to find an ancient, primitive, or more "natural" spiritual tradition that predates organized religion. SBNRs lean towards a type of "perennialism," a contemporary assumption that each of the world's religions converge on a few common principles, whether that is love, compassion, "brotherhood," or others. They often feel proud to have outgrown the imprisonment of these principles in particular religions.

To them, what is most important are their individual thoughts and choices. Many insist they can stay in tune with the universal energy by practicing "positive thinking," drawing to themselves what they project from their minds. However, many avoid using terms like "good" and "bad," insisting that these are relative and judgmental. Ironically, however, during the interview process nearly 100 percent began their comments by saying,

"Everyone is born good." They explained that individuals only slip into dysfunction when something has damaged them therapeutically or biologically, such as bad parenting or mental illness.

Community

As for community, many SBNRs I meet seek it out from time to time, but most do not find long-standing commitment essential for spiritual growth.[11] When I asked interviewees who supports them spiritually, many answered, "I do." Some hoped to find a group where everyone could believe and practice as they chose, without peer pressure. However, the anti-institutional bent meant that few had found – or felt they needed – a group of like-minded people for the long haul.[12]

In spite of the individualism, this is not a population of "lone rangers." Many will commit to causes, participate in charitable or political-action groups, and be motivated to serve, even if only on a case-by-case basis. Rather than the seedbed for a new spiritual organization, however, this is a developing subculture without, as yet, an identifiable center. Its ethos is passed around through low-cost or no-cost things, such as informal discussion groups, popular books, internet sites, 12-step and therapy groups, and alternative spiritualties such as Reiki. It also is disseminated on the back of capitalism through such businesses as yoga classes, fitness studios, boot camps, and self-improvement programs. These feed on and spread the gospel of individual self-fulfillment, sometimes with other participants encouraging each other's personal spiritual journeys.[13]

Afterlife

When I ask SBNRs about their views on afterlife, the theme of individuality and self-fulfillment usually shows up again. In fact, some insist they have access to their "past lives" and/or expect ongoing continuation of their individuality after death. Although a few insist that death is the end of everything, many others have a general belief in reincarnation. It is a very American brand, however, promising endless lives of progress. SBNRs also mention karma – the idea that "what goes around, comes around." It is seen as a process that regulates harm, replacing a God who judges or the universality of human sin.

One may hear, in the SBNR ethos, echoes of earlier themes in American religion, such as theosophy, transcendentalism, spiritualism, positive thought, romanticism, Swedenborgianism, etc. However, the SBNRs I meet are not consciously adopting or are in touch with these traditions. Even so, this growing group could be called the new "metaphysicals" or the "liminals" because they sense a fragile place between material and spiritual reality.[14] No matter what term is used, however, the SBNR ethos provides some footholds for a theology.

Theological footholds

It is beyond the scope of this chapter to determine whether a systematic theology for SBNRs is feasible, much less to develop one. Yet there are a few theological starting places, as well as issues needing further development, that can provide room for the insights of religious thinkers.

Spiritual experience

The focus on spiritual experience gives a likely foothold. Exploring those times when a sense of fullness or peace or deep connection happens can put words to experience without automatically invoking religious doctrine. SBNRs seek a sense of "cosmic consciousness," seeing it as the location of internal divinity. They often equate feelings of awe, wonder, mystery, and gratitude with spiritual experience. One connecting point, then, can be something like Schleiermacher's "feeling of absolute dependence" or Tillich's understanding of "ultimate concern." At least one theologian is trying to bridge this gap by developing the concept of "love beyond belief" (Thandeka 2018).

On the other hand, theologians can explain that unmediated experience of any kind is an impossible goal, because everything is filtered through bodies, contexts, and history. After all, we all swim in a sea of culture. The fact that many SBNRs – sometimes with puzzlement – claim to feel inspired by religious architecture and music is one way to make this point. Theologians can contribute by discussing the ideas and beliefs behind these inspiring creations – and the sensations they evoke – especially because SBNRs often value artistic creativity.

Moreover, it must be asked whether spiritual experience is an end in itself or a route to something greater? One way to explore this question would be to examine the recent interest in dramatic bodily practices to see whether self-transcendence, self-fulfillment, or sheer stimulation is the experience sought. This could include such things as extreme sports (such as free climbing and BASE jumping), ideologically based dietary regimens, self-imposed pain or markings (such as tattoos, piercings, or body suspension on hooks), or pilgrimage treks (such as the Camino de Santiago in Spain).

The natural world

A starting place with wider appeal is the natural world, especially the environment and its nonhuman inhabitants. For SBNRs, nature is very often revered as a likely site of spiritual experience, with assertions like, "I find more spirituality in a sunset (out on a hike, at the ocean, etc.) than I do in a religious service." The increasing focus on domestic pets can sometimes function as spiritual source for SBNRs as well. Although SBNRs are unlikely to understand the natural world as God's creation, they do sense a sacredness in the Earth. This links well to their sense of holism and oneness and the energy that permeates everything.

Perhaps because of this, SBNRs are often quite concerned with the degradation humans have caused the Earth. Sometimes their response is restricted to dietary and lifestyle changes. But this is limited. Instead, this concern can be linked with their often-expressed belief that the common ground of all religions is compassion. Having compassion for the Earth and all its inhabitants can motivate to action, for there is no expectation that a savior will come to rescue humans from their mess.

Yet the Earth crisis also forces us to realize that we all have erred in some way, becoming unconsciously complicit in the Earth's suffering. This moves the discussion beyond a simple assertion that "we are all born good" and individual freedom as the highest value. Instead, it raises issues of the reality of evil and human wrongdoing beyond a mere therapeutic explanation. It opens the door to exploring the different approaches religions take on human finitude, fallibility, and vulnerability.

Thinking about the Earth's suffering – and how that affects humans – suggests that we have inherited wrongdoing, catching it like a disease. Often without realizing it, we perpetuate it, but at times, we also knowingly cooperate with harm or fail to act in the face of it. This would not necessarily push SBNRs to a theological idea such as original sin, although it could be analogized with the genetic determinism of popular views on alcohol addiction. Instead, connecting the Earth's suffering with the SBNR focus on individual responsibility and the power of positive thought can lessen feelings of powerlessness and inspire action.

The authentic self

The SBNR focus on the authentic self, rather than socially imposed roles, can also link with many religions' emphases on the false self versus the true self. This, too, may help promote responsible activism. Beyond that, if SBNRs believe they can connect with cosmic consciousness or allow the universal energy to propel action, so much the better. One need not go as far as proposing God's grace or the Holy Spirit as this consciousness or energy, but pointing out the similarities might help SBNRs better appreciate religion and promote solidarity in action.

Issues needing work

Attention must be paid to the important issues needing further development. A few key ones can be mentioned here. One is the SBNR paradox between control and conformity. Do individual thoughts control reality in an interesting twist on "you reap what you sow?" Or must one conform to – become one with – the cosmic or universal energy source by removing blocks, clearing pathways, and staying attuned?

Another is the tension between individual and group. If individual authority is primary yet one seeks holism, oneness, and compassion for all, how does this tension get resolved in real life? This paradox has not been lost on advocates of the SBNR ethos, even if they are secular humanists. One leader of a humanist group affirmed the need for life-meaning beyond self-absorption and mundane goals. He stressed the need to inspire "nones" to move toward altruism and community. The problem to be overcome, he said, is "relative absence of inspiration, of potent means to climb out of our self-centric existences to something greater than ourselves, something more edifying than me, here, now."[15]

The perennialist attitude towards world religions also needs more work. Although advocating tolerance, this view does not recognize the deep particularities of each religion. In addition, tolerance is more "live and let live" than deep reconciliation or mutuality, factors that could promote solidarity and cooperation in the face of current crises. One could even consider the random borrowing from practices, rituals, and/or beliefs of other religions – without permission, firsthand knowledge, or a legitimate guide from the particular religion – to be akin to "poaching" or stealing. SBNRs need to reflect more deeply on this practice. Does it reflect hubris, privilege, simple tolerance, a colonialist sense of entitlement, or an actual effort to embrace the "other?"

In addition, SBNR alternative spiritualties often pay insufficient attention to the very hard questions of life, issues such as imposed suffering, victimization, cruelty, abuse, and other harms that seem more intentional than inadvertent. Affirming that all individuals are born good or that we should keep a positive attitude is not an adequate formula that reaches the depths of actual or unexplainable evil. As an example, when the internet was formed, many assumed it would automatically be a force for connection and good. Where were the conversations about its unexpected "sorcerer's apprentice" type effects, such as election manipulation, the spreading of lies, or its potential to enhance human division?

Finally, more work needs to be done on ideas of afterlife. Is there a trajectory for this, an endpoint? Do humans endlessly and individually progress, or do they ultimately get absorbed into the oneness? If individuals transition into and out of life and a new body takes the place of the old one, if the brain dies with the body, how does reincarnation really work? If karma keeps order and restricts random harm – and if its cold justice extends to all – where is the place for compassion, love, forgiveness, or mercy, themes that SBNRs insist are common wisdom?

New grounds for dialogue

It is possible the SBNR movement indicates many are becoming fed up with the pervasive cynicism, irony, and suspicion of genuine emotion that permeates contemporary culture (Mercadante 2017a). As SBNRs take more seriously what they are for, rather than simply against, they may be willing to reconsider the hope and truth-claims found in religions. By working on the hard questions suggested earlier and seriously grappling with human frailty, willfulness, and vulnerability, they may realize it is the cracks that let the light in.[16] But this will not happen automatically. Theological tools are needed. Therefore, it is important to recognize the footholds available for envisioning a theology for SBNR people.

It is also critical to include faith communities in this work. Historic religious traditions, writings, and informed participants contain a wealth of millennia-old reflection, showing both meaning and mishaps, offering wisdom, cautions, and the long lived experience of putting beliefs into action.

Rather than eschewing belief and focusing on experience, the starting point of an SBNR theology should be, as Philip Sheldrake contends, "to actually have the courage and ability to make our implicit beliefs and values more explicit and balanced and then to live a principled and harmonious life more effectively" (Sheldrake 2012, 120). The first task of theologians, then, is to help SBNRs excavate their buried beliefs and recognize that a disharmony here often hinders fulfillment, community, and spiritual growth.

At this moment, the focus on self-authority, individualism, and distrust of institutions stands in the way of creating an SBNR theology that could be widely accepted. However, history shows that oftentimes things happen that make humans realize they have to organize, agree, and rally to the same vision. Hopefully, this will not be some cataclysmic event, but will come about organically as we try to save our home the Earth, promote peace instead of violence, and increase our respect for "the other."

Notes

1 The Pew Forum is replete with articles and statistics on the rise of SBNRs and "nones."
2 For more on spiritual capital, see the *Spiritual Capital Research Project* (2018).
3 Thanks to Jeanine Diller for pointing out that this is more a "gerrymandered set" or "demographic" than an actual cohesive group. Email correspondence Dec. 27, 2018.
4 I found much evidence for this in my qualitative research. See Mercadante (2014).
5 This has been noted before, e.g., see Asma (2018, 3): "The dismissal of religion . . . is often a luxury position of prosperous and comfortable groups. . . . Perhaps they have not suffered much. . . . For the rest of us, religion is vital to our well-being. There are many forms of suffering that are beyond the reach of any scientific or secular alleviation. Religion is a form of emotional management, and its value does not lie in whether it is true or false, but whether it consoles and humanizes us."
6 See, e.g., Mercadante (2017b), DeGruyter.com
7 For a full rundown of beliefs rejected and proposed see Mercadante (2014).
8 Rabbi Abraham Joshua Heschel said as much: "Religion declined not because it was refuted, but because it became irrelevant, dull, oppressive, insipid. When faith is completely replaced by creed, worship by discipline, love by habit . . .

when religion speaks only in the name of authority rather than with the voice of compassion – its message becomes meaningless" Heschel (1976), Kindle location 325.

9 I've noticed this problem even in seminaries, but as for the wider culture, see e.g., Merritt (2018).

10 This obviates an excellent definition of the work of theology and culture: "the process of seeking normative answers to questions of truth, goodness, evil, suffering, redemption, and beauty in the context of particular social and cultural situations" Lynch (2005, 36).

11 Some earlier New Agers are quite harsh in condemning this SBNR feature. See, e.g., Brian Wilson's summary of the change from New Age communal solidarity, such as characterized by the Fetzer Institute, to the current emphasis on the self: "From the beginning the Fetzer Institute's mission was . . . global spiritual transformation . . . [but this] has fallen out of step with more recent developments within the New Age movement. . . . The New Age moved on . . . to the point that many contemporary observers see it as a shorthand for spiritual shallowness and reject the label outright. Many prefer instead the label 'spiritual but not religious' . . . although SBNRs tend to be just as hyper individualistic and shallow as the New Agers they decry" Wilson (2018, 211–212).

12 There are some exceptions, such as the Fetzer Institute, or popular retreat centers, such as Esalen in Big Sur, California.

13 See, e.g., the marketing of the fitness studio "System of Strength." Its website proclaims: "The System™ was created and a community of inspiring, like-minded badasses was built. . . . We'll sweat together. We'll struggle together and we'll leave feeling proud, together."

14 See, e.g., Parsons (2018) and Bender (2010). A history of this can be found in Albanese (2007). Another history traces the foundation of this emerging population in liberal religion – see Schmidt (2012).

15 Krattenmaker (2017); also phone conversation 10/9/18. Krattenmaker is on the board of the Yale Humanist Community.

16 From Cohen's (1992) lyrics in "Anthem": "There is a crack in everything. That's how the light gets in." From the 1992 album *The Future*. Columbia.

References

Albanese, Catherine L. 2007. *A Republic of Mind & Spirit: A Cultural History of American Metaphysical Religion*. New Haven: Yale University Press. doi:10.2307/25094968

Asma, Stephen T. 2018. "Religion is Emotional Therapy." *Tikkun*, September 16. www.tikkun.org/religion-is-emotional-therapy-by-stepen-t-asma

Bender, Courtney. 2010. *The New Metaphysicals: Spirituality and the American Religious Imagination*. Chicago: University of Chicago Press.

Chaves, Mark. 2017. *American Religion: Contemporary Trends*. 2nd ed. Princeton: Princeton University Press.

Cohen, Leonard. 1992. "Anthem." *The Future*. Columbia.

Heschel, Abraham J. 1976. *God in Search of Man: A Philosophy of Judaism*. New York: Farrar, Straus, Giroux.

Krattenmaker, Tom. 2017. "The New Secular Moment." *TheHumanist.com*, February 21. https://the humanist.com/magazine (accessed October 19, 2018).

Lynch, Gordon. 2005. *Understanding Theology and Popular Culture*. Malden, MA: Blackwell Publishing.

Mercadante, Linda. 2014. *Belief Without Borders: Inside the Minds of the Spiritual but Not Religious*. New York: Oxford University Press. doi:10.1093/acprof:oso/9780199931002.003.0008

Mercadante, Linda. 2017a. "'Cheesy' and the Church: Cultivating Space for Authentic Emotion." *Bearings Online, Collegeville Institute*. July 20. https://collegevilleinstitute.org/bearings/cheesy-and-the-church/.

Mercadante, Linda. 2017b. "How Does It Fit? Multiple Religious Belonging, Spiritual but Not Religious, and Dances of Universal Peace." *Open Theology* 3 (1): 10–18. doi:10.1515/opth-2017–0002

Merritt, Jonathan. 2018. "It's Getting Harder to Talk About God: The Decline in Our Spiritual Vocabulary Has Many Real-world Consequences." *The New York Times*, October 14. www/nytimes.com/2018/10/13/Sunday/talk-god-spirtuality-christian.html (accessed October 20, 2018).

Parsons, William B., ed. 2018. *Being Spiritual but Not Religious: Past, Present, Future(s)*. New York: Routledge.

Putnam, Robert D. 2001. *Bowling Alone: The Collapse and Revival of American Community*. New York: Simon and Schuster.

Schmidt, Leigh E. 2012. *Restless Souls: The Making of American Spirituality*. 2nd ed. Berkeley: University of California Press.

Sheldrake, Philip. 2012. *Spirituality: A Very Short Introduction*. Oxford: Oxford University Press.

Spiritual Capital Research Program. 2018. "What is Spiritual Capital?" www.metanexus.net/archive/spiritualcapitalresearchprogram/what_is.asp.html (accessed December 28, 2018).

Taylor, Charles. 2007. *A Secular Age*. Cambridge: Belknap Press of Harvard University.

Thandeka. 2018. *Love Beyond Belief: Finding the Access Point to Spiritual Awareness*. Salem, Oregon: Polebridge Press.

Wilson, Brian C. 2018. *John E. Fetzer and the Quest for the New Age*. Detroit: Wayne State University Press.

Part V

Expanded confessional theologies

Introduction

Jerry L. Martin

Even the most open-minded, interreligiously educated theologian may feel adrift without the boundaries of a well-defined tradition. Moreover, there may be potential, both tapped and untapped, within a confession for accommodating experiences and ideas from other traditions. "Without walls" means without distorting the insights from the other traditions by forcing them to conform to the grids of one's own confession. In Theology Without Walls discussions, expanded confessional theologies have always been recognized as one of the options.

No one has done better in accommodating insights from other traditions – even accepting their diverse "salvations" – while placing them within a confessional frame than S. Mark Heim in *The Depth of the Riches*. In the present piece, he poses sharp questions about any attempt to "give full credit" to "all religious data" with a "simultaneous, impartial, and comparative assessment." "Who knows what all the data are," he asks, "and what it means to consider them appropriately?" Can one approximate a "blank slate" in an "unrestricted field of hypotheses and sources"? Does Theology Without Walls (TWW) exclude those already practicing particular paths? In seeking "the maximally comprehensive and practicable religious understanding," TWW assumes that "this maximal integration does not yet exist." In fact, openness to the full range of religious data is intrinsic to the universal intent in each confession. "The God believed in is the God of all." "The horizon of universality can only be approached by transforming engagement with the other religions," which honors their diversity. This activity is "animated by confidence that Christian understanding can expand to accommodate and be transformed by insight and truth in other religious sources." "Clear where it is working *from*," Heim concludes, "such comparative theology has no predetermined limit on where it might *go*."

Francis X. Clooney's sensitive, nuanced studies of Hindu and Christian texts have provided models for comparative theology, virtually defining the field. Here he argues forcefully that the Catholic tradition already provides "a solid foundation for finding God present in the wide world" precisely because of "a distinctive Catholic dynamic: the universal in tension with the

DOI: 10.4324/9780429000973-23

Jerry L. Martin

particular (the Catholic and the catholic), a hierarchical tradition with settled doctrines, a commitment to rational and systematizing inquiry alongside openness to the imaginative and intuitive, the freedom of the individual amid a strongly ordered community." Clooney reminds us of the Church's history of "accommodation and engagement with cultures," rooted in a "Logos theology" attesting that God's wisdom is "everywhere implicit in the human reality, which is therefore intelligible and accessible to reasoned inquiry." The Catholic sense of sacramentality suggests that "particular things and actions can be sites of the sacred," inviting us to "recognize God in the particulars of other traditions." Setting aside doctrine does not necessarily make us "more open." We might just become "directionless, aimless." It would be a mistake to give up on doctrine for the sake of an "idealized complete, unlimited openness to everything." "What is needed," he concludes, "is a theology with walls, a home with foundations and walls and windows and doors, a roof held up by the walls and – why not, a welcome mat at the entrance."

Christianity is not the only religion with a capacity for teaching beyond its walls. Perhaps all religions can. Here Jeffery D. Long argues that the Vedanta tradition of Ramakrishna is already a Theology Without Walls. The founding figures of multiple traditions – such as Jesus and Buddha – might be avatars. Universal in its aspirations, Vedanta remains one tradition among others. It affirms universal ideas, such as "a divine reality which manifests Itself to human beings" but renders this idea concrete in, for example, Ramakrishna as the avatar of our current historical epoch, whose mission is "to teach the harmony and the ultimate unity of all religions." The aim of Vedanta is the realization of the divine in every being. According to Sri Aurobindo, the Buddha is a divine incarnation who chooses to set aside his divinity in order to show us the path to realizing our inherent divinity. Jesus, too, is regarded as divine. Perhaps the Jesus who says, "I am the way, the truth, and the life; no one comes to the Father but through me" is the same "I" who, as Krishna, says, "In whatever way living beings approach me, thus do I receive them; all paths lead to me."

Rethinking a religion through cultural forms different from those in which it was originally articulated may create unanticipated possibilities. Christian theology developed in part by articulating the Jesus event through the categories of Greek and Roman philosophy. As Christianity has settled into Asia, it is beginning to articulate itself in different cultural forms. Witness the remarkable story of Hyo-Dong Lee. Born in South Korea, Lee's spiritual life began in an atmosphere of "diffuse religion" – ancestor veneration and spirit worship alongside Buddhist, Confucian, and Daoist practices. Becoming an evangelical Protestant in his youth, Lee was still attracted to Daoism, but saw no way to reconcile the two. Influenced by Rahner and Moltmann, his thinking came to have "a decisively pneumatocentric orientation," which led him to Hegel's Absolute Spirit and then back again to Daoist thought and neo-Confucian metaphysics, with reality as the dynamic interaction of psychophysical energy (qi) and pattern (li). Lee discovered the Korean philosophy of qi of Yulgok and Nonmun, which envisioned the ultimate as a kind of, using Spinoza's term, *natura naturans*, as "the Daodejing did." Incorporating insights from Whitehead, Deleuze, and Catherine Keller, he turned to the Korean tradition of Donghak, or Eastern Learning, according to which Ultimate Qi is also a personal deity, Lord Heaven, who is both within and outside the human self and, when encountered, makes one a "bearer of Lord Heaven" with democratic, egalitarian, and liberationist implications. Lee's chapter, he says, could well be called "My Path to a Confucian–Daoist–Donghak–Christian Theology of Qi." That characterization signals the creative possibilities of Theology Without Walls.

18 More window than wall

The comparative expansion of confessional theology

S. Mark Heim

Is it possible to do a "Theology Without Walls" (TWW) in any meaningful sense while existentially or conceptually committed to a particular religious path? Is it not precisely the limitations of such adherence that free-range religious inquiry seeks to escape? Such incompatibility is certainly the case, if we conceive of TWW as an omnibus totality, an "all at once" performance that somehow combines awareness of and openness to all religious data with a simultaneous, impartial, and comparative assessment of it. Stated so flatly, this theoretical extreme seems as unrealistic in practice as an extreme particularist approach seems uninterested in principle.[1] Who knows what all the data are and what it means to consider them appropriately? Jerry L. Martin says "ideally the theologian without walls gives full credit to all religious data, to all spiritual epiphanies, whatever their source or auspices."[2] Does this mean that such a theologian treats all such data *ab initio* as grist for the mill of assessment, all boundaries as only circumstantial artifacts, on the way to reaching some specific and located spiritual conclusion? Or does it mean that such a theologian must end as well as begin with a perspective that resembles or relies upon no existing religious perspective more than another? A settled religious conviction can bring a distorting lens to unfamiliar sources and perspectives. But the fragile innocence of an intensely interested but entirely undecided approach to the complete set of religious phenomena is both hard to attain and difficult to preserve.

If we apply the "full credit" assumption in the candidacy phase of personal decision making, it describes a necessarily transient phase of spiritual and intellectual practice – one that must quickly give way to at least some working judgements and theories reflecting one's own experiences and reasoning. TWW stands apart from strictly descriptive and academic comparative study by virtue of its frank normative interests and personal engagement. Its major purpose is to seek to make sense of and give meaning to the data from a specific interpretive stance, one that implies personal application and commitment. Any emerging TWW would build by selection and evaluation. Its practitioners end by themselves constituting part of the "data," adherent to and participant in some particular religious approach, however traditionally or nontraditionally defined. From this

DOI: 10.4324/9780429000973-24

view, TWW is a novelistic religious journey, more about the traveler than the destination.

What of those who cannot pretend to approximate a blank slate starting point or a dramatically composite one? It would be odd if a search whose premise is an unrestricted field of religious hypotheses and sources were in some way to exclude those already seriously practicing any of the particular paths within that field or those whose quest had led them to some operative conclusions. We could take the "full credit" dimension of TWW as pointing not so much to a departure point as to a horizon. It is an aspiration to integrate all of the religious data within the most maximally comprehensive and practicable religious understanding. What distinguishes TWW from exclusivists in current religions or individuals with a definitive syncretic solution to religious diversity is the conviction that this maximal integration does not yet exist. It is not evident that it can be had simply by making a choice among existing religious options as they stand, nor among academic interpretations as they stand. TWW is energized by the possibility of a new, collective, religious option for thought and practice. It seeks an interpretation that sees or elicits something new in the religions, a perspective of understanding and practice not fully on offer elsewhere, one that is unrestrictedly open for all to adopt. In this sense, it is not only an additional perspective on the religious data but a new addition to them. This is TWW as pioneering discovery, more about the destination than the traveler. In this respect, it is parallel to the origination of certain religions, like Ba'haism or Sikhism or (by some historical accounts) Islam, which explicitly understood themselves to be an integration of other existing religions (as known in their context).[3] In fact, there is no reason that the horizon point should not turn out to be a new version of an existing faith: a revitalized Ba'haism, an inclusive Hinduism, an expanded Christianity or Islam.

If we consider TWW in this light, it need not preclude participation by people as soon as they have drawn any religious conclusions. Some of the most developed works of thought prototypical of TWW – the writings of Robert Neville, or Keith Ward, or Raimon Panikkar – have a particularist profile (their thought begins from a Christian background) but "come down" on many controverted issues among the religions without necessarily conforming to Christian authorities. Such works have a somewhat indeterminate constituency, in that their thought does not "belong" to a specified religious community or correspond to the practice of any. The key emphasis in TWW is not on neutrality, but on the effort to build thicker, deeper, and presumably more comprehensive religious perspectives. This constructive work can be done from a specific location, because its constant effect (and aim) is to produce a more richly specified religious perspective from which the process then continues. We need not exclude confessional forms of TWW if we think of TWW less in terms of a binary state that is on or off and more in terms of incremental approximations.[4] No theology lacks walls, as no complex organism lacks a body plan and no cells lack membranes. Many theologies may be distinctive and fruitful by virtue of their removal of *some* walls.

A Theology Without Walls might measure itself by the assumptions that it removes, dropping exclusive appeal to scriptures from one religion, or definitive appeal to reason and logic as defined in one cultural tradition rather than another. But it can also develop through the expansion of horizons. The impetus within a confessional religious perspective that drives toward consideration of the full range of religious data stems from the intrinsic universal intent in that faith. On one side, that universal intent expresses itself in a mode of witness, the missional conviction of Buddhists or Christians or Muslims that the truth they know is available and relevant to all people. On another side, that universal intent is expressed as "faith seeking understanding." This is less the sharing out from the tradition to others than the working in of the truth, beauty, and wisdom whose reality "outside" the tradition requires connection with that inside. The God believed in is the God of all. Understanding of that God through revelation and reflection extends to all aspects of the world. A living confessional faith hopes to more fully understand truth that one already partially grasps, to understand new things that one had not previously grasped, and to discover coherence across a more and more comprehensive field of human and natural phenomena. In fact, this hope is part of a larger eschatological imagination and expectation for what is not yet manifest. An existing life of faith can throw up barriers of prejudgment. But it is also a powerful instrument of tacit knowledge in the process of understanding others, a defining part that suggests an unrealized whole.

Christian revelation and faith are understood as integral steps in the flourishing and realization of the world meant (in addition to their healing and liberating effect) to make the world more intelligible and to be most fully intelligible themselves in the most comprehensive context of human experience. This conviction is often a matter of tension, but theology has largely been defined by the universal project it defines, whether the wider context was provided by Greek philosophy, historical analysis, or modern science. Though people often speak of religious faith "walling itself off" from the results of, say, historical study or scientific investigation, theology in principle holds there can be no wall between truths in one area and those in another. Religion might be thought to be the one exception to this, the one area where Christian theology has all the answers and no questions. But the matter is quite different if one understands the religious sphere as a realm of God's providential engagement. "In many and various ways God spoke of old" and "The Spirit blows where it will."[5] Before the rise of separated distinct disciplines of historical or scientific study, what we call religion and philosophy were the primary realms in which this search for universal breadth and correlation was exercised. To leave the religions aside would be to default on the "faith seeking understanding" conviction about the comprehensive character of that understanding.

Plainly, the extension of the theological quest into the religions depends in major part on convictions adopted within that part of theology called the theology of religions. There are theological teachings that discourage any expectation of value in the study of other religions and those that encourage or even mandate it. Even theological authorization or encouragement of such learning is no substitute for the actual demonstration of it. This vision of a permeable framework is what John Cobb called a picture of "mutual transformation" between the religions. The horizon of universality can only be approached by transforming engagement with the other religions. And if "universality" itself is a dangerous ideal without diversity and complexity, then the effort to approach it comparatively from various located, confessional spaces has a decided virtue: it works with and honors that diversity.

Comparative theology is the best current concrete demonstration of that learning and the best example of TWW as an expanding confessional perspective.[6] It might be considered a bilateral Theology Without Walls, a "reading together" of sources from two (or more) religious traditions, typically one from a "home" tradition and one from another tradition in which one has some level of learning or participation. A comparative theologian embraces their confessional location, seeking to enrich and expand the truth found there. One "passes over" into immersion in the study of another and returns with enriched perspectives to be shared with the home community.[7] What distinguishes such activity from TWW is clearer in theory than in practice, largely defined by the hypothetical depth of the change that may result from comparative study. In its contemporary form, comparative theology practitioners are predominantly Christians, operating from an acknowledged Christian confessional or even institutional standpoint, but scholars from other traditions increasingly take part as well.[8]

A comparative theologian typically identifies with one religious tradition and undertakes intensive study of a particular source in their own tradition and some particular source in another. For a Christian, this work is part of a search for the most universal shape of Christianity. It is animated by confidence that Christian understanding can expand to accommodate and be transformed by insight and truth in other religious sources.[9] And it is animated equally by humility: the recognition that this fuller understanding does not yet exist. God's nature far exceeds our categories, and the religions resist assimilation into our existing forms precisely because they contain truth about the divine and the world not sufficiently grasped by our operative terms. Such comparative theology is driven less by the apophatic conviction that God so exceeds description as to make distinctions between religions meaningless and more by the positive impetus suggesting that what we have known of God draws us to the expectation of a fuller coherence.

Comparative theology is a kind of "retail" TWW. It does not address walls in general, only in particular. Its most common format is concrete and limited. It does not compare Christianity and Hinduism, but reads together two specific texts – for instance, the *Essence of the Three Auspicious*

Mysteries by the Hindu writer Śrī Vedānta Deśika and the *Treatise on the Love of God* by St. Francis de Sales, to take an example from the work of Francis X. Clooney.[10] This encounter is impossible without some attention to the fact that de Sales is a Catholic, not a Protestant; French and not English or Spanish; and that this text is both similar and different to his more famous work *Introduction to the Devout Life*. All these bear upon an understanding of the text. Likewise, one must attend to the fact that Vedānta Deśika was a Vaishnavite, not a Shaivite; wrote in a variety of Indian languages; and was an artist as well as a teacher. In other words, there are countless specific things that distinguished each of these writers from others of the same "religion" in their time and after, as well as the things that united them. And there are elements – images, topics, language – that resonate with each other across the two texts, as well as things that contrast or that simply fail to connect. These mazes of similarity and difference disarm our conceptual generalities.

Rather than erasing an entire border between two entities, "Hinduism" and "Christianity," the theologian has pierced one specific wall: the one separating the backyards of these two individuals, the convention that had meant the readers of one text were never readers of the other. Despite their irreducible specificity, each of the writings is also woven into a wider framework, looking back to earlier texts in their traditions and drawing upon prior commentators and practices in forming their own voices. A Christian reader who wants to follow Vedānta Deśika's line of thought must look sympathetically with him through the lens of prior Hindu writers toward the Vedas and their assumed subjects. In both traditions, reading is itself a religious act. To attentively take up the *Essence of the Three Auspicious Mysteries* is in some measure to participate in that act with its writer. Francis X. Clooney called his early studies "experiments," whose results could be gleaned only after the fact, in assessing how his Christian attitudes and insights had been permanently shaped by exposure to the comparative text.[11]

A different work of comparative theology, by Clooney or another scholar, will lower yet another specific wall and beat a small path of conversation and questioning back and forth across that line. And so on. This process may or may not be accompanied by an extensive theological statement on the principle of treating revered texts of other religious traditions as theological sources. As liberation theology puts primary emphasis on praxis, so, too, does comparative theology in its way. Its practice is focused on repeatedly crossing very concrete boundaries, breaching small walls. Clear where it is working *from*, such comparative theology has no predetermined limit on where it might *go* or on how much the theology and faith of the home tradition may be transformed.

Comparative theology will necessarily include work of wider scope than I have just described, though more limited than the large-scale projects of writers like Neville. An example would be my own recent work drawing upon a classic Buddhist text to develop an extended comparison between the path of Christ and the path of the bodhisattva (Heim 2019b). Such "middle-level" discussions are necessary if key learnings are to be incorporated into the doctrinal source code of a religious tradition and that tradition transformed into a more universal version of itself by means of the TWW dynamic.

Comparative theology is not, in practice, the omnibus enterprise that TWW can appear to be. It is never global, in the sense of addressing "all religious data" at once. It addresses that "all" in a slow, cumulative manner. It is dialogical and concrete, considering not what all religions, or even two traditions, as such have to say about divine–human relationships, but what it is like to read particular Christian hymns to Mary in connection to some particular Hindu hymns to specific goddesses or what it is like to see the work of Christ in light of the path of the bodhisattva.[12] This concreteness is further specified in that one end of the comparison is always located closer to "home," in one's own tradition, though not necessarily in what one has hitherto taken as its most prominent or central sources. Comparative theology is particular theology seeking a steadily greater universality.

A TWW could be taken to be a theology with no "inside," no shape or structure to frame it or to order a life lived in accordance with it. But in truth as TWWs develop – whether in individual scholars or as collective endeavors – they will necessarily either take on some such structure or inherit and maintain it. A comparative Christian theology is a home with plentiful windows, and new ones being constantly added. Such an expansive confessional theology, one that seeks its newer and more universal form, could be taken by those outside to be "walled in," with no true access to the widest religious world. And critics within the confession in question will warn that the expansion constitutes a drastic renovation and threatens the load-bearing integrity of the entire structure. My hope is that these cautions prove to be similar to the assumptions of a pre-gothic architecture, assumptions that could be definitively reversed only with the actual realization of buildings that are more window than wall. Comparative confessional theologies of this ilk have an important role to play in the TWW discussion.

Notes

1 More could be said about this as a reservation or question for TWW as a whole. See Heim (2016).
2 Jerry Martin, in a personal communication, August 10, 2018.
3 On Islam, see Donner (2010).
4 In this chapter I focus on the extent to which Christian theologians might participate in a Theology Without Walls, but many of the observations may hold for other locations as well.
5 Heb 1:1 and Jn 3:8, respectively.
6 For a summary, see Heim (2019a).
7 Some scholars appreciative of comparative theology challenge this paradigm, in that they question whether one needs a "home" location to engage in it, or

whether the location might be defined other than by identification with an exist-ing communion. This is clearly relevant to the TWW discussion, but because I want to focus here on the possible role for explicitly confessional theology, I limit my discussion in this chapter to comparative theology of that type. For more on comparative theology without a "home" tradition, see the Introduction in Brecht and Locklin (2016). Also see Corigliano (2016).

8 See for instance the essays by Muna Tatari and Shoshana Razel Gordon-Guedalia on Muslim and Jewish examples in Clooney and von Stosch (2018).

9 That search can be seen to have an implicit apologetic dimension – expressed in John Cobb's hope for a fruitful competition among religions over which could prove most adept at honoring and incorporating the truths of others. See Cobb (1990).

10 See Clooney (2008).

11 See Clooney (1993).

12 The former example is from Clooney (2005).

References

Brecht, Mara, and Reid B. Locklin. (2016). *Comparative Theology in the Millen-nial Classroom: Hybrid Identities, Negotiated Boundaries. Routledge Research in Religion and Education.* New York: Routledge, Taylor & Francis Group. doi:10.4324/9781315718279

Clooney, Francis X. 1993. *Theology After Vedanta: An Experiment in Comparative Theology (Suny Series, Toward a Comparative Philosophy of Religions).* Albany: State University of New York Press. doi:10.1177/002071529803900413

Clooney, Francis X. 2005. *Divine Mother, Blessed Mother: Hindu God-desses and the Virgin Mary.* Oxford; New York: Oxford University Press. doi:10.1093/0195170377.003.0005

Clooney, Francis X. 2008. *Beyond Compare: St. Francis De Sales and Sri Vedanta Desika on Loving Surrender to God.* Washington, DC: Georgetown University Press. doi:10.1017/s0360966900008069

Clooney, Francis X., and Klaus von Stosch. 2018. *How to Do Comparative Theol-ogy.* New York: Fordham University Press.

Cobb, John. 1990. "Beyond Pluralism." In *Christian Uniqueness Reconsid-ered*, edited by Gavin D'Costa. 92–93. Maryknoll: Orbis Books. doi:10.1017/s0036930600046044

Corigliano, Stephanie. 2016. "Theologizing for the Yoga Community? Commit-ment and Hybridity in Comparative Theology." In *Comparing Faithfully: Insights for Systematic Theological Reflection*, edited by Michelle Voss Roberts, 324–350. New York, NY: Fordham University Press. doi:10.5422/fordham/978082 3278404.003.0016

Donner, Fred M. 2010. *Muhammad and the Believers: At the Origins of Islam.* Cam-bridge, MA: The Belknap Press of Harvard University Press.

Heim, Mark S. 2016. "Of Two Minds About a Theology Without Walls." *Journal of Ecumenical Studies* 51 (4): 479–486. doi:10.1353/ecu.2016.0043

Heim, Mark S. 2019a. "Comparative Theology at 25: The End of the Beginning." *Modern Theology* 35 (1): 163–180. doi:10.1111/moth.12450

Heim, Mark S. 2019b. *Crucified Wisdom Theological Reflection on Christ and the Bodhisattva.* New York: Fordham University Press. doi:10.2307/j.ctv75d9z2

Selected Bibliography

Brecht, Mara, and Reid B. Locklin. 2016. *Comparative Theology in the Millennial Classroom: Hybrid Identities, Negotiated Boundaries*. Routledge Research in Religion and Education. New York: Routledge, Taylor & Francis Group.

Clooney, Francis X. 2008. *Beyond Compare: St. Francis De Sales and *Sr*I Vedanta Desika on Loving Surrender to God*. Washington, DC: Georgetown University Press.

———. 2005. *Divine Mother, Blessed Mother: Hindu Goddesses and the Virgin Mary*. Oxford; New York: Oxford University Press,.

———. 1993. *Theology after Ved*Anta: An Experiment in Comparative Theology*. Suny Series, toward a Comparative Philosophy of Religions. Albany: State University of New York Press.

Clooney, Francis X., and Klaus von Stosch. 2018. *How to Do Comparative Theology*. New York: Fordham University Press.

Cobb, John. 1990. "Beyond "Pluralism"." In *Christian Uniqueness Reconsidered*, edited by Gavin D'Costa. Faith Meets Faith, 81–95. Maryknoll: Orbis Books.

Corigliano, Stephanie. 2016. "Theologizing for the Yoga Community? Commitment and Hybridity in Comparative Theology." In *Comparing Faithfully: Insights for Systematic Theological Reflection*, edited by Michelle Voss Roberts, 324–350. New York, NY: Fordham University Press.

Donner, Fred McGraw. 2010. *Muhammad and the Believers: At the Origins of Islam*. Cambridge, MA: The Belknap Press of Harvard University Press.

Heim, S. Mark. 2016. "Of Two Minds About a Theology Without Walls." *Journal of Ecumenical Studies* 51 (4): 479–486.

Heim, S. Mark. 2019a. "Comparative Theology at 25: The End of the Beginning." *Modern Theology* 35 (1).

———. 2019b. *Crucified Wisdom Theological Reflection on Christ and the Bodhisattva*. New York: Fordham University Press. https://TE6UZ4HK6Z.search.serialssolutions.com/ejp/?libHash=TE6UZ4HK6Z#/search/?searchControl=title&searchType=title_code&criteria=TC0002059624.

19 Strong walls for an open faith

Francis X. Clooney, SJ

The Catholic tradition throughout history shows us how confessional commitments provide a solid foundation for finding God present in the wide world around us. The Church is, briefly put, catholic (global, worldwide) as well as Catholic (an institution centered in Rome); but if it is not Catholic, it ceases also to be catholic. I admit that the Church's narrative of itself is tainted with self-regard and rarely leaves room for the full self-articulation of the other. Nevertheless, there is a distinctive Catholic dynamic: the universal in tension with the particular (the Catholic and the catholic), a hierarchical tradition with settled doctrines, a commitment to rational and systematizing inquiry alongside openness to the imaginative and intuitive, the freedom of the individual amid a strongly ordered community. This dynamic provided a fertile ground wherein interreligious learning can occur, because of the specificity of the Catholic manner of being in the world and not despite it. This firm structure – support walls, floors and roofs, doors and windows – has a contribution to make in an interreligious context, and indeed is arguably preferable to the ideal of an entirely open space.

A great tradition

In this short space, the best way to proceed is by hearkening to the great story the Church tells about itself, even if this story, like any such fond account, is best heard with a touch of skepticism.

As the Church thinks of itself, its history is a history of accommodation and engagement with cultures. The history of Israel combined a strong sense of vocation with endless engagement with surrounding cultures and with all the virtues and pitfalls of trying to balance openness and fidelity. The Church of which I speak is, of course, the *Roman* Catholic Church, which moved from its Jewish roots to an engagement with Greek and Roman cultures. The empire was hostile to the Christian message, but then became the vehicle of Christian identity and community. The Church was, from its beginnings to its self-realization (for a time), in the context of empire.

To speak of the development of the field of comparative theology with attention to Catholic roots in recent centuries is in part to rehearse

DOI: 10.4324/9780429000973-25

Catholicism's own narrative of how Catholic tradition has worked from the beginnings of the Church until now: that history has always been an interreligious history. In a sense, the history of the Church is conducive to comparative theology. But we must both hear this self-account and consider it with some skepticism.

But first, a few words are in order with respect to the general background in which an open, interreligiously attentive Catholic theology might arise and flourish. The Catholic tradition adheres to the view that the world is essentially good. Nature speaks of God, and cultures, too, in their essential goodness speak of the divine, a truth and beauty that are never entirely obscured. The proper disposition is to expect to find the divine everywhere. The Catholic tradition is full of examples of how confessional commitments provide a solid base for noting the presence of God in the world around us, times and places rich in at least implicit epiphanies of Christ. The tradition of Logos theology attests that God's word and wisdom are everywhere implicit in the human reality, which is therefore intelligible and accessible to reasoned inquiry. Seeds of the Word are scattered, nonsystematically, in all the world's traditions.

The expectation that the Logos is discernible, if not everywhere, nevertheless in places near and far from centers of Christian culture, and thus at work and to be discovered amid the cultures of the world, may be taken also to highlight the characteristic rational current of Catholic tradition, a tendency that encourages both conversation and argument. Cultures and religions are intelligible, commensurable, and open to intelligent and spiritually meaningful exchange. This openness – instantiated again and again throughout history – is in turn accompanied by a more focused and narrow confidence that one can sort out the good from the bad, highlighting what is productive while refuting what one judges to be inadequate. Broad-ranging intellectual inquiry facilitates the maturation of the faith, even as it provides the conditions for apologetics, which at times lapse into polemic. Missionaries through the ages have been energized by various forms of the expectation that we can, with discernment, find God already present in the other. The Church is, briefly put, catholic as well as Catholic in both its dispositions and in its metaphysical and epistemological expectations.

The Catholic sense of sacramentality is also germane here, at least intuitively, because the idea that particular things and actions can be sites of the sacred opens the way for a deep reverence for reality as a whole. Versed in sacrament and liturgy, Catholic tradition fosters the dispositions by which one can recognize the presence of God in the *particulars* of other traditions, in the holy manifest in certain times and places. For Catholic tradition is thoroughly liturgical: words are never merely words, books never merely books. Rather, what we learn is enacted in Church and world, and by analogy, interreligious learning, even as a form of study, is always more than "merely" reading a book. The expectation of finding God in all things has a materiality and concreteness to it. There is, to put it simply, a catholicity to the Catholic view of the world that, doctrinal and ecclesial restraints notwithstanding, has nevertheless allowed the Catholic tradition to learn interreligiously over and over again.

Such dispositions open the way to learning, intended or unintended, in which whatever the doctrinal limits may be, but there is also there is fluid exchange across cultural and even religious boundaries. But such exchange also indicates, on a practical level, the probability of apologetics: we can argue the truth with them, showing the rationality of the Christian and the irrationality of systems that clash with the Christian. Openness and argument go together. All of this creates a frame in which comparative theological learning, as comparative and theological, is possible and religiously significant.

Edifying examples

The story takes on new life and significance in the Middle Ages, as the maturation of the great Catholic theological traditions of the West learn to anticipate and experiment in receiving wisdom from traditions outside the West. An intensely Catholic commitment to reason and to the Catholic faith as universally true and locally realized has quite often been productive of interreligious learning. Thomas Aquinas (1225–1274) is one of the supreme explicators and defenders of Christian doctrine in the history of Christianity, and at times he had hard things to say about non-Christians. No surprise. But as David Burrell showed decades ago (e.g., Burrell 1986, 1993), Aquinas also was an avid reader of Aristotle, as made available to the Christian West by Arab Muslim writers. He engaged in thinking through and arguing with Aristotle and his Arab interpreters, while likewise engaging and arguing with Jewish thinkers such as Maimonides. Aquinas's mind was capacious, to be sure, but there seems to be little evidence to sustain the view that he would have been more intellectually open had he a looser, permeable sense of doctrine: his quest for a right understanding of God's world led him to be open to truth wherever it was to be found. Nicholas of Cusa (1401–1464), a cardinal of the Church, plumbed deeply the mysteries of Christian faith in his brilliant philosophical and theological writings, and in works such as *De Pace Fidei* and *Cribratio Alkorani* he was also an extraordinary pioneer in imagining the conditions for interreligious learning, and how such learning might proceed, by way of the actual study of texts such as the Qur'an. Seen from the vantage point of the twenty-first century, this medieval learning was modest, fraught with misunderstandings, and less open than it might have been. But the thrust of this learning, grounded in a Christian commitment to the truth of reality and the truth of the faith, models the substantive and tough interconnection of faith and reason for which I have been arguing.[1]

In early modernity, the Catholic story went global in a new way. The support walls of faith and convictions regarding the narrow gates to salvation structured homes from which the early Jesuit missionaries in Asia (if I may stick to examples I know well) into a very creative learning wherein mission and intellectual openness fueled one another.[2] Francis Xavier (1506–1552) was certainly negative toward other religions but nevertheless found himself having to learn to deal with cultural differences, precisely to continue the missionary work he felt himself obliged to: mission drove him to cultural experimentation, as when he re-presented himself for the sake of the learned Japanese leaders he wished to influence. Roberto de Nobili (1579–1656) re-created himself, as it were, in the course of his mission in south India. He changed his dress and customs, mastered the Tamil language, and sought ways to express the faith in accord with Tamil ways of moral and religious thinking.[3] He was steadfastly critical of idolatry and harsh in finding moral depravity in Hindu mythology, but he did not abandon his intellectual project. Rather, he combined selective openness and selective negativity.

But not all missionaries are alike. An interesting contrast can be made with a Jesuit several centuries later. Constantine Beschi, SJ (1680–1747), also working in south India, did not disown Catholic doctrine, but in the potent chemistry of missionary fervor and a sense of the need for a new way of presenting the faith, he turned out to be a creative writer who could freshly re-envision the faith. He mastered the Tamil language and studied its literatures, among those a marvelous and unparalleled epic, *Tempāvani* (*The Unfading Garland*), which tells the story of the Incarnation – and much of the Bible – in high Tamil poetry, and from the perspective of St. Joseph. His turn to the literary provided him ways to re-express the faith without hammering it home and without giving it up. Yet he is the same Beschi who argued vociferously with the nearby Lutherans. His catechetical writing – for example, the *Manual for Catechists* – is primarily about habituating people to the faith, rather than attacks on the Hindu. And even in the *Tempāvani*, a negative attitude toward the pagan can be seen.

The nineteenth century is a sobering caution to my optimism regarding the Catholic manner of openness, because it does not give us very good examples of Catholic interreligious learning. This may have been due to the defensiveness of a Church feeling itself to be threatened by the hostility of rationalism in a skeptical Europe. Every claim made in the missions about non-Christian religions had to be received and restated with a mindfulness of how this new knowledge would be used in Europe, where reports about the non-Christian world might variously aid or undermine Catholic faith. Typical of a defensive Church were the polemical works of scholar/practitioners such as Leo Meurin, SJ (1825–1895) in Bombay (see his lecture, "God and Brahm"). In the West, Catholic writing was marginal to the developing fields of comparative religion and comparative theology was and primarily resistant to the swiftly changing intellectual cultures of the West. In the United States, Augustus Thébaud, SJ (1807–1885) wrote the weighty *Gentilism* and *The Church and the Gentile World at the First Promulgation of the Gospel*, a learned investigation of the origins of religions and their relationship to Christianity, which in retrospect seems more concerned about the West's encroaching rationalism than the pros and cons of actual interreligious learning. But more research needs to be done on the little-studied Catholic attitudes toward interreligious learning in the nineteenth century.

We see the revival of a more nuanced yet still very Catholic view of other religions late in the nineteenth century. Interestingly, it was a convert to Catholicism who was instrumental in this new venture. William Wallace (1863–1922)[4] rethought his Christian identity rather dramatically through his encounter with Hinduism and, as a result, became a Catholic and then a Jesuit. A staunch Catholic resentful of both Anglicanism and empire, Wallace turned out to be a vigorous Catholic defender of Hinduism against its detractors. He insisted that the next generation of Jesuits had to study Hinduism deeply, with the necessary linguistic tools in place. As a result of his efforts, there flourished in Calcutta in the early twentieth century a school of Jesuit Indology under the notable leadership of Pierre Johanns (1882–1955), Georges Dandoy (1882–1962), Robert Antoine (1914–1981), Pierre Fallon (1912–1985), and Richard de Smet (1916–1997). Johanns and Dandoy cooperated in the famous "To Christ through the Vedānta" essays, published serially in *The Light of the East*. Here, too, we see formidable learning, harnessed for the sake of understanding positively major streams of Hindu intellectual thought, yet by the measure of the theology and philosophy of Thomas Aquinas, which provided both narrow restraints and a defining focus for new learning. Their commitment to Aquinas provided a coherent frame and confidence that progress in an interreligious theological understanding could be achieved; perhaps they would have been more open-minded without reference to Aquinas and the tight hold of Thomistic thinking, but more likely they would not have undertaken such study at all.

We might continue this exploration by paying attention to still other figures who can be honored as icons of the prehistory of comparative theology. I have in mind figures such as the innovative contemplatives Jules Monchanin (1895–1957) and Henri Le Saux (1910–1973). In the late 1940s, in deep south India, they founded the Saccidananda Ashram (Abode of Being, Consciousness, and Bliss), which came to be known more popularly as Shantivanam. Both took very seriously the truths of the Catholic faith and would not discard them. Confident in the adaptability of their Catholicism, however, they sought to free it of its Western cultural baggage in order to reimagine Christian contemplative life, and deeply root it, as they said, in Indian soil. Each in his own way delved deeply into Vedānta and Hindu texts, seeking both to find Christ in the mystery of Hindu spirituality and to rediscover Christ through Hinduism. Their struggles, intellectual (in finding common ground between Hindus and Christians), spiritual (in becoming intimate to Hindu learning in its depths while still a Christian), and practical (in setting up and maintaining the ashram), characterize them as persons; were they not Catholic, they probably would not have come to India at all.

Monchanin and Le Saux would not have labeled themselves comparative theologians; they feature what are virtues necessary to the work of comparative theology: sustained study and doctrinal commitments, yet without letting Christian doctrines turn into the tools of a priori judgments about other religions. Here it suffices to say that these figures represent nicely the holistic nature of modern Catholic learning, such as that which infuses comparative theology. Of course, similar representations of the roots of comparative theology might be set forth with respect to other parts of the world as well.

We can also think in this regard of Thomas Merton (1915–1968), whose sustained and deepening interest in other religions remained even to the end in service to the renewal of Christian contemplative identity. Raimon Panikkar (1918–2010) deserves attention too, as a figure whose experience and aspirations are closely aligned with the work of comparative theology. In his own signal fashion he brings together the riches of Hindu and Christian traditions, transforming his own religious identity in the process. His "imparative theology" reflects some of the same confidence and hope, and commitment to reading practices, that inspires comparative theology.

In the twentieth century, we witness more Catholic scholars coming to the fore and contributing to comparative study *outside* the mission fields. Here I can mention just a few of the notable figures. The twentieth century abounds in figures who exemplify Catholic learning at its best. Louis Massignon (1883–1962) was a seriously committed Catholic even as he became one of the greatest scholars of mystical Islam.[5] Henri de Lubac (1896–1991),[6] no theological pluralist, silenced by the Church in mid-career but later in life in a position of rejecting the honor of becoming a cardinal of the Church, studied Buddhism in some depth. He went far beyond the needs of apologetics, determined as he was to find a way of connecting its wisdom with Christian revelation, casting it as a highest form of natural questing for what had been given to Christians fully as God's gift. We can also think in this regard of Thomas Merton (1915–1968), who sought to deepen Christian identity in and through bold interreligious openness.[7]

And so on. Such examples could be multiplied and must be deepened beyond this series of honorable mentions, but my point is precisely to evoke an array of witnesses: learned, believing Catholic Christians who also crossed boundaries and learned interreligiously. None of these figures was doing precisely the work we need to do today, in part because our attitudes and expectations (regarding both Christian and non-Christian) have changed, and in part because they, like us, were ever responding to the particular historical moment wherein their thinking and writing took shape. But possessed of very strong religious convictions, they managed to exemplify serious interreligious learning and creative engagement across religious borders, and thus exemplify the style of being Christian that is still needed today.

On doctrine

We must now step back and take a closer look at the foundations of this tradition of real and persisting openness. The examples in themselves are telling: that these figures are all Catholic merits some further consideration if the point is to be more than anecdotal and inspirational. All these figures, from the early Church up to contemporary Catholic thinkers engaged in interreligious learning, worked within a clear doctrinal frame, engaging in truths not of their own making. I suggest that if we understand doctrine properly, we will not be inclined to think them better off had they left doctrine behind.

The theological texts most worth reading are those written with both seriousness and humility, respectful of the power of words that direct our attention to truth and urge us to think and judge after our minds have conformed to that truth. The combination of faith – its doctrinal formulation clearly asserted and stubbornly held so as to be productive of inquiry, not stifling of it – remains potent. Doctrinal words can work, provided they do not draw attention to themselves and in that way become obstacles.

The relation of words, learning, and doctrines – and claims of truth – of course remains complex, and an adequate assessment of doctrine is well beyond the scope of this small chapter. Even if the broad lines of doctrinal claims are clear in creed or catechism, new information constantly and properly upsets settled ways of learning, while explanations that aim at smoother understanding inevitably end up complicating things in new ways. Making doctrine meaningful and fruitful is never a matter of mere application, but rather the discovery of a creative ground. This careful compounding of faith and understanding – inquiring faith, humble understanding – has its own intensity. It drives a truly open search that brings commitments and doctrines, dearly held, into contact with what is true and holy in other traditions, precisely because (in many cases) such doctrines are seen to be competing for the same space. As a result, there is always new work to be done, to make sure that our words, individual and communal, do not drift away into side issues near or far. But this ought not distract us from the work of study. The solution is not the abandonment of doctrine, but a more careful use of doctrine to open up a perspective on the world rather than closing it down.

Wesley Hill's reflections on the purpose of creeds sheds light on the power of careful, insistent, yet humble writing with respect to realities beyond words:

> The Creed safeguards the mystery and wild freedom of God; it does not box it in and tame it. The point of the Creed isn't that its words are satisfactory. It's that those words refuse our inveterate preference for premature theological satisfaction.
>
> (Hill 2016, 15)

Doctrinal reflection is not so much a matter of making things perfectly clear as instead ruling out bad alternatives that drain our words of God's mystery:

> Approaching Jesus in *this* way [attentive to doctrine] turns *language back on itself, exposing our poverty.* Confessing what is beyond language, *the creeds use the words least likely to diminish the mystery* while at the same time *gesturing at its depths.* To say otherwise, to reject the Creed as so much rationalist mystery-refusal, is to get things exactly backward. It is the Creed, not the heresies it proscribes, that dares to confess God in Christ *uncontainable, unclassifiable, and incomprehensible.*
>
> (Hill 2016, 16)

The words I have italicized serve us well interreligiously. The disciplined words of creedal statements do not block the path to interreligious learning, but inculcate virtues of mind and heart that direct us properly toward the mystery of our own tradition and, I suggest, the mystery of the other as well. Without doctrine, we have no guarantee that we will simply be "more open," because we might just as well become directionless, aimless.

Truth in its doctrinal form focuses inquiry, helping inquiry to avoid losing its way and ceasing to be real interreligious learning. A serious commitment to the truths of religious traditions can guide interreligious learning. This is so if we do not make too much of our carefully chosen words. We would be foolish to reduce the mystery of God to what we can say about it by the best words of theologians. But we would *not* be better off were we to decide that our encounter with truth is better fostered by leaving behind even the positive doctrines of traditions, as if unlimited verbal and mental fluidity would be a better base for taking other traditions seriously.[8]

These reflections on doctrine are implicitly couched in Christian terms. But this disciplined and even austere attitude toward our words and the received truths of received faith claims applies also to thinking about the truths of the Hindu traditions we encounter in great Hindu theological texts. Non-Christian masters of theology also know that words must be used skillfully and without inflated importance, crafted so as to disencumber the reader, put aside wrong ways of reading and using words: very specific and rigorous rules for thinking, reading, and writing at the service of formulating a correct view of the world. Hindu thinking, for example, will not be driven by a Gospel imperative, but there are pertinent and parallel universalizing trajectories in Hindu thought that both drive and constrain Hindu views of the religious other.[9]

Vatican II's opening up of a Christ-grounded space

A Catholic grounding for interreligious learning is not merely a wish, detached from the harder realities of the Church. The Catholic attitude

I have been presenting thus far is in harmony with the direction of Church teachings today.[10] Vatican II (1962–1965) in particular opened up new space for a Catholic interreligious learning, and in the typically Catholic way that combines depth, focus, and a consequent openness.[11] Though not all the conciliar statements were equally interreligiously open, *Nostra Aetate*, approved in the last session of the Council, turned out to be most capable of showing a way to learn from the religious other. Here is the key text from n. 2 of the document:

> The Catholic Church rejects none of the things that are true and holy in these religions. She regards with sincere attentiveness those ways of acting and living, those precepts and doctrines which, though differing in many aspects from the ones she holds and sets forth, nonetheless by no means rarely reflect the radiance of that Truth which enlightens all people.

This is a limited openness, a nonrejection of the true and holy, rather a full embrace of Hinduism and Buddhism, but it is a deeply founded positive regard for other traditions. The images of light refer to John 1.9, which presents Christ as light and truth: "The light shines in the darkness, and the darkness did not overcome it. . . . The true light, which enlightens everyone, was coming into the world" (Jn 1:5, 9). This is a matter of the light of Christ, not a generic light, and it shines from within the religions, not as a harsh light of judgment on them.

The next statement draws explicitly on John, and it can be read so as to serve to undergird and justify, rather than narrow, the deep reverence with which Catholics are to approach religious traditions:

> Truly she announces, and ever must announce Christ "the way, the truth, and the life" (Jn 14:6), in whom humans may find the fullness of religious life, in whom God has reconciled all things to Himself.
>
> (2 Cor 5: 18–19)

This text may be read as very narrow: *only* Christ. But I have always found it to be rather universal in disposition: wherever there is truth, Christ is there; wherever people are on the way to God, Christ is there; where people are fully alive, Christ is there, not as an add-on, but as deep within the truths, ways, and lives of people of all traditions and none.

What is notable, too, about *Nostra Aetate* n. 2 is its lack of a priori judgments and already-settled conclusions about what other religious traditions are to mean. Study and inquiry are necessary. It stands exceptionally on a middle ground, neither conservative nor liberal, free of many of the theological constraints and a priori conditions common to the other documents, and yet without stepping away from Christian commitments. Written in the space of dialogue, expecting to be read by people of many faith traditions, it stands open and receptive in the presence of the other, expecting listeners and hence conversations rather than monologues, true learning rather than confirmations of what we already know. It is the harbinger of a new era of the Church and a new Catholic style in the world.

The authors of *Nostra Aetate* were not independent operators, unaware of or unsympathetic to the cautions posed in other documents of the Council, and a Catholic cannot choose merely the parts of documents she or he likes. Still, this declaration shifts from *talking about* to *inviting* listeners to learn something: listen, find, learn. Christian witness remains essential; it is possible because Christ is the way, the truth, and the life; it is this witness that indicates respect for and openness to all that is true and holy in the world's religious traditions, illumined by the light of Christ shining from within. In a sense, *Nostra Aetate* sets for the entirety of Vatican II documents their interreligious application: how they are to be used in our era.

The Council and its forward-looking daring prompted fresh thinking interreligiously by Catholic theologians, with many figures daring to chart new paths forward. By my judgment, the soundest strand has been that of the new, post-conciliar inclusivism, promoted in an incipient fashion by Karl Rahner (who did not study other religions)[12] and then most famously by Jacques Dupuis. This project, not so much as "-ism" as an "including" theology, has been dedicated to achieving a balance between fidelity to tradition and the core revelation of Christian faith – in Christ, in the mystery of the Trinity – on the one side and, on the other, a radical openness to God at work in the world, in Christ, in the Trinitarian dynamic, particularly that of the Spirit.[13] The hard edge of such work, of course, lies in a refusal to give up on doctrine for the sake of an idealized complete, unlimited openness to everything.

Monsignor John Oesterreicher, a convert to Catholicism from Judaism who was a leading figure at the Council and thereafter, reflected as follows on *Nostra Aetate*:

> We must not be satisfied with some general knowledge of them [i.e. non-Christian religions]; the Declaration rather demands a deeper knowledge of the ways of God and men. The more we penetrate into the convictions and religious practices of non-biblical origin, the more we shall perceive God's gentle, almost shy action everywhere. . . . It is the greatness of those sections of the Declaration dealing with the various non-Christian religions that they praise the omnipresence of grace.
> (Oesterreicher 1967, 93)

This is the inquiring spirit that motivates much comparative theology as well.

Here, too, it would be disingenuous to be ignorant of limitations and counterexamples. How doctrine is used is unsurprisingly varied, and not every usage facilitates openness. The conservative authors of *Dominus Iesus*

(2000), the document from Rome's Congregation for the Doctrine of the Faith, were determined to rein in Catholic speculations on pluralism, binding very tightly together Creed, Gospel, Church, and salvation, all in the light of Christ, and for this purpose the declaration became a handy litmus test for orthodoxy, and unfortunately a set of justifications for not actually engaging in interreligious learning and for rejecting insights gained interreligiously.[14] Still, the Creed remains the bedrock for many, if not most, of the constructive Catholic theologians who engage in interreligious learning in a faithful and open manner and likewise do comparative studies. That there are truths of faith grounded in scripture and tradition, truths regarding God, Christ, the Spirit, the world, and the Church, enables those of us committed to interreligious openness to be open and yet maintain and refine ever more definitely a frame within which to receive and welcome the religious other. This delicate balance is deeply indebted to a robust understanding of the Trinitarian God.

Walls yes, and with door and windows that open

The paradox of a strong version of Roman Catholic doctrine and practice, instantiated always in the lives of Catholics who did learn interreligiously, has to do with the rigor and boundaries of the tradition and its simultaneously adaptation, over and over again, to new circumstances: the Church is in a position of having constantly to modify itself globally because it is dedicated to the good news of God's kingdom; it can be fruitfully open, ever on the edge of crossing sanctioned borders, because it has borders and limits and works only with a sense that God has already been present in the Church, as it has already been. But this focused-open dynamic makes sense. Religions are not like properties with boundary markers, fences that keep people in or out. They are places in which to dwell, houses, homes. These have walls that making dwelling within them possible. One doesn't remove the walls if one wants to dwell there. Rather, we seek to ensure by the use of windows that light and fresh air can enter and by the use of doors that dwellers in the home can go out and come back.

I have thus far said nothing about "Theology Without Walls," even if, by contributing to this volume, I am hoping to make evident my respect for Jerry L. Martin's best instincts regarding openness while resisting his way of putting it. I am suggesting that we do well to pay closer attention to how traditions work and, in this instance, how Christian tradition works. If we do, we come to see that walls need not, should not, be torn down, because doing so would be in danger of removing the very support walls that make religions able to be robustly universal. I therefore distance myself from the particular framing of the project as Jerry L. Martin puts it:

> Often theology is defined as the articulation of the beliefs about the divine reality within one's own tradition. In light of the widespread

experience of finding spiritual insight in other traditions as well, that definition seems inappropriately limited. Surely, the aim of theology should be to learn all we can about ultimate reality, regardless of the source of the insights. Even comparatively theology, when it is regarded as finally confessional, limited to asking what light other traditions throw on my own, stops short. What is needed is a Theology without Walls, without confessional boundaries, without blinders, as it were. That does not mean that we do not stand somewhere, but that our sense of our goal is not limited to where we stand at the outset.

I therefore rewrite Jerry's words like this:

Often and rightly theology is defined as the articulation of the beliefs about the divine reality within one's own tradition and from there, outward into the world around us. In light of the widespread experience of finding spiritual insight in other traditions as well, that definition may seem inappropriately limited, because it fails to indicate more directly how the articulation of beliefs also reaches out to other traditions. Surely, we see now that the aim of theology should be to learn all we can about the revealed truths of the faith, without confusing the insights with any particular cultural framing of them. Even comparative theology, which is confessional at the beginning and end, does well to explore what light other traditions throw on my own, so as to change my relation to my own tradition, without denying the roots of that tradition and without reducing the religious other merely to an instrument of self-improvement. It does not stop short for the sake of a hoped-for unrestricted openness. What is needed is a theology with walls, a home with foundations and walls and windows and doors, a roof held up by the walls and – why not, a welcome mat at the entrance.

Notes

1 For a thoughtful, though guarded, assessment of Cusa's approach to pluralism, see "Nicholas of Cusa's *De pace fidei* and the Meta-Exclusivism of Religious Pluralism" by Aikin and Aleksander (2013, 219–235).
2 I choose here simply several of the Jesuit figures I have read in recent years and without prejudice against the fact of other Catholic and Christian instances of creative interreligious adaptations.
3 On de Nobili's real but limited openness, see Clooney (2007, 51–61).
4 See my essay, "Alienation, Xenophilia, and Coming Home: William Wallace, SJ's *From Evangelical to Catholic by Way of the East*" (Clooney 2018a, 280–290).
5 See Krokus (2017).
6 See Grumett and Plant (2012, 58–83).
7 On Merton, see my essay, "Thomas Merton's Deep Christian Learning Across Religious Borders" (Clooney 2017, 49–64).
8 I have spoken of the use of words in crafting "liberating doctrines." But the point – submission to tradition, focus, particularity as a base for universality – illumines

also the value of rituals, particular sacramental rites that significantly open up perspectives on material and human realities without restriction, and likewise the value of strong communities with defined identities that have the resources to support venturing forth, learning from the other, and substantive returns home: these help ensure openness, rather than thwarting it.

9 See Clooney (2003). Also guest editor of this thematic issue.
10 I must, however, leave aside here the many controversies among Catholics today about the true legacy of Vatican II.
11 See my essays, "How Nostra Aetate Opened the Way to the Study of Hinduism" (Clooney 2016, 58–75) and "Nostra Aetate and the Small Things of God" (Clooney 2018c, 305–316).
12 See Rahner (1971, 161–177).
13 See Dupuis (2002), Heim (2000), and a recent essay of mine explaining how this including theology works as the desired alternative to pluralism: "Fractal Theory, Fractal Practice: Theology of Religions, Comparative Theology" (Clooney 2018b).
14 For a balanced set of assessments of *Dominus Iesus*, see Pope and Hefling (2002).

References

Aikin, Scott F., and Jason Aleksander. 2013. "Nicholas of Cusa's *De pace fidei* and the Meta-Exclusivism of Religious Pluralism." *International Journal of the Philosophy of Religion* 74: 219–235. doi:10.1007/s11153-012-9367-0

Burrell, David B. 1986. *Knowing the Unknowable God: Ibn-Sina, Maimonides, Aquinas.* Notre Dame, IN: University of Notre Dame Press.

Burrell, David B. 1993. *Freedom and Creation in Three Traditions.* Notre Dame, IN: University of Notre Dame Press. doi:10.1017/s0034412500019648

Clooney, Francis X. 2003. "Hindu Views of Religious Others: Implications for Christian Theology." *Theological Studies* 64 (2): 306–333. doi:10.1177/004056390306400204

Clooney, Francis X. 2007. "Understanding in Order to be Understood, Refusing to Understand in Order to Convert." In *Expanding and Merging Horizons: Contributions to South Asian and Cross-Cultural Studies in Commemoration of Wilhelm Halbfass*, edited by Karin Preisendanz, 51–61. Vienna: Austrian Academy of Sciences Press.

Clooney, Francis X. 2016. "How Nostra Aetate Opened the Way to the Study of Hinduism." In *Nostra Aetate: Celebrating 50 Years of the Catholic Church's Dialogue with Jews and Muslims*, edited by Pim Valkenberg and Anthony Cirelli, 58–75. Catholic University of America Press. doi:10.1353/acs.2018.0002

Clooney, Francis X. 2017. "Thomas Merton's Deep Christian Learning Across Religious Borders." *Buddhist-Christian Studies* 37 (1): 49–64. doi:10.1353/bcs.2017.0005

Clooney, Francis X. 2018a. "Alienation, Xenophilia, and Coming Home: William Wallace, SJ's from Evangelical to Catholic by Way of the East." *Common Knowledge* 24 (2): 280–290. doi:10.1215/0961754x-4362469

Clooney, Francis X. 2018b. "Fractal Theory, Fractal Practice: Theology of Religions, Comparative Theology." In *Incarnation, Prophecy, and Enlightenment*, edited by Paul Knitter and Alan Race. Maryknoll, NY: Orbis Books.

Clooney, Francis X. 2018c. "Nostra Aetate and the Small Things of God." In *Catholicism Engaging Other Faiths: Vatican II and Its Impact*, edited by Vladimir

Latinovic, Gerard **Mannion**, and Jason **Welle,** 305–316. London: Palgrave Macmillan. doi:10.1007/978-3-319-98584-8_18

Dupuis, Jacques. 2002. *Toward a Christian Theology of Religious Pluralism.* Maryknoll, NY: Orbis Books.

Grumett, David, and Thomas Plant. 2012. "De Lubac, Pure Land Buddhism, and Roman Catholicism." *Journal of Religion* 92 (1): 58–83. doi:10.1086/662206

Heim, Mark S. 2000. *The Depth of the Riches: A Trinitarian Theology of Religious Ends (Sacra Doctrina: Christian Theology for a Postmodern Age).* Grand Rapids, MI: Wm. B. Eerdmans Publishing Co. doi:10.1017/s0360966900009919

Hill, Wesley. 2016. "God's Strangeness." *First Things* 259: 15–16.

Krokus, Christian. 2017. *The Theology of Louis Massignon: Islam, Christ, and the Church.* Washington, DC: Catholic University of America Press. doi:10.2307/j.ctt1p6qppr

Oesterreicher, John. 1967. "Declaration on the Relationship of the Church to Non-Christian Religions." *Commentary on the Documents of Vatican II* 3: 93.

Pope, Stephen J., and Charles Hefling. 2002. *Sic et Non: Encountering Dominus Iesus.* Maryknoll: Orbis Books. doi:10.1017/s0360966900000293

Rahner, Karl. 1971. "Anonymous Christianity and the Missionary Task of the Church." *Theological Investigations.* trans. David Bourke. London: Darton, Longman and Todd. doi:10.1017/s003441250000648x

20 A Hinduism without walls? Exploring the concept of the avatar interreligiously

Jeffery D. Long

Introduction: the universal and the concrete

Jerry L. Martin has defined a Theology Without Walls as "a theology that takes all sources of revelation, enlightenment, and insight into account, without (to the extent possible) privileging our own." He has further characterized this approach as "a cooperative, constructive, trans-religious theological project," based on the observation that "[p]eople who engage in serious study beyond their own tradition frequently find revelation, enlightenment, or insight into ultimate reality in multiple traditions. In light of this experience, restricting theology to the articulation of truths within one's own tradition seems unduly restricted" (Martin 2018).

The Vedanta tradition of Ramakrishna is a Hindu tradition that one might expect not only to embrace the idea of a Theology Without Walls but also to suggest that this mode of theologizing describes precisely what its adherents have been doing all along; for from the inception of this tradition in the multireligious spiritual practices of its founding figure, it has been rooted in the idea that ultimate reality and the truths leading to it cannot be confined to a single tradition. To its adherents, Vedanta is, in short, already an example of a Theology Without Walls. In the words of Pravrajika Vrajaprana, "Vedanta is the philosophical foundation of Hinduism; but while Hinduism includes aspects of Indian culture, Vedanta is universal in its application and is equally relevant to all countries, all cultures, and all religious backgrounds" (Vrajaprana 1999, 1).

Even as it aspires to universality, though, Vedanta is also, in practice, one tradition among others. The organizations founded by Swami Vivekananda and charged with promulgating this tradition – the Ramakrishna Order and Mission and the Vedanta Societies – have their own specific practices, observances, beliefs, and so on. There is a distinctive Vedantic worldview that, even as it seeks to integrate the insights of many traditions into its universal vision, is nevertheless different from these other traditions in many respects.

As a scholar-practitioner in this tradition, I can say that it is precisely its breadth of vision, its aspiration toward universality, that was one of the main factors that drew me to it.[1] A religious tradition, though, must also

DOI: 10.4324/9780429000973-26

make the universal concrete if it is to mediate universal concepts and transcendental realities to living practitioners. In the words of Alfred North Whitehead:

> Religion should connect the rational generality of philosophy with the emotions and purposes springing out of existence in a particular society, in a particular epoch, and conditioned by particular antecedents. Religion is the translation of general ideas into particular thoughts, particular emotions, and particular purposes; it is directed to the end of stretching individual interest beyond its self-defeating particularity. . . . Religion is an ultimate craving to infuse into the insistent particularity of emotion that non-temporal generality which primarily belongs to conceptual thought alone.
>
> (Whitehead 1978, 15, 16)

To take Vedanta as an example of this principle, Vedanta as a spiritual practice tied to a tradition and an institution affirms universal ideas, like the idea of a divine reality that manifests Itself to human beings at various points in history but also renders this idea concrete in the form of the image of Ramakrishna as the avatar, or divine incarnation, of our current historical epoch, whose primary mission has been to teach the harmony and the ultimate unity of all religions. The idea of Sri Ramakrishna as an avatar is, of course, distinctive to the Ramakrishna tradition: an affirmation that differentiates this tradition not only from other religions but also from other forms of Hinduism, for not all Hindu traditions accept the avatar doctrine, and not all that do would affirm the idea of Ramakrishna as an avatar. But although this doctrine serves to differentiate the Ramakrishna tradition as one historical tradition among others, it also serves for its adherents to render concrete the far more abstract ideal of divine love: a love willing to manifest itself in time and history in order to draw humanity ever nearer to the realization of its divine potential.

The concept of the avatar

The necessity of the concrete manifestation of divinity in a human form is affirmed in many places by Swami Vivekananda, according to whom we, as human beings, can only relate to a highly abstract reality such as the Infinite if we can approach it through the medium of a human form. In one passage, using the metaphor of light, he says,

> The vibration of light is everywhere in this room. Why cannot we see it everywhere? You have to see it only in that lamp. God is an Omnipresent Principle – everywhere: but we are so constituted at present that we can see Him, feel him, only in and through a human God. And when

these great lights come [that is, avatars, or divine incarnations], then man realizes God.

(Vivekananda 1979b, 122)

The ideal of the avatar is part of the Vaishnava tradition of Hinduism. It is first affirmed in a text that is foundational both for Vaishnavism and Vedanta: the *Bhagavad Gītā*. In the seventh verse of the fourth chapter of this text, the Supreme Being, or Bhagavān, Lord Krishna, tells his friend, the hero Arjuna: "Whenever *dharma* declines and when chaos and evil [*adharma*] arise, I manifest myself" (*Bhagavad Gītā* 4:7, translation mine). Interestingly, the word *avatāra* itself does not actually appear in the *Bhagavad Gītā*, though it is clear from the subsequent textual tradition that this is the idea being expressed. In the *Bhāgavata Purāṇa*, a central Vaishnava text, many avatars are listed and described (*Bhāgavata Purāṇa* 1.3). Although the avatars are sometimes said to be countless in number, there are several lists of these avatars in various Hindu texts. The best-known list includes 10 avatars, though there is also a list of 24 and another list of 108.[2]

Hindu sources describe the attributes of an avatar, thus making it possible to determine if a particular individual might be one. How has Sri Ramakrishna been proclaimed an avatar by his followers? According to the accounts of his life – the Bengali *Kathāmṛta* and *Līlaprasaṅga* – he was filled at a very early age with a deep longing to see God: to perceive divinity directly. This longing intensified after he became a priest at the temple of Kali, the Divine Mother, at Dakshineshwar, near Calcutta. After many days of intense prayer and profound emotional turmoil, Ramakrishna experienced the Goddess Kali as a living reality, who manifested to the young priest as "a limitless, infinite, effulgent Ocean of Consciousness" (Nikhilananda 1942, 14). In the months that followed, Ramakrishna conceived a desire to experience divinity in as many forms as possible, taking up the disciplines of various Vaishnava, Shaiva, and Shakta traditions of Hindu spiritual practice. It was in the course of these *sādhanas*, or spiritual disciplines, that a woman called the Bhairavi Brahmani became his guide:

Day after day she watched his ecstasy during the kirtan [singing of sacred hymns] and meditation, his samādhi [a profound state of meditative absorption which he was capable of entering spontaneously], his mad yearning; and she recognized in him a power to transmit spirituality to others. She came to the conclusion that such things were not possible for an ordinary devotee, not even for a highly developed soul. Only an incarnation of God was capable of such spiritual manifestations. She proclaimed openly that Sri Ramakrishna, like Sri Chaitanya [a medieval Vaishnava saint proclaimed an avatar in the Gauḍīya Vaishnava tradition], was an Incarnation of God.

(Nikhilananda 1942, 19)

The Bhairavi Brahmani's faith that Ramakrishna was an incarnation is widely held in the tradition based on his life and teachings. But this tradition has no dogma or creed. Individuals in the Vedanta tradition are thus free to express skepticism about this teaching. One such skeptic, in fact, was Swami Vivekananda himself, who, in his youth, frequently expressed doubts about the idea of his teacher's divinity (Nikhilananda 1942, 72). Although he would later come to believe in his teacher's divinity very deeply, he never insisted that adherents of Vedanta accept this idea, and he discouraged others from insisting "too much" on it (Vivekananda 1979c, 81). He did not want it to become a bar to people accepting the more fundamental teaching of Vedanta, of the inherent divinity within *all* beings. In contrast with mainstream Christianity, Vedanta is not primarily about belief in the divinity of a particular teacher, but about the realization and manifestation of the divinity within us all.

Indeed, one can observe that there is some tension between the idea of the avatar and the idea that all beings are divine. Again, the ultimate aim of Vedanta is the realization of the divine potential in every being. What, then, is an avatar, according to this worldview? One could suggest that an avatar is simply a person who has fully realized and manifested this divine potential. We will all someday be avatars from this point of view.

There is a distinction, though, in Hindu traditions between one who *ascends* to the level of enlightenment and becomes God-realized – literally *jīvanmukta*, or liberated in this lifetime – and a *descent*, or *avatāra*, of the Supreme Being. The idea of the avatar clearly points to a distinct form of divine manifestation in the world that is different from the more general inherent divinity of all beings that practitioners of Vedanta are seeking to make manifest.

The avatar is the assumption of a concrete form by the Paramātman, or Supreme Self – the Infinite Being, or Supreme Reality – for a specific purpose, or mission. The classical avatars of the Vaiṣṇava tradition all come to, as Krishna says in the *Bhagavad Gītā*, destroy evil and restore the good. This typically takes the shape of their destroying demonic beings who embody *āsuric*, or negative, qualities that keep us from God-realization: qualities such as egotism, greed, hatred, and lust. Avatars such as the Varāha, or Boar Avatar; the Narasiṃha, or Man-Lion Avatar; Vāmana, the Dwarf Avatar; and Rāma, or Rām, destroy demonic beings called, respectively, Hiranyaksha, Hiranyakashipu, Mahābāli, and Rāvaṇa. Other avatars, such as Paraśurāma and Krishna, destroy human beings who exhibit demonic qualities.

In the interpretation of Sri Aurobindo, the Buddha avatar – the ninth in the standard list of ten avatars – is a divine incarnation who chooses to set aside his divinity in order to show human beings, by example, the path to the realization of their inherent divinity. By setting aside his divine power and living as a human seeking freedom from suffering, he shows us the way to this freedom.

Significantly, the Buddha avatar is himself a good example of Hindu traditions operating after the manner of a Theology Without Walls, with an
openness to the sacred figures and teachings of other traditions; for the
Buddha in question is, of course, the historical founder of Buddhism, a tradition with which Hindu traditions were often in a relationship of antago-
nism for much of the history of Buddhism in India. To be sure, the original
concept of the Buddha avatar was not at all friendly to Buddhist traditions;
for the Buddha is represented as deluding ignorant and demonic persons
into not performing Vedic rituals. This negative assessment was not to pre-
vail, however. In Jayadeva's *Gītagovinda*, for example, it is said that the
Buddha avatar only taught his followers to avoid those Vedic rituals that
caused harm to living beings: the animal sacrifices that have been enjoined
in certain rituals and in certain regions during certain periods of history.
He thus plays a positive role, from a Vaiṣṇava perspective, in establishing
the central Vaiṣṇava value of ahiṃsā, or nonviolence in thought, word,
and deed. This is seen as the primary mission of this avatar in the Vaiṣṇava
tradition. In the modern period, Swami Vivekananda teaches that there
is nothing in the Buddha's doctrine contrary to the teachings of Vedanta,
as found in the Upanishads, even as he rejected some aspects of the more
ritualistic practices of the Vedas. According to Swami Vivekananda, "Buddha brought the Vedanta to light, gave it to the people, and saved India"
(1979a, 2.139).

What is Ramakrishna's mission as an avatar, according to his tradition?
This mission is, importantly, closely connected with the idea of the Ramakrishna tradition as a Theology Without Walls; for Ramakrishna's mission
as an avatar is widely believed to have been the establishment of the idea
of the harmony and unity of religions on a practical, experiential basis.
In his pursuit of God-realization through many traditions, Ramakrishna's
multireligious disciplines can be seen as an embodied, practical version of
a Theology Without Walls. Indeed, Ramakrishna sought not only "revelation, enlightenment, or insight into ultimate reality in multiple traditions"
but also direct realization, a profound inward encounter with divinity, in
multiple traditions.

Ramakrishna experienced divinity through varied Hindu systems of practice – Vaishnavism, Tantra, Advaita Vedanta, and so on. But his quest was
truly "without walls," for he engaged in Islamic and Christian practices as
well. These practices similarly culminated, as his Hindu practices had, in a
direct realization of God.

The Hindu avatar and the Christian incarnation

As a result of Ramakrishna's explorations of both Islam and Christianity,
the Ramakrishna tradition sees not only the avatars listed in Vaishnava texts
and Ramakrishna himself as divine incarnations but also figures from outside the Hindu tradition, such as Jesus Christ.

Jesus, of course, as traditionally understood in Christianity, is a singular divine incarnation, "the way, the truth, and the life" (Jn 14:6), faith in whom is necessary for salvation.

Ramakrishna never came to believe that Jesus *alone* was divine. Ramakrishna's sensibility was far closer to that expressed in a *Bhagavad Gītā* verse cited by Swami Vivekananda in his famous welcome address at the first World Parliament of Religions in Chicago in 1893: "In whatsoever way that living beings approach me, thus do I receive them. All paths lead to me" (*Bhagavad Gītā* 4:11).

Ramakrishna did not deny that Jesus was divine, and indeed accepted the possibility that he was, himself, a manifestation of the same divinity that had previously walked the Earth not only as Rama, Krishna, and Buddha but as Christ as well. Ramakrishna did not proclaim himself to be an incarnation of Christ; but there were Christians in Ramakrishna's time, and subsequently in the Ramakrishna movement, who believed this to be the case, and he did not contradict them when they expressed this view (Saradananda 2003, 910).

A "test case" of a Theology Without Walls arises if one encounters claims made by religious traditions that at least appear to contradict one another. The Hindu idea of many avatars, in contrast with that of a singular divine incarnation found in Christianity, would appear to be such a case.

It is significant, too, that this is not a peripheral or trifling issue – at least for Christians. If one takes seriously the idea that Jesus is "the way, the truth, and the life" and that no one comes to the Father but through him, then the conclusion one reaches on the issue of multiple incarnations or only one could be a matter on which one's eternal salvation hinges.

From a Hindu perspective, this issue seems easily resolvable. The one divine being who is the way, the truth, and the life, without whom salvation is impossible, has incarnated many times. There is no contest between Jesus and Krishna, because both are incarnations of the same divine reality. If the "I" who says, "I am the way, the truth, and the life; no one comes to the Father but through me," is the same "I" who says, "In whatever way living beings approach me, thus do I receive them; all paths lead to me," then the contradiction is resolved. The divine being who has come as Jesus Christ is the only way to salvation, and that same divine being has also come as Rama, as Krishna, as Buddha, as Chaitanya, as Ramakrishna, and as many more such beings.

One can imagine the verses from John's gospel and from the *Bhagavad Gītā* that one might normally take to be contrary to one another as two halves of a new verse, or *navya śāstra*:

> *I am the way, the truth, and the life; no one comes to the Father but through me. And in whatever way living beings approach me, thus do I receive them; all paths lead to me.*

This is not the way Christians would typically address this issue, unless the idea were to become available to them that the same divine Word, the same cosmic Christ, who walked the Earth as Jesus of Nazareth, also walked the Earth as these other figures. One appeal of this idea for Christians might be that it helps resolve, in a very elegant way, the question of the salvation of non-Christians. The idea that most of humanity is damned for eternity for following teachers other than Jesus is difficult to reconcile with the idea of the loving God proclaimed in the gospel.

Conclusion

The idea of a singular divine being with multiple incarnations – with Christianity giving greater emphasis to the singularity side of the equation and Hindu traditions emphasizing the plurality side – is an example of how a Theology Without Walls can draw traditions to appreciate one another's insights, moving toward a more inclusive vision of truth.

Notes

1 I was raised in the Roman Catholic tradition of Christianity.
2 There are at least two versions of the standard list of ten avatars. In the older one, the ninth avatar, after Krishna, is listed as Krishna's brother, Balarama. A somewhat more recent and better-known version replaces Balarama with the Buddha.

References

Martin, Jerry L. 2018. *Theology Without Walls: What Is TWW?* http://theology withoutwalls.com/what-is-tww/ (accessed October 6, 2018).

Nikhilananda, Swami. 1942. *The Gospel of Sri Ramakrishna*. New York: Ramakrishna Vivekananda Center.

Saradananda, Swami. 2003. *Sri Ramakrishna and His Divine Play*, trans. Swami Chetanananda. St. Louis: Vedanta Society of St. Louis.

Vivekananda, Swami. 1979a. *Complete Works, Volume Two*. Mayavati: Advaita Ashrama.

Vivekananda, Swami. 1979b. *Complete Works, Volume Four*. Mayavati: Advaita Ashrama.

Vivekananda, Swami. 1979c. *Complete Works, Volume Five*. Mayavati: Advaita Ashrama.

Vrajaprana, Pravrajika. 1999. *Vedanta: A Simple Introduction*. Hollywood, CA: Vedanta Press.

Whitehead, Alfred N. 1978. *Process and Reality: An Essay in Cosmology*. Corrected edition. New York: Macmillan.

21 My path to a theology of Qi

Hyo-Dong Lee

The Theology Without Walls (hereafter TWW), as I understand it, is "a theology without confessional restrictions."[1] It is a theology in a mode of trans-religious inquiry that engages the resources of multiple traditions without prioritizing any single one among them. As such, it is a more experimental and perhaps daring form of theology, given the widely accepted customary definition of theology as "the articulation of religious truths as held by a particular tradition" (Martin 2016). Further, precisely as such it diverges from comparative theology, which Francis X. Clooney defines as consisting in "acts of faith seeking understanding which are rooted in a particular faith tradition but which, from that foundation, venture into learning from one or more other faith traditions" (Clooney 2010, 10). The prevailing understanding of comparative theology – as championed by Clooney and Paul Knitter, among others – assumes one's rootedness in a single home tradition from which one undertakes the adventure of passing over to other traditions and coming back with a deeper understanding of the home tradition. TWW is premised on more complicated patterns of religious affiliation (or nonaffiliation), which do not presume one's rootedness in a single home tradition. Whether affiliation is envisaged as belonging in the sense of membership in particular religious communities or as participation in certain religious practices, the practitioners of TWW in principle do not give more authority and weight to one tradition over others with which they affiliate themselves (Thatamanil 2016b, 355).[2] Hence, the issue of multiple religious belonging or multiple religious participation accompanies the theoretical endeavor of TWW as its existential and practical horizon.

As a Christian comparative theologian who grew up in East Asia (South Korea), I have found the underlying premise of comparative theology, that is, that the comparative theologian is rooted in a single home tradition, most challenging to make sense of. I was born into a family without membership in an organized religion but committed to Confucian ritual and ethical obligations, particularly the ritual of ancestor veneration. The religious landscape was characterized by what is called "diffuse religion" – the ancient practices of ancestor veneration and spirit worship that over time became amalgamated with basic elements of Buddhism, Confucianism, and Seondo

DOI: 10.4324/9780429000973-27

(a Korean form of Daoism), in which it was common for an individual or family to participate in religious rituals or practices that suited the occasion (Esposito, Fasching, and Lewis 2012, 495). Before Christianity arrived on the scene, "religions" in the sense of organized communities with exclusive membership did not really exist. Although different people might be respectively more committed overall to the practices of one tradition over the others, in most cases they treated one another with respect and in that sense can be said to have accepted a loose concept of multiple religious belonging (Kim 2016, 79). Regarding the sense of religious identity and religious ethos in such a context, Chung Hyun Kyung put it best:

> When people ask what I am religiously, I say, "My bowel is Shamanist. My heart is Buddhist. My right brain, which defines my mood, is Confucian and Taoist. My left brain, which defines my public language, is Protestant Christian, and overall, my aura is eco-feminist." . . . As a Korean woman, I was raised in the 5,000-year-old Shamanist tradition and the 2,000-year-old Taoist-Confucian tradition, with 2,000 years of Buddhist tradition, 100 years of Protestant tradition, and twenty years of eco-feminist tradition. So, my body is like a religious pantheon. I am living with communities of Gods, a continuum of divinity, and a family of religions.
>
> (Kyung 2009, 73–74)

The fact that I was baptized a Christian – more specifically, an evangelical Protestant – in a cultural-religious milieu of "diffuse religion" that assumed a loose sense of multiple religious belonging complicated my relationship to the other traditions. The evangelical Protestant church of which I became a member at the age of 16 demanded an exclusive allegiance to it – I was supposed to regard Christianity as my only "home" and the rest of the religious landscape as consisting in "others." But that was an impossible demand, for however much I formally repudiated Confucianism, Buddhism, etc., as "pagan" and "heathen," I could not disown or erase the childhood and teenage-year memories of taking part in the house rituals of venerating my grandfathers and grandmothers or accompanying my relatives in fun-filled Sunday picnics to nearby Buddhist temples where the sound of the monks' chanting was a soothing music to my ears. Those memories formed an indelible part of who I was as a person; and one could even argue that, in the language of comparative theology, by being baptized a Christian, I was actually leaving "home" to embark on the adventurous journey of crossing-over into a "foreign" tradition.[3]

Such a complex pattern of religious affiliation perhaps explains the sense of ease and safety with which I explored Confucian and Daoist philosophies in my college years in South Korea, despite my formal consent to the doctrinal stance of my church that declared them to be error-filled human creations, if not the work of the devil. I was especially attracted to the teachings of the *Daodejing* (or *Laozi*), the earliest and foundational scripture of Dao-ism, although at the time I had no intellectual frame or tools to reconcile, if possible at all, its teachings of Dao, "self-so" (自然 *ziran*) and "non-self-assertive action" (無爲 *wuwei*) with my church's thoroughly Western, missionary-brought theology. I started studying the *Daodejing* in earnest during my graduate studies of theology in Canada and the United States, when I was preoccupied with the question of how to reduce the distance I felt existed between the glorified Trinity and the fallen creation in much of classical Christian theology.

My theological quest then had a decisively pneumatocentric orientation, having been influenced by Rahner's dictum, "the immanent Trinity is the economic Trinity and vice versa"; Moltmann's revamping of Barth's trini-tarian history of God as virtually coinciding with the history of creation's redemption, emancipation, and healing; and ultimately, Hegel's grand vision of the consummation of the absolute in the divine–human–cosmic unity of the *Geist*, Spirit. It was an attempt to reconceive God's transcendence – or God's own being, traditionally captured by the notion of the "immanent" Trinity – so as to find it right in the midst of, not apart from, the com-mon history of God and creation.[4] Following Hegel, I wanted to re-envision God's ultimate being as Spirit, understood as the all-encompassing divine–human–cosmic unity, which unceasingly worked at the liberation and ulti-mate consummation of itself.[5]

With its paradoxical conception of the Dao (Way) as both the unnamable Dao and the Mother of the world, the *Daodejing* offered me a resonant account that located the ultimate squarely at the heart of a divine–human–cosmic whole, while retaining a sense of the Dao's ultimate transcendence of that whole as a kind of *natura naturans*.[6] Moreover, the *Daodejing* pre-sented a vision of the pre-civilizational undercurrent of nature beneath the human world as most perfectly aligned with the movement of the Dao. In other words, it proffered a counterthrust to Hegel's anthropocentrism and Eurocentrism, that is, his prioritizing of human culture, especially in its modern European Enlightenment version, as the most privileged locus of divine–cosmic reconciliation.

The fact that I turned to classical Daoist thought to find intellectual resources for the task had certainly a lot to do with the familiarity and comfort with which the ancient Daoist texts spoke to me, as if I was hearing my own voice. At the same time, it was also due to the dawning awareness on my part that Christian theology had never had its "own" intellectual frameworks and conceptual tools that enabled it to safeguard its orthodoxy. From its very beginning, Christianity in its theoretical self-articulation relied on the intellectual resources of classical Greek and Hellenistic thought, and in that sense had always harbored "others" within itself that rendered the boundaries of its self-identity permeable. If one is to apply the previously mentioned logic of comparative theology for a Christian convert whose home coincides with a "mission field," what happened to Christian theology early on was as much the Greek-speaking gentiles leaving their home base to cross over into a foreign Jewish tradition and returning, having been transformed in the process, as Christianity leaving its Jewish home to pass over into the alien world of Greek thought and coming back changed. This bidirectional logic of comparative theology indicates that if there is to be double religious belonging as a version of multiple religious belonging, such a belonging should be understood as symmetrical, not asymmetrical.[7] Further, it also implies that the long-running debate in ecumenism and missiology about contextualization of theology should expand its understanding of the "inculturation" of theology to include the so-called "grafting" model, according to which the Christian gospel is the shoot (guest) and the local culture the stock (host) onto which the gospel is grafted.[8]

After my first comparative (Christian–Daoist or Daoist–Christian) theological project culminated in a PhD dissertation on Hegel and the *Daodejing*, my attention turned to the resources of Confucianism, particularly allured by the conceptual rigor and the grandeur of the vision of Neo-Confucian metaphysics. What drew my attention to it was the way the most historically influential school of Neo-Confucian metaphysics,[9] following its founder Zhu Xi, dynamically structures all of reality in terms of the relationship between psychophysical energy (氣 *qi*) and pattern (理 *li*). Psychophysical energy is the primordial energy of the universe that constitutes whatever exists, whereas pattern is the ultimate ideal principle of coherence and order which is logically, ontologically, and normatively prior to psychophysical energy and upon which the cosmic creativity of the latter is dependent. In other words, the dominant school of Neo-Confucian metaphysics places the very energy and "stuff" of the universe within an ontologically hierarchical, binary relationship with its *raison d'être*, its ground of being, its *suoyiran* (所以然). At the same time, in contrast to the substantialistic portrayals of the metaphysical ultimate as unchanging divine substance found in the dominant strains of classical Western theism and the Indic tradition, the Neo-Confucian metaphysics treats *li* as a dynamic ontological creativity – that is, as an incessant activity of patterning, structuring, and harmonizing at the very root of the cosmos.[10]

Given my continued theological quest to find a better intellectual framework to articulate God's transcendence as God's deepest immanence in creation, I was attracted to the subtle manner in which the Neo-Confucian metaphysics positioned the metaphysical ultimate – *li* – as a dynamic and creative "force" at the root of the universe itself. At the same time, I was both intrigued and flummoxed by the somewhat incongruous idea of the ultimate ideal principle of coherence and order – a kind of lure, guideline, or in some instances, schematic – seemingly functioning as the "agent" of ontological creation. Shouldn't *li* as dynamic ontological creativity be construed also as a kind of energy rather than strictly as an ideal principle if it is to serve as the "cause" of ontological causation in the least restrictive sense of the term? This ambiguity in the overarching metaphysical architectonic of the dominant Neo-Confucian position drew my attention to the Korean philosophy of *qi*, represented by Yulgok and Nongmun, a sixteenth- and an eighteenth-century Neo-Confucian figure, respectively. What arrested my interest was their move outside the orbit of the "orthodox" school of Zhu Xi that interpreted *qi* quasi-dualistically as the dynamic material principle subordinate to *li*. Especially in Nongmun's conception of it, *qi* can be said to designate none other than ultimate reality itself, because it has two modes: 1) the cosmic energy that coalesces to become the material and ideal "stuff" of every concrete entity and 2) the original *qi* that permeates the world of concrete entities to make them creative and living by providing them with a fundamental inclination toward order and value (which is the source of novelty in the universe). This "layering" of *qi* provides a sense of ontological depth and radically immanent transcendence to the primordial energy of the universe. For Nongmun, *li* is merely a name for the original *qi* to designate specifically the latter's ordering and governing of creative processes.[11]

Yulgok and Nongmun's philosophy of *qi* suggested to me a way to envision the ultimate as a kind of *natura naturans* like the Daodejing did, but with a more conceptually robust articulation of the relationship between its world-immanence and world-transcendence. I was inspired to articulate my theological thesis, that the trinitarian God is first and foremost Spirit, as meaning that God is first and foremost the primordial Energy of the universe, without simultaneously being forced to make a distinction between God's unknowable essence (*ousia*) and God's experienced energy (*energeia*) – like some Eastern Orthodox theologians had done – in order to safeguard divine independence and freedom from creation.[12] This theological development spurred my transition from a chiefly Hegelian standpoint to one that incorporated insights from Whiteheadian and Deleuzean thoughts. My view of God as some kind of primordial yet all-pervasive creative energy resonated with Whitehead's definition of the ultimate metaphysical ground as the very cosmic process of creative advance into novelty, on the one hand, and Deleuze's notion of *chaosmos* (i.e., the orders of the universe "bubbling up" from the chaotic background of virtuality), on the other. Catherine Keller's work of creatively blending the two intellectual giants also gently nudged this God as the primordial Energy into the heterogeneous beginning and tehomic depth of the universe and in so doing enabled me to complete the identification of divine radical transcendence with divine radical immanence.[13]

I cannot end this chapter without mentioning Donghak, or Eastern Learning (today called Choendogyo). Donghak is another "home" tradition of mine whose intellectual resources inspired and enriched my theological journey. Donghak is the first indigenous organized religion of Korea born of the crucible of late nineteenth-century Korea in which the traditional teachings of Confucianism, Buddhism, Seondo, and shamanistic folk religion clashed and wrestled with the new arrival, namely, Christianity or Western Learning. The Donghak understanding of ultimate reality has two poles. The ultimate is first *jigi*, or Ultimate Energy (that is, Ultimate Qi). At the same time, Ultimate Energy is a personal deity called *haneullim* (Lord Heaven), who is both within and outside the human self, identified with the human heart–mind yet coming to meet it from outside as the larger cosmic heart–mind to which the individual heart–mind is called to be attuned. The experience of the personal encounter with Ultimate Qi as Lord Heaven makes one a "bearer of Lord Heaven" who has become one with the rest of the universe and whose entire psycho-physical being shares in the cosmic creative-transformative agency of Ulti-mate Energy. By conferring a clear sense of divine subject agency to the spontaneous and pluriform creativity of the cosmic *qi* whose harmoniz-ing power is not predicated on some kind of transcendent metaphysical unity, Donghak developed a view of the divine that is both one and many, divine and creaturely, and impersonal and personal. At the same time, as a social movement it worked toward the creation of a free, egalitarian, and inclusive society of "the bearers of Lord Heaven," eventually culminating in the first attempt at democratic revolution in Korean history in the late nineteenth century.[14]

Donghak teachings have helped me overcome a major obstacle in con-structing a theology of Spirit while drawing on my East Asian religious and intellectual heritages – that is, the fact that, largely speaking, Confucian-ism and Daoism are philosophically nontheistic. The polar conception of the ultimate as both Ultimate Energy and Lord Heaven has enabled me to think of God as Spiritual Energy – that is, both the energy of my existence and the object of my prayer and worship. If the spirits of my ancestors who responded to my family's invitation to take a seat at the altar of ancestor veneration to bless us consisted of the same *qi* of which I was also made, God as Spiritual Energy also responds to my call for help from the cha-otic depth of my being and provides succor by "energizing" my *qi*, that is, by strengthening my sinews and bones and stirring in my mind and heart visions of liberation and healing.

Furthermore, Donghak is an East Asian theological source that, however compromised and diluted by sociopolitically dominant traditions, still rep-resents the voice "from the underside of history." Hence, my engagement of it answers the liberationist impulses that have always been present in my theological quest, while helping me respond to the demand of the new generation of comparative theologians that we attune ourselves more to the marginalized voices within the major religious traditions or "outsid-ers within."[15] Donghak's ecological and political ideas, as the product of what may be called subversive subaltern reinterpretations of the historically dominant Neo-Confucian ideas, practices, and institutions, have provided suggestive pointers for developing my pneumatocentric reconstruction of the doctrine of the Trinity into a full-blown ecopolitical theology – one that is attuned to the cries of the oppressed, exploited, and marginalized, both human and nonhuman.

As I mentioned earlier, I have come to reject the universal applicability of the idea of asymmetric belonging so as to allow for a bidirectional conception of the operational logic of comparative theology. Does this mean that I have come to embrace TWW in earnest insofar as it eschews the idea of the primary religion to which one belongs? Perhaps. Yet if the account I have presented here of my path to a theology of *qi* is any indication, my theologian self does not escape being encumbered and propelled forward by the weight of the historical layers of traditions accumulated and embedded in my body. This explains why, although a chance glance at Augustine's *City of God* or Nongmun's *Miscellaneous Writings from the Deer Hut* can get my theological mind and heart all worked up and beating, it is only with an intentional effort that I pick up Sankara's *Brahma Sutra Bhasya* to receive a fresh insight about God. Hence, the version of TWW that I can accept is one that allows room for a theological thinking spontaneously – and even confessionally – tethered to, but not arbitrarily restricted by, a certain number of concrete teachings and practices as a result of one's existential and historical embeddedness in particular traditions. Such a TWW would raise no objection if I renamed my chapter *My Path to a Confucian–Daoist–Donghak–Christian Theology of Qi*, except for the unwieldly nature of the new title.

Notes

1 This phrase was taken from Jerry Martin's initial proposal for this volume. He articulates the definition and ethos of transreligious theology more fully in his programmatic statement to a section of *Open Theology* dedicated to the topic (Martin 2016).

2 Whether religious affiliation is to be understood as (identity-shaping) belonging in the sense of membership in religious communities or as participation in certain religious practices is an important distinction drawn by John Thatamanil (Thatamanil 2016a, 9–15).

3 I put the word in quotation marks because Christianity was already a well-established part of the religious landscape of Korea, though with a much shorter history and, most importantly, an intellectual – theological – foreignness.

4 Peter Hodgson has very helpfully coined the term "pre-worldly Trinity" for the immanent Trinity and "worldly Trinity" for the economic Trinity to clarify the distinction between the two (Hodgson 1994, 151).

5 For this I am deeply indebted to Peter Hodgson's Hegelian interpretation of the Trinity. See his *Winds of the Spirit* (Hodgson 1994, 151–172).

6 I am referring to the famous distinction made by Spinoza between *natura naturans* (nature naturing or active nature) and *natura naturata* (nature natured or passive nature). *Natura naturans* is nature taken as the free cause of itself – that is, as God – whereas *natura naturata* is the same nature seen as contingent, dependent on, and existing in God. (Spinoza 1993, 25). In the Daoist interpretation suggested here, the unnamable Dao as *natura naturans* implies that *natura naturans* transcends any unity or order, including the divine-human-cosmic whole (*natura naturata*) to which it has given birth.

7 According to Heup Young Kim, the notion of asymmetrical belonging advanced by Catherine Cornille, which makes a distinction between the primary religion

to which one belongs and others with which one identifies, is suspected of harboring the religious, cultural, and philosophical imperialism of the West, especially if the primary religion happens to be Christianity Kim (2016, 82).

8 The "grafting model" is suggested by Kyoung Jae Kim in his *Christianity and the Encounter of Asian Religions: Method of Correlation, Fusion of Horizons and Paradigm Shifts in the Korean Grafting Process* (1994, 135–141). Here Kim is relying on the ideas of Ryu Dong-sik, one of the pioneers of Korean *tochakhwa* theology. In the "grafting" model both the Christian tradition and the local function as theological subjects taking part in the creative process of theological indigenization or inculturation.

9 I am here referring to the "orthodox" lineage of the so-called Cheng-Zhu School, whose founding figure is Zhu Xi (朱熹 1130–1200 CE) of the Chinese Southern Song Dynasty.

10 I have presented this account more fully in my book, *Spirit, Qi, and the Multitude: A Comparative Theology for the Democracy of Creation* (Lee 2014, 62–82).

11 For a fuller account see *Spirit, Qi, and the Multitude* (Lee 2014, 142–173).

12 For the Eastern Orthodox distinction between divine essence and divine energy, especially that of Gregory Palamos, see Lossky (1974, 52–56). Mary-Jane Rubenstein convincingly argues that the distinction ultimately collapses, because of the intrinsically self-revelatory – that is, relational – nature of divine life (Rubenstein 2011, 38–41).

13 See *Spirit, Qi, and the Multitude* (Lee 2014, 174–210).

14 See *Spirit, Qi, and the Multitude* (Lee 2014, 211–243).

15 See Roberts (2010) and Tiemeier (2010).

References

Clooney, Francis X. 2010. *Comparative Theology: Deep Learning Across Religious Borders*. Malden, MA: Wiley-Blackwell. doi:10.1002/9781444318951

Esposito, John L., Darrell J. Fasching, and Todd T. Lewis, eds. 2012. *World Religions Today*. 4th ed. Oxford and New York: Oxford University Press. doi:10.3366/swc.2007.13.3.301

Hodgson, Peter C. 1994. *Winds of the Spirit: A Constructive Christian Theology*. Louisville, KY: Westminster John Knox Press. doi:10.1177/004057369605300314

Kim, Heup Y. 2016. "Multiple Religious Belonging as Hospitality: A Korean Confucian-Christian Perspective." In *Many Yet One? Multiple Religious Belonging*, edited by Peniel Jusudason Rufus Rajkumar and Joseph Prabhakar Dayam, 75–88. Geneva: World Council of Churches Publications.

Kim, Kyoung J. 1994. Christianity and the Encounter of Asian Religions: Method of Correlation, Fusion of Horizons, and Paradigm Shifts in the Korean Grafting Process. Zoetermeer: Uitgeverij Boekencentrum. doi:10.1163/157254395x00072

Kyung, Chung H. 2009. "Seeking the Religious Roots of Pluralism." In *Christian Approaches to Other Faiths: A Reader*, edited by Paul Hedges and Alan Race. 73–74. London: SCM Press. doi:10.1111/j.1467–9809.2011.01112.x

Lee, Hyo-Dong. 2014. *Spirit, Qi, and the Multitude: A Comparative Theology for the Democracy of Creation*. New York: Fordham University Press.

Lossky, Vladimir. 1974. *In the Image and Likeness of God*, edited by John H. Erickson and Thomas E. Bird. 52–56. Crestwood, NY: St. Vladimir's Seminary Press. doi:10.1017/s0034412500009094

Martin, Jerry L. 2016. "Is Transreligious Theology Possible?" *Open Theology* 2 (1): 261. doi:10.1515/opth-2016-0021

Roberts, Michelle V. 2010. "Gendering Comparative Theology." In *The New Comparative Theology: Voices from the Younger Generation*, edited by Francis X. Clooney. 109–128. New York: Continuum.

Rubenstein, Mary-Jane. 2011. "The Fire Each Time: Dark Energy and the Breath of Creation." In *Cosmology, Ecology, and the Energy of God*, edited by Donna Bowman and Clayton Crockett. 38–41. New York: Fordham University Press. doi:10.5422/fordham/9780823238958.003.0003

Spinoza, Baruch. 1993. *Ethics and Treatise on the Correction of the Intellect*, trans. Andrew Boyle. London: J. M. Dent Orion Publishing Group and Rutland, Vermont: Charles E. Tuttle.

Thatamanil, John J. 2016a. "Eucharist Upstairs, Yoga Downstairs: On Multiple Religious Participation." In *Many Yet One? Multiple Religious Belonging*, edited by Peniel Jesudason Rufus Rajkumar and Joseph Prabhakar Dayam, 9–15. Geneva: World Council of Churches Publications.

Thatamanil, John J. 2016b. "Transreligious Theology as the Quest for Interreligious Wisdom." *Open Theology* 2 (1): 355. doi:10.1515/opth-2016-0029

Tiemeier, Tracy S. 2010. "Comparative Theology as a Theology of Liberation." In *The New Comparative Theology: Interreligious Insights from the Next Generation*, edited by Francis X. Clooney. London and New York: T & T Clark. doi:10.1111/j.1467–9418.2012.01050.x

Index

Note: Page numbers in *italics* indicate figures and in **bold** indicate tables on the corresponding pages.